D1528188

AMONG THE ANTHROPOLOGISTS

Among the Anthropologists

History and Context in Anthropology

ADAM KUPER

THE ATHLONE PRESS
London & New Brunswick, NJ

First published in 1999 by
THE ATHLONE PRESS
1 Park Drive, London NW11 7SG
and New Brunswick, New Jersey

© Adam Kuper 1999

British Library Cataloguing in Publication Data
*A catalogue record for this book is available
from the British Library*

ISBN 0 485 11536 0

Library of Congress Cataloging in Publication Data

Kuper, Adam.
  Among the anthropologists : history and context in anthropology /
Adam Kuper.
    p.   cm.
  Includes bibliographical references.
  ISBN 0-485-11536-0 (alk. paper)
    1. Ethnology.   2. Ethnology–Africa, Southern.   3. Africa,
Southern–Social life and customs   I. Title.
GN325.K89   1999
306′.0968–dc21   99-14802
                                                                    CIP

Distributed in the United States, Canada and South America by
Transaction Publishers
390 Campus Drive
Somerset, New Jersey 08873

Typeset by Bibloset
Printed and bound in Great Britain by
Cambridge University Press

Contents

Preface

Rereading, selecting and revising essays published over a decade obliges one to take stock, and it is tempting to impose a retrospective order on whatever it is that one thinks one has been doing. These essays reflect a point of view about how theories in anthropology emerge and are put to work, and (it follows) a strategy for going about research. Nevertheless, I cannot pretend that I have followed a conscious plan. Particular projects have crept up on me unawares, sustained themselves for a few years, then given way to new projects.

Moreover, the work I have done has always followed two distinct tracks: studies in the intellectual history of anthropology on the one hand, essays in the ethnography of Southern Africa on the other. (There have also been occasional deviations, often enjoyable, such as the work on dreams, particularly appropriate for an unplanned detour, which is touched on in chapter six.) These two tracks have met up from time to time, although they might appear to lead in very different directions. In the seventies and early eighties I was engaged in research on Southern African systems of kinship and marriage. At the same time I worked up a historical critique of lineage and alliance theory.[1] Yet while these studies helped to sustain each other, I would not wish to suggest that they fit together in an efficient whole, a dialogue between 'theory' and 'ethnography'.

In any case, that is not how research in anthropology proceeds. The issues that we argue out in a series of discursive conversations are usually only roughly to be distinguished in these terms. There are few coherent theories, and not many takers, and we are insistently told that there are no innocent (or finished) ethnographies. What we have are simply more or less interesting contributions to a broad conversation that may draw in philosophers, sociologists, historians, regional specialists, planners, and local informants.

Distinctive accents seldom rise clearly above the babble of conversation. Most individual contributions to debates reflect a point of view that is shaped by collegial affiliations. From time to time new voices chip in, or are introduced, and heard out, sometimes reluctantly. The network is open-ended, one reason the conversation is always changing. But it does not approximate very closely to the rational debate of informed equals that Habermas recommends. Schools and parties form, but represent currents of opinion rather than coherent theoretical positions. Tentative conclusions come to be accepted, but these are shaped as much by the context of the conversations as by the immediate subject of the argument, and they establish themselves through the insidious workings of prestige and patronage as well as for more elevated reasons. (Big Men have always mattered in anthropology.)

Theoretical excursions and field studies must accordingly be situated, their authors treated individually, but also placed within a loose, local community of experts, or a cosmopolitan network of intellectuals, or perhaps, at times, as participants in a social movement. There is, accordingly, a case to be made for the ethnohistory of anthropology, not as a separate speciality but as the context within which our work must be read. Yet there is room for criticism as well as interpretation. As ethnographers, we expect Zande beliefs about causality to make sense, but we do not treat them as contributions to science or to logic, contenting ourselves with the demonstration that the ideas hang together, cope with the experience of the Zande, and sustain other ideas and even social relationships. However, even confirmed relativists are inclined to think they can deliver a true and reliable account of how their colleagues delude themselves. The implication is that at some point, once the ideas are decoded and situated, the bias of the descriptions exposed, there are further questions to be asked about the reliability, accuracy, and value of particular contributions to the historically formed debates in which we are engaged. As new data and fresh arguments are introduced, the conversation can take a fresh turn. Often this happens by way of reintrepretations of classic ethnographic cases, our common point of reference, and by the rereading of our intellectual history.

An ethnohistorical approach to theory yields a double perspective, which is a powerful antidote to the pressures of intellectual fashion, the messianism of graduate schools, and the inhibitions imposed by political correctness. First, it imposes an awareness of alternatives, and also the sense that new theories grow out of an intellectual climate that is overwhelmingly powerful for a time but which is bound to change, leaving its adherents shivering as the wind shifts. Second, it leads one to read ethnographies as tentative syntheses, local historical processes seen through the lens of current ideas, but always refractory, raising their own questions, unsettling the observer. (Ethnographies must therefore be read, in conjunction with other accounts, as contributions to a multivocal, interdisciplinary discussion of what is going on here.)

This, then, is the point of view that informs the essays in this book. Theories and descriptions in anthropology are time and culture bound, historically conditioned, provisional. To grasp what they mean involves an exercise in the historical (or ethnographic) imagination. Yet at the same time they have certain qualities as theories that can be evaluated with reference to the work they do. Theories may encode political slogans, or rework popular prejudices, but they are also more or less helpful when it comes to designing and executing and analysing and comparing ethnographic studies. Ethnographic studies are themselves informed by particular historical circumstances, political forces, intellectual fashions, those of the ethnographer and those of the subject, but they can nevertheless be interrogated for information that can be turned against their own theoretical agendas, or pressed into use as data for other empirical projects. And anthropologists and ethnographers are again historical constructs, and must be understood in context, ethnographically and historically. Nevertheless, their ideas and their findings may also be interpreted, criticised, and put to use, if only for the time being.

We should therefore be prepared to turn our traditional methods on ourselves. They may help us to understand our collective project, and even to further it. We have to ask where an argument, or a description, comes from, and what it means. But in the end we have to face up to two further questions. Does this make sense? Does it work? Less than a theory, rather perhaps a strategy, these at any rate are the propositions to which the following essays are dedicated.

Adam Kuper
London, July 1998

Notes

1 See Kuper, A. (1982) *Wives for Cattle: Marriage and Bridewealth in Southern Africa*, London: Routledge and Kuper, A. (1988) *The Invention of Primitive Society: Transformations of an Illusion*, London: Routledge.

1
A Conversation with Charles Stafford –
About Culture and Anthropology

The conversation which follows took place in London in 1996, and provided the basis for an interview published in the *Newsletter* of the European Association of Social Anthropologists. Charles Stafford came from the USA to Britain to study anthropology, and he teaches at the London School of Economics. He specialises in the ethnography of China and is the author of *The Roads of Chinese Childhood* (Cambridge: Cambridge University Press, 1995). The conversation focused on the value of a historical approach to anthropology, and on the book I was writing at the time. (*'Culture': The Anthropologists' Account*, Cambridge, MA: Harvard University Press, 1999.)

CS A lot of your work focuses on the history of anthropology and of anthropological concepts. Why do you think it is important for anthropologists to be aware of their intellectual history?

AK It's a kind of personal deformation. When I try to understand a theoretical problem, I can really only get at it when I understand its development. Some people think in this way and others don't. When I was a student, trying to get some sort of grip on economics, the book that stuck in my mind was Joseph Schumpeter's *History of Economic Analysis* (London: Allen and Unwin, 1954). Once I could locate arguments historically, I also began to understand – or thought I could understand – why academics become captivated by some very odd questions.

When I came into British anthropology, the central debate was about lineages and lineage theory. It only

made sense when I learnt enough about the history of
the subject to realise that there was a long tradition of
thought according to which primitive societies all over
the world had the same kind of social system, based
on blood ties. The implication was that human beings
naturally organise on the basis of common descent.[1]
Kinship theory, lineage theory, alliance theory, they were
all at bottom theories about the origin of human society,
about what Lévi-Strauss called 'the elementary systems'
(ambiguously, since this could be read to mean that these
systems were the logical basis for all others, a sort of
Cartesian starting-point, or that they were the historical
point of origin). And so you could see debates about
lineage theory as the fag end of a very old argument
about the nature of human groups. Because these were
theories about human nature, they conveyed political
messages. I also began to see lineage theory as a sort
of metaphor of the Apartheid ideology in South Africa,
with which I had grown up. That may seem far-fetched,
but the theory tells us that prehistoric – or primitive –
societies were rooted in blood relationships, that these
are the fundamental social ties.

Perhaps what I try to do could be glossed as an
ethnographic approach to theory, as much as a historical
approach. But in any case recognising where the ideas
come from, grasping the context that shaped them, con-
sidering what ideological work they might be doing, all
that is only a start. We still need theories to work with as
anthropologists. We have to find out which theories work
for us. You have to ask whether the original question that
the theory addressed still matters. And then, wherever
the theory comes from, you have to come to a view about
how much it helps us to make sense of what people are up
to. But I can't get into those questions until I have some
idea what the theory means, and for me that involves
getting a grip on it historically – or ethnographically, if
you like.

CS Speaking of context and use, I was once paid by a
management consultant to compile a list of definitions of

'culture', so that he could then sell them to corporations as part of a survey of their corporate culture.

AK What a great story! One of the interesting questions, once you begin to look at it historically, is why culture has become such a major issue again. In the United States today, culture explains what is right with America and what is wrong with America. Why is there crime in the inner city? It's no longer about racial discrimination and prejudice, or poverty and unemployment, it is all down to culture! Samuel Huntington [Professor of International Relations at Harvard] recently came out with a theory about global conflict that created a huge fuss in America.[2] He said, the Cold War is over, we're not going to have these big fights over ideology, we're not going to fight over territory or markets, that's all going to be sorted out in international organisations. What is the history of the next generation going to be? It's going to be the history of cultural wars, wars between civilisations. You have to ask: what happened to the United States in the late 1980s, the early 1990s, which made people believe that culture is the big question? (And I do not believe that a cultural analysis will provide the answer. You must consider political changes, like the end of the Cold War, the great secular changes in education and employment, patterns of immigration, demographic shifts . . . .)

CS I suppose that your own interest in this particular issue had something to do with your background as a South African.

AK Most people, coming into anthropology as young people, confronted with the study of culture, see it as a liberating idea. And it can be a liberating idea because it says, look, the differences between people are not caused by race but by culture. Very welcome news, certainly for many liberal Americans. It is also a liberating idea if you've got political ambitions to change things. Culture is learned, so you can change things, things aren't fixed the way they are by nature.

I was presented with the idea of culture in completely

the opposite situation, as an argument for retaining the system of racial domination in South Africa. People said, of course we've given up the old, terrible idea that South Africans are naturally divided by race, this was a crude idea. In fact, they are divided by culture! Culture is fixed, given. It is the real basis of identity. Even though you might not like what goes on in another culture you've got to leave it the way it is. That's the way these people go about things. Admittedly, some African leaders were saying that they did not want to stick to the old traditional ways of doing things. But that's because they've lost touch with their real culture. The authentic people haven't!

So in South Africa a theory of culture served as a central pillar of the ideology of a terrible political system. In the liberal universities in South Africa this view of culture was constantly contested. My anthropology teachers imbued me with a deep suspicion of all essentialist arguments about culture.

CS Marshall Sahlins discusses the contrast between the German notion of *Kultur* and the French *Civilisation*. And he holds it up as a very positive thing that people were willing to grant a kind of validity to various cultures and examine them on an equal basis.[3] But you're suggesting that he may be oversimplifying the use to which that kind of culture concept may be put.

AK All I'm saying is that my own experience left me with a deep suspicion of the political uses of the idea of culture, whereas for Americans of my generation, on the contrary, the idea of culture was liberating and a good political idea, that could be used to fight discrimination and so on. Ideas about culture have different uses in different contexts, and I don't think you can judge an idea by the uses to which it is put by political activists. But anthropologists do have to be aware of the political uses of their concepts in order to understand some of the political charge, the emotion that goes with arguments about culture, and not only within anthropology. After all, virtually everybody now talks the language of culture. Today wherever anthropologists go in the world some version of culture theory is fed back to them, and it helps if they understand something about the history of this discourse. But after working out the history of a theory, and specifying its ethnographic context, we still have to ask another kind of question. If we take one or other of the more refined ideas about culture and we put them to work, what are the consequences? These are questions that I work through in my new book on culture theory. Having traced the history of these ideas, I take the notion of culture that crystallised in the mid-twentieth century in America, the idea of culture as a symbolic system for speaking about values, norms and ideas. The mainstream discourse in modern American anthropology suggests that culture (in the sense of ideas, values, norms, symbolic forms, particularly language) is actually the system that controls behaviour. It determines perceptions and determines the choices that people make, and even determines personality and the very emotions you feel. I try to see what happens when sophisticated scholars put this notion to work in the analysis of social processes. Let's look in detail at the work this concept does in their studies. In the end, an anthropological judgment has to be based on that. What are the analytic consequences – the gains and losses analytically?

Looking at the best work of modern American anthropologists, I came to the conclusion that they face two problems that they do not always recognise, and that they cannot deal with. One is that it becomes more and more difficult to see how you fit back this idealist aspect of social life which you've isolated and called 'culture', how you fit this back into the process of social and political history. Unless you take care, you are led very quickly to say that culture is everything that is happening – everything is in the realm of ideas, norms, values and symbolic communication. Even power is really a matter of ideas. Economics. And so on and so forth. Obviously, a whole lot of other things get locked out, often the very things that explain the particular form that ideas and values and norms have taken. Some writers are more sophisticated than others, and the best are very much aware of the difficulties and try to cope with them. But it doesn't seem to me that you can cope with it once you've made the opposition between culture and social structure, or culture and action, and then decided that culture is the driving force.

The second danger is that this kind of cultural determinism – because that is what it amounts to – inevitably suggests that the world is very different when seen from different cultural perspectives. This leads to the belief that there are in effect different types of human beings, who are programmed to think and feel and act in very different ways. Someone plucked from culture A and a person plucked from culture B would have the greatest difficulty in understanding one another. One is led to an idea of a world which is really divided into these blocs which according to Samuel Huntington are going to be engaged in a great conflict for the forseeable future. All this seems to me to be based on a totally false perception of what cultural difference means. It certainly does not help one to undertand the interrelations between people of so-called different cultures in a particular social field, as in London, say. And it also exaggerates the distance between people who live in different parts of the world. Even on the furthest periphery, people are brought into contact with others through trade or migration, or simply by films and TV and music and sport and fashions in dress. And they seem on the whole to manage these inter-cultural exchanges, or at least to grasp what the others are up to. Certainly immigrants and traders make sense of other cultures in a very practical way. The proof is that people quickly learn to operate in other cultural contexts, to make a living, to cope with the police, to organise churches in their new homes, and so on. Incidentally, my image of the ethnographer is as a kind of immigrant. Why should he not be as successful as any other sharp and hungry immigrant in picking up how things operate?

CS Culture can be as categorical as race.

AK The terms easily become mutually interchangeable. There's a very nice ethnography from a man called Michael Moffatt about a students' hostel at Rutger's University in New Jersey.[4] Black and white students living together in the 1970s. Lots of tensions, etc., but they're not allowed to use the word race. One or two students whispered the word race to the ethnographer. But they would talk in *exactly* the same way about culture. We can't mix with them because their culture is very different; their culture makes them eat food we don't like, that smells; we can't dance to the music of their culture. . . . These are precisely the same arguments that their parents would have made, but in terms of race. In the USA, as in South Africa, race and culture become mutually interchangeable in the popular discourse. And I think the same is true for many Europeans.

CS Can you imagine a time when anthropologists could do without the culture concept?

AK A generation ago, most British anthropologists did without this concept, or marginalised it. Edmund Leach has a passage where he says, well, culture is the way in which we symbolise social relations. In one society, when people get married they wear white, when they go to a funeral they wear black. In another society it's black for weddings, white for funerals. I take that for granted, Leach says. The important issue is, what constitutes marriage?[5] It is the rights and duties, the social and economic ties, that really shape peoples lives. That is what we should be comparing across societies. Today that seems a rather extreme point of view, but anyway there was a major school of British social anthropology that did without an idea of culture.

CS In your book you talk about the very different ways of thinking about culture and civilisation . . . .

AK It is conventional to distinguish three main ideas. The one is the progressive version, the French idea of civilisation, which comes into anthropology through Tylor. All human beings have essentially the same culture, but just more or less of it. And they're all advancing along the same

trajectory, in the direction of greater technological
sophistication, better scientific understanding, higher
morality, more effective and satisfactory government.
All these things are interlinked and they're moving in
the same kind of way, onwards and upwards, rationality
being the main motor of progress.

As against this there is the Romantic idea, which
developed in Germany, partly in reaction against the
French, partly in reaction against the Francophile courts
in the little German states, and partly as an expression
of a German nationalist movement which argued that
all the separate German states should be united since
the Germans were culturally and ethnically one people.
We're run by these Francophile courts which speak
French, we should be represented by people of our
own culture. Norbert Elias writes very well about this.[6]
And so they developed the idea that each *Volk* has its
own history and its own destiny. And the culture of each
Volk expresses the genius of the people – the *Volksgeist.* It
is expressed in the language, in the laws, in the religion.
However, the *Volksgeist* has been corrupted by two things.
First, by an elite which is cosmopolitan, which rejects it,
which is foreign to it, which brings in incompatible ideas.
Secondly, it's been undermined by foreign technological
and material values that are coming in and undermining
it and changing it. So how do you combat these forces?
You have to go back to the wisdom of the people,
peasants, that's where the culture really lies. That's where
the *Volksgeist* expresses itself with greatest purity. So folk
music should provide the inspiration for high music. Folk
literature – the Grimm brothers are collecting these tales
– will provide the material for new epics. The folk law
should provide the principles for the legal system. The
job of the ethnographer was to dig up the authentic
culture. Once it was brought to light it would show you
how things should be. And it's different from the culture
that you might find anywhere else. You must protect it
from foreign infiltration and from elite cosmopolitan
corruption.

There is also a third, humanist idea, of culture, although it can be linked with the other two. The humanist idea says that throughout the history of civilisation a few people of genius create wonderful works which are for all time. There is no progress. Virgil is not an advance on Homer, Chaucer is not an advance on Virgil, Shakespeare is not an advance on Chaucer. But occasionally a genius comes along who hits these high points. Culture is an anthology of their works. The man of culture works to preserve and to understand and to appreciate the best that has been thought and said, which is Matthew Arnold's phrase. Educated people in every society must hang on to that, because these are the highest achievements of human beings. And culture in this sense is supposed to be cosmopolitan and universal. If you were to educate Chinese people – they would realise that there is only one culture, to which a few Chinese geniuses have also contributed!

What is the enemy of this culture? Again, partly materialism, utilitarianism. Matthew Arnold argues against the Philistines, as he called them, whose God is Mammon. The other enemy, which is the enemy that people like T.S. Eliot and F.R. Leavis worried about, is mass culture, popular culture. Most people can't appreciate true culture, so they mass produce rubbish. And there is always the danger that it may corrupt the real culture.

I think these ideas all have something in common. They're all statements about what is the most important value in human life. And these ideas are really statements about what it is that human beings live for, in other words, they are religious dogmas. The best that has been thought and said, the greatest achievements of the human soul, that's what you must dedicate your life to. Or it is progress, the rational progress of civilisation and technology. Or it is the particular inborn values of a particular people which must be fought for.

Anthropology is partly about understanding one's own society. And these are major ideologies, both at a popular level and among intellectuals, and they have been diffused around the world. Anthropologists should contribute to understanding them. At the same time they must re-examine their own ideas. By all means study popular ideas of culture, but study the anthropological concepts of culture in the same way.

CS Your comments about elite culture bring to mind a current Sinological debate. One of the things Maurice Freedman and others pointed out was that Chinese elites never paid much attention to popular culture. And because of Chinese history in *this* century it's been very complicated for anthropologists to do fieldwork. Now it's becoming more feasible. But simultaneously there's a move in Chinese studies to say it is sheer romanticism to look for some authentic Chinese culture in the heartland among these peasants. In fact the really fascinating thing to study about China now is the Chinese diaspora. And so you have people arguing that the core of Chinese cultural creativity now at the end of the twentieth century isn't along the Yellow River, it's in Hong Kong, Taiwan, New York, London.

One of the reasons this debate comes up in Chinese studies is because young people who got sent to the countryside during the Cultural Revolution are now writing novels about it. And a lot of them are saying we went to the countryside thinking we would find the authentic China and we didn't find it. So now there's this debate in China, and the anthropologists are tagging along with it.

AK That's just as romantic an idea! They are still peddling an essentialist idea of Chinese destiny.

CS The irony for me is that once again the masses get ignored. There's a devaluation of anybody ever paying attention to what these farmers in these obscure provinces are doing. And there are lots of them! 800 million or something. And that gives me a kind of sympathy for this old German idea of *Kultur* – as this thing being sustained by pure, authentic peasants. It seems to me that to ignore *Kultur* is to ignore something terribly important.

AK I think you might be the victim of early leftist indoctrination! The humanist view was elitist. Only the elite possess true culture. It follows that only people who possess high culture are elite. This idea generated an alternative view, which was put about by Gramsci and Raymond Williams and Pierre Bourdieu and other people. They say that elite culture has a political function. People defer because they believe that the elite have superior knowledge, even higher ideals. The left-wing answer is to insist that there may be a greater value – a more accurate statement about what the world is really like, and what matters in it – in the cultural productions of the masses of people, if only you could find it. The whole premise of the argument seems bizarre if you're an anthropologist. If you're an anthropologist you should not be asking who in the population has the authentic culture. We ask: how are people living, how are they getting on with their lives? Can we understand the way in which they're organising themselves, thinking about it, planning, plotting? Can we make some kind of coherent sense of it? We put ourselves in their position in order to understand why they act as they do. In their situation, we realise, we would probably act in a similar way. That's the result of a good ethnographic analysis.

CS Last night I saw *Shanghai Triad*, which is set during the Nationalist era, and it precisely juxtaposes the corruption of Shanghai and the authenticity and sincerity of the countryside. All these gangsters from Shanghai end up hiding out on a remote island where they encounter some genuine Chinese peasants. Anyway, we've gone way off the track here.

AK Let me go back to your concern that we will not be able to do justice to all those Chinese peasants. My uncle, Leo Kuper, a sociologist, was very dedicated all his life to the view that social science should serve social justice. He always used to reproach me for being totally negative. What idea is your next book going to demolish? I have to admit when I look back that I do have a tendency to try to unpick ideas. And then the reaction is exactly the reaction you had – well, what are we going to do then if we don't have 'culture', can we have anthropology?

What can we offer people? And I'm always thrown by
that question. Because it seems to me that if you put
in question a false and perhaps even dangerous idea,
that's an important thing to do. After all, the greatest
achievement of modern anthropology was to get rid of
the idea of race. (Pity that it was replaced by culture,
though. . . .) I do not agree that hanging on to a bad
idea is better than a confession of ignorance or even
impotence. I am not bothered by the charge that I may be
depriving a technician – your management consultant,
say, or a social reformer – of a good but slightly faulty
tool which they should be able to use if only you can fix
it up a little bit here and there.

CS This I agree with completely. But it's interesting because
I think of you – I know at the end of your article
about Leach you say perhaps it's time for a cycle of
neo-positivism, and that would be a good thing[7] – I
think of you as being for the most part uninterested in
fashionable ideas. Trying to do something more serious
that relates to the longer term in anthropology. But to
some extent the work you do – if you used a different
language – could easily be seen as deconstruction and
so on. And anti-positivist. You certainly deconstruct concepts and you've done a lot of reflexive anthropology by
proxy, you've done it for the discipline.

AK But you're assuming that a positivist perspective must be
unreflexive, unselfcritical and so on. That's preposterous.
If you believe that it's possible to get more or less
accurate representations, and more or less defensible
analyses, then you can only do that by worrying about
the concepts, what they mean, where they come from,
what consequences they have when they're put to use. I
don't see this as being in opposition to a more scientific
programme.

CS I don't think anybody would question that it's a valuable
thing to write histories of disciplines and of disciplinary
concepts.

AK What do you mean nobody would question it! People
have been questioning it all the time! Violently.

CS I suppose the point I'm making is you might have put it in much more fashionable language.

AK Yes, I see that. But I think there's a kind of bloody-mindedness, which I've got to accept as part of myself, which makes me very suspicious of received ideas. A lot of people make good, strong criticisms of work that one does, it could be better, it should take this or that into account. But a lot of people just react against what they see as the nihilist message. They say, you can't just be critical. But I also try to apply ideas to explain ethnographic observations . . . .

CS In trying to teach your stuff, I never get that reaction from students – that it's a dead-end, something that stops thinking. It's a good way of figuring out how things fit together. You can trace the connection between ideas. By contrast I constantly have students come in who are hitting a dead-end because of interpretivism and post-interpretivism and the feeling that you have to put every word in quotes . . . . They come out feeling negative and disheartened. Unable to understand how we understand anything. I find myself seriously having conversations with students: look I fly to Beijing, I take the train to the northeast, here's a house. There are all kinds of things I can say about it: there's a *kang*, you sleep on the *kang*, there's a fire, the fire from the stove heats the *kang*, people have all these ideas about the connection between the fire, the stove, the heat, and the *kang*. These are facts!

Notes

1 These issues are the subject of my book, *The Invention of Primitive Society: Transformations of an Illusion* (London: Routledge 1982).

2 Samuel P. Huntington (1996) *The Clash of Civilizations and the Remaking of World Order*, New York: Simon and Schuster.

3 Marshall Sahlins (1993) 'Goodbye to *Tristes Tropes*: Ethnography in the Context of Modern World History', *Journal of Modern History*, 65: 1-25.

4   Michael Moffatt (1989) *Coming of Age in New Jersey: College and American Culture,* New Brunswick: Rutgers University Press.
5   E. R. Leach (1954) *Political Systems of Highland Burma,* London: Bell and Sons, pp. 16-17.
6   Norbert Elias (1978) *The Civilizing Process: The Development of Manners. Changes in the code of conduct and feeling in early modern times,* New York: Urizen Books. (First German edition, Basel, 1939.) Volume one.
7   This is the conclusion to the paper, reprinted here, 'Cambridge, Post-modernism, and The Great Kalahari Debate'.

2
Post-Modernism, Cambridge and the Great Kalahari Debate

I

In what may have been the last essay that he wrote before his death in 1989, Edmund Leach reviewed Clifford Geertz's *Works and Lives: The Anthropologist as Author* (Stanford: Stanford University Press, 1988). It is a characteristic Leach polemic, but although he accused Geertz of jumping on his students' bandwagon just before it ran him down, the piece ends quite unpredictably, with what reads like an endorsement of a strong post-modernist position.

> An ethnographic monograph has much more in common with an historical novel that with any kind of scientific treatise. As anthropologists we need to come to terms with the now well-recognised fact that in a novel the personalities of the characters are derived from aspects of the personality of the author. How could it be otherwise? The only ego I know at first hand is my own. When Malinowski writes about Trobriand Islanders he is writing about himself; when Evans-Pritchard writes about the Nuer he is writing about himself. Any other sort of description turns the characters of ethnographic monographs into clockwork dummies.

And again: 'Ethnographers as authors are not primarily concerned with factual truth; they convince by the way they write.'[1]

This is a striking declaration, given its source. It is surely startling that propositions of this sort should emanate from one of the most distinguished students of Malinowski. With characteristic boldness, Leach scorned to qualify his endorsement, or to reconcile it with his earlier theoretical statements, but while this is a clear and strong statement of one possible post-modernist claim, Leach was hardly an orthodox spokesman for post-modernism in general, or even for the anthropological version of post-modernism that became current in the United States in the 1980s. In France, post-modernism appeared as a transformation of both structuralism and Marxism, which had competed for the domination of Parisian intellectual life in the fifties and sixties. Translated to American academia, its context and content altered subtly but significantly, and again it took a very particular form in the context of American cultural anthropology. Disputed as it is between a biological scientism and a relativist tradition, American cultural anthropology has always been a very different enterprise from European social anthropology. We situate ourselves within the social sciences, while American cultural anthropology has traditionally been detached from sociology, and has largely ignored the traditions of Durkheim and Weber. What it took from Parsons was the news that 'culture' could – as a preliminary step perhaps even should – be treated separately from 'society', 'biology' and 'personality'.

Each of these anthropological traditions sustains different research programmes, and each will give a characteristic spin to any idea that is brought in from outside. Post-modernism in American anthropology addresses the study of culture in the tradition of the humanities. Moreover, the definition of culture that it uses has becomes increasingly specialised and restrictive. Today the orthodox definition is Geertz's (derived from Parsons). Culture is a symbolic system, a web of meanings. The anthropologist is trying to understand and communicate from one web to another, a personal, probably ultimately impossible, but nevertheless worthwhile endeavour, comparable to the attempt to translate a Japanese haiku into English. Except at the most elementary level, such an enterprise cannot be judged to be correct or incorrect.

Leach did not, of course, represent this tradition, but his apparent surrender to relativism is perhaps therefore all the more interesting. Moreover, his formulation is valuable because it is so clear and uncompromising. Leach could cut through the fat of any argument to bare its essence, while more cagey academics hedge and cover themselves, dodging (often with maddening insouciance) from a strong to a weak formulation of their claims. This is a familiar trick of the post-modernists. Whenever a critic reads their texts in a strong sense, they are accustomed to crying foul.

Carrithers, for instance, is surely not alone in his reading of Geertz's essay in post-modernism, *Works and Lives*, and also of James Clifford's *The Predicament of Culture* (Cambridge, MA: Harvard University Press), both of which appeared in 1988:

> They conceive that anthropologists are first and foremost writers, and 'writers' they understand on the model of fiction. What anthropologists do is create for themselves writerly personae with more or less authority, and that authority derives from the text itself and its style of presentation . . . . And in consequence the reliability of the knowledge anthropologists pretend to is of far less interest than the inventiveness (Clifford) or persuasiveness (Geertz) of their texts.[2]

This seems to me to be a fair reading of the strong thesis that is present in the texts of Geertz and Clifford. Geertz, however, repudiated it as a complete misreading of his position.

> I do not believe that anthropology is not or cannot be a science, that ethnographies are novels, poems, dreams, or visions, that the reliability of anthropological knowledge is of secondary interest, or that the value of anthropological works inheres solely in their persuasiveness. I do, indeed – doesn't Carrithers – think that rhetorical effectiveness has something to do with who gets believed and who doesn't and that it matters a bit who says what, where, when, and to what purpose . . . .[3]

Thus when challenged Geertz falls back on a weak reading of his thesis, insisting, ironically, that this is the only admissible reading of his famously suggestive prose.

Any thesis can be formulated in a strong or a weak form. Generally, in its strong form it is interesting but obviously wrong, in its weak form, rather obvious but sometimes right. Formulated weakly, Geertz's claims are true but not very interesting. The fieldworker is certainly limited by his or her upbringing, gender, age, status; the fieldworker's social and political situation will certainly condition his or her results; any monograph can be read to reveal hidden assumptions, and its author will surely make use of rhetorical tricks. But as Roth has argued, 'literary analyses of ethnographic texts, although they may document an interweaving of style and perspective' – which he sees as a virtue of Geertz's *Works and Lives* – 'leave unanswered and untouched the epistemological questions with which this debate began, viz, how properly to warrant claims from within a chosen perspective and how to assess the political import of one's position.'[4]

But while the weak version to which Geertz retreats is banal, Leach's unambiguous, strong version of anthropological post-modernism remains dangerous and interesting. His thesis is that what ethnographers produce is fiction, if not propaganda. He is asserting that objective truth, accuracy, even reliability cannot be expected from ethnography, though it may yield insights of a kind we might normally associate with serious works of fiction. And he should know – which is a second reason for paying attention to his formulation of the argument. He produced ethnography that is widely admired within the profession, and he has criticised and reworked the ethnographies of others.

My own first reaction to Leach's challenge was perhaps appropriately personal, even reflexive. I found myself thinking back to my initiation within the Cambridge department of social anthropology, in which Edmund Leach was himself one of the central figures. This is my final, personal reason for taking up Leach's argument: and a fashionably post-modernist reason it is too. (The most obvious attraction of post-modernism is surely the licence it provides for selective autobiography in the guise of honest scholarship.)

II

I fetched up at King's College, Cambridge, in 1962, at the age of twenty, as a research student in social anthropology. This was still very much the pre-modern Cambridge, and for a young foreigner it was exotic and more than a little unnerving.

The department of social anthropology presented special problems for the newcomer. There were only perhaps a dozen research students, of whom four or five would be away in the field at any one time. There a few Cambridge graduates (Andrew Strathern in my year), graduates from other English universities (Maurice Bloch, for instance, coming from the LSE), and several foreigners, mainly Americans, although Peter Rigby who had come up the year before me was, like myself, from South Africa. There were only seven or eight members of the academic staff, the dominant figures being the professor, Meyer Fortes, and the Reader, Edmund Leach. Jack Goody and Stanley Tambiah were their respective lieutenants. For very different reasons, Audrey Richards and Reo Fortune, famous anthropologists, were marginal figures in the department.

Both Fortes and Leach were fellows of King's, and in my first week Leach invited me to lunch. Gigantic and dishevelled, he looked me over at the table. 'I try to get people to work in South East Asia', Edmund said as we hacked at the petrified potatoes on our plates. 'The professor, of course, is interested in Africa.' I explained that, given my background, I was keen to do research in South Africa. He considered me kindly, writing me off but willing to soften the blow. 'Well, perhaps I can tell you something about Cambridge,' he said. 'Professor Fortes – for all his insight into Ghanaian society – has never really understood the place. The thing to grasp about Cambridge is that it is essentially lower middle class.'

A few days later, Meyer Fortes had me to lunch at King's. 'You'll be working in Africa, of course. Southern Africa? You will have to look up Schapera in London.' He then turned to other matters. 'Let me tell you something about Cambridge. Nobody else will tell you this – people like Edmund probably wouldn't even know it – but never forget that they don't like Jews.'

Both these characterisations turned out to be true, and helpful to the foreigner. But the most important thing I learnt from my lunches was that there was a serious rift between the two leading Cambridge anthropologists. The reasons underlying the quarrel are neither here nor there. The fact was that a new research student had to commit himself or herself to one camp or the other. This had to do in part with where one wanted to work. In general, Fortes and Goody directed the Africanists, while those travelling East of Suez worked with Leach or Tambiah. (The rest of the world was divided up as convenient.) But this initial choice entailed an intellectual orientation as well, since the Africanists were all expected to work in the tradition of Radcliffe-Brown and Fortes, while Leach and Tambiah were experimenting with structuralist ideas, under the influence of Lévi-Strauss.

A university like Cambridge is an efficient engine of acculturation. The department itself impressed a very specific academic identity on the new recruit. Within a couple of terms it would turn out a fledgling Fortesian Africanist or a structuralist South Asianist, armed with some ideas but above all with strong loyalties. These ideas were inculcated with a minimum of direct instruction. One had to pick up a great deal on one's own. That also perhaps made one less likely to rebel. There was little explicit control, though it is significant that when we tried to establish a small seminar of our own Fortes did his best to nip it in the bud.

We also all imbibed the faith that field research in the manner of Malinowski, by participant observation, would yield a more accurate view of another way of life that any other method. Indeed, it was hardly worth reading books about the societies we intended to study if their authors were not followers of Malinowski. (On the other hand, an extreme but not exceptional view held that if a Malinowskian had worked in a region – even in the same country – then it had been 'done' and one had best go somewhere else.)

I say we imbibed this faith, but it was imbibed without conscious effort, like mother's milk. There was no instruction in the methods of fieldwork by participant observation. This provoked a certain nervousness as the moment approached to depart for the field. We began to solicit instruction. Several of us were on the point of going out to Africa, New Guinea, Madagascar, Mexico . . . . Couldn't we be given some tips about procedures?

At last Jack Goody consented to talk to us. We met in his rooms in St John's College one evening in the early summer, after dinner. My image of that occasion is still vivid, for there was a May Ball at St John's that night, and we slipped into Goody's rooms past young men in evening dress and young women in décolletée silk gowns; and while we sat talking we could hear the dance music across the lawn. This was the image of England that haunted Edwardian travellers as they dressed for solitary dinners in deserts and jungles. However, we did not, I am afraid, learn a great deal directly that evening. Jack Goody explained that there was no real method, nothing that could be taught. The important things to bear in mind were that one had to remain healthy and on good terms with the authorities, and keep duplicates of one's notes, sending copies home as often as possible, in case one died.

This was the established tradition. The veterans boasted that they had gone into the field without any directions, or at best with risible and conflicting pieces of advice on matters of etiquette. Evans-Pritchard claimed that Seligman told him only to keep his hands off the local girls, while Malinowski's one piece of advise was to take a native mistress as soon as possible. And yet, of course, the directions were in their way explicit enough, perhaps all the more powerful for being purveyed through indirection and, especially, by way of personal anecdote.

III

It was natural enough that I should have chosen to do research in Southern Africa. I was a South African, and this was a time when African states were becoming independent, with all that this seemed to promise for the future of South Africa itself. And for similar reasons it seemed obvious that I should study politics. The South African government ethnologist, N.J. van Warmelo, met me in his office and spent an hour courteously discussing my plans for research, before telling me, with a slight inclination of his head towards the office where the more political staff of the Department were housed, that I would never be permitted to do research in South Africa. Accordingly I decided to work in one of the British protectorates in the region, and settled on the Bechuanaland Protectorate. The authority on Bechuanaland was Isaac Schapera, and he suggested that I consider fieldwork among the Kgalagari, a remote, little-known congeries of peoples on the western fringe of the famous Tswana states.

I did the conventional minimum of preparation: read the main books on the neighbouring Tswana and took lessons on SiKgalagari from an authority on Southern Bantu languages whom I was fortunate enough to discover at the School of Oriental and African Studies. And I approached the colonial authorities for permission to do research. The British administration in Bechuanaland was undermanned and remote. Its headquarters were actually in another country – in Mafeking, in South Africa. They were ready to let me go into the field, but were unable to provide any information at all about the distribution of Kgalagari communities in the west of the country.

Physically getting into the Kalahari seemed to pose the most daunting initial problem, but fortunately my aunt – the anthropologist Hilda Kuper – wrote to say that a couple of anthropologists from Harvard were going into the Kalahari to look for Bushmen groups, and that they had a Land Rover and would give me a lift if I met them at the Rhodes-Livingstone Museum in Northern Rhodesia. Their names were Irven DeVore and Richard Lee. Together we went into the Kalahari, accompanied by a baby baboon which DeVore had found beside its mother, who had been killed by a leopard. Soon we hired an interpreter, a man who had been employed as a gardener by the archaeologist

Desmond Clark in Livingstone, and who was trilingual in Naron, Tswana and English.

DeVore was already an established figure, who had conducted path-breaking field studies on primates in East Africa. Lee was like myself a graduate student, but we had been trained in very different schools, and we came to the Kalahari in 1963 with two very different projects. Both DeVore and Lee were evolutionists, but of somewhat different schools. The Bushman study was conceived by DeVore as a logical development from African archaeological research and from his own primate studies. It would provide a further point of reference for theories about the transition to modern humans in eastern Africa. Lee was influenced more by Julian Steward's cultural ecology, with its emphasis on adaptation to specific local conditions, but he also assumed that his ethnographic research would be relevant to the great evolutionary questions. The first hunters and gatherers had evolved in the East African plains, and it should be possible to gain insights into that process by studying the ecology and subsistence of primate groups and hunter-gatherers in the East African savannah today. 'My hunch was that research on contemporary hunter-gatherer groups – subject to critical safeguards – could provide a basis for models of the evolution of human behaviour.'[5]

Lee was not much interested in social structure, and so far as his thesis was concerned, the crucial data were biological and ecological. Accordingly he made detailed observations on food collection and nutrition, and conducted censuses and mapped group movements, relating these to ecological conditions. The research was guided by an hypothesis. He did not believe that the hunter-gatherer way of life was necessarily or even normally precarious, particularly since DeVore and others had found that non-human primates did themselves rather well. In the field Lee established what he had suspected, that the !Kung sustained themselves quite comfortably with surprisingly little effort, even in the marginal environment of the Kalahari. This suggested that the conventional reasons given for the transition to farming would have to be reconsidered. In 1966 Lee and DeVore

organised a conference on 'Man the Hunter' to discuss this
new conception of hunting and gathering, and Marshall
Sahlins famously announced that the !Kung were the original
affluent society.[6]

IV

My own research was much less well-organised, but after a
while I also began to focus on a body of data. The Kgalagari
were pastoralists, horticulturalists and migrant labourers,
living in compact village communities. The public affairs of
the village were debated and ordered in the *kgota*, the village
council. I attended all the meetings, took detailed notes,
discussed the proceedings with the councillors, and in due
course found myself with a systematic body of materials about
village decision-making, which formed the basis for my thesis.
I had decided to study politics before going into the field, but
I could also tell myself – with some cause – that I was obeying
Evans-Pritchard's famous, if rather imprecise, injunction, to
'follow the grain of the culture', since the affairs of the *kgota*
were clearly central to the villagers themselves.

   Though innocent of a coherent theory, let alone a clearly
formulated hypothesis, I did take some organising ideas into
the field. The British Africanists had two models of political
systems: there was the 'state', exemplified in Botswana by
the Tswana states of the east, and there were kinship based
political systems, taking the form of bands (as among the
Bushmen, so it was said) or segmentary lineage systems,
as operated by the Nuer and the Tallensi – or so we then
believed. There were no segmentary lineages in the Kalahari,
however, and no states either, for the Kgalagari villages were
small, equivalent in scale to a ward of a Tswana town. The
village in which I spent most of my time had a population of
three to four hundred. Kinship relationships were politically
important, but the administrative structures were based on
locality and residence.

   The theoretical notions I took into the field with me suggested a question: what was the role of kinship in Kgalagari

village politics? This was the theme of my doctoral disserta-
tion, submitted in the summer of 1966. But my own political
preoccupations also made me interested in the relationship
between the village and the District Administration, and in
the political changes that presaged the independence of
the country from Britain, eventually consummated in 1966.
There was a strong Malinowskian tradition that the ethnographer should take at least two bites at the cherry. Accordingly,
I returned to Ghanzi district in the newly independent state
of Botswana after completing my thesis, to study the changes
that the independence of Botswana precipitated at village
level, and to fill in the many gaps that had become apparent
in the process of writing up. It was difficult to know how to
analyse the impact of external political and social processes
in the rather hermetic terms imposed by the established
models of British social anthropology, but I struggled with
the problem and emerged, at least with a political moral.
The Kgalagari had democratic political institutions (up to
a point, excluding women and Bushmen), and they were
active in a sophisticated manner in district and national
politics. [7] This was in itself significant. The South African
government was arguing that so-called tribal peoples could
not operate democratic institutions, that their identity was
bound up with chiefly authority, and that authentic rural
Africans were not inclined to meddle in affairs beyond the
boundary of the tribe.

V

There is a case for concluding that both Richard Lee and
I saw what we were programmed to see. I would argue,
however, that our personalities and our opinions on politics
or ethics were less significant than features of our formal
education. Specifically, we had both been trained – we
had, perhaps, up to a point, *elected* to be trained – to study
social behaviour in particular ways, within explicit theoretical
frameworks. Ours were not idiosyncratic, personal projects.
We were both eminently dispensable. Similar projects were

very likely to emerge within the disciplinary traditions that
we represented. Indeed, on a journey in the Kalahari in
1965 I met a young Japanese anthropologist, Jiro Tanaka,
who was beginning a study of a Central Kalahari Bushman
group designed on the lines of Japanese primate studies. His
project was very like DeVore's.

Our methods had also been inculcated during our training, and in Tanaka's case this involved a radical experiment.
His initial object was to study Bushmen in the same way
as Japanese primatologists studied monkeys. Therefore, he
decided not to get involved in distracting and intrusive personal relationships, or even to learn the language. Coming
from a British university, I had, of course, begun with a
blind faith in the conventions of Malinowskian participant
observation. It seems to me today that the decisive feature
of his method was not a command to go native, to think and
feel and to experience life as a Trobriander. Malinowski's
method did not provide a license for romantic subjectivity.
Rather, the anthropologist had to come off the veranda so as
to see how the Trobriander really behaved, instead of being
content to hear him describe how he should behave. In order
to achieve this intimacy of observation, it was necessary to
be accepted as part of the community. The anthropologist
therefore participated in order to be able to observe without
intruding. Participation was less a means of observation that
a way of gaining access to opportunities to observe.

But these features of participant observation had to be
learnt the hard way. Since nobody had explained to me
precisely what it entailed, I fumbled and worried, eschewing
interviews – or at any rate interviewing only with a guilty
feeling that I was breaking the rules. But it was a robust
method, to the extent that one knew at least that one had
to learn the language, forge bonds of trust and friendship,
fit into the community as best one could, and hang about.
In doing these things one picked up information that turned
out to be increasingly reliable. Gradually I initiated a series
of dialogues. Hypotheses were discussed with villagers. I
found myself trying little experiments, predicting responses
to particular happenings.

The particular American tradition of anthropology from which Richard Lee came was more eclectic and less unswervingly committed to one method of data collection, but participant observation was by now an accepted feature of ethnographic fieldwork in American anthropology. Despite his primary interest in measurable forms of behaviour, Lee increasingly engaged in participant observation as his study developed. He spend a further twenty months in the field in the years 1967-9, in partnership with his wife, the demographer Nancy Howell, and he recorded the shift in his methods with characteristic precision. 'The first fieldwork had been about 70 per cent interviews and 30 per cent observation. This time the ratios were reversed, with much more of my time spent visiting people in their camps and sharing long morning and afternoons of conversation.'[8] More remarkably, Tanaka was also converted to participant observation. He became enthusiastically involved in local life, picked up the language, and increasingly operated like a good Malinowskian.[9] It seems that the imprecise and apparently unteachable method imposed itself even on sceptics.

VI

Lee later expanded the range of his enquiries and began to organise longitudinal studies of group movements, seasonal nutrition and other issues. And soon the research group at Dobe began to grow. Over the following two decades Lee returned to the field several times, and a stream of fieldworkers trained by himself and DeVore carried out other cultural, psychological, nutritional and archaeological studies of the Dobe !Kung.[10]

Other scholars were working at the same time on other Kalahari Bushmen groups, notably George Silberbauer, an employee of the Bechuanaland administration, who had been studying the Central Bushmen for some years before Lee and I entered the Kalahari. Silberbauer and I collaborated on a small study of Bushmen serfs in the Kgalagari village, and he, Lee and DeVore had extended discussions about Bushman ethnography. It was on the basis of this indirect contact that I was able to supervise the fieldwork of Alan Barnard, when he began to study the Nharo, using the theoretical framework of British social anthropology. Later another American anthropologist, Ed Wilmsen, began a long-term study of the !Kung. And in due course, what was called a revisionist thesis developed on the !Kung, and on the Bushmen or San more generally.

The essence of the revisionist case is that the evolutionist model tore the !Kung from their historical and current social context. The archaeological record shows that Kalahari foragers were in intimate contact with pastoral groups for perhaps a thousand years. For some two centuries they have been a part of an integrated Southern African system that bound together Portuguese, Dutch, Bantu-speakers and San in complex relationship of exchange. Typically the San had aspirations, intermittently realised, to a establish a pastoral economy, but they always remained at least on the margins of the pastoral economies of their neighbours, by whom they were often dominated and exploited. They cannot be taken to represent (in a phrase of Lee's which Wilmsen throws back at him) 'foragers in a world of foragers'.[11] They do not represent a stage in human evolution, but rather, Wilmsen suggested, an adaptation to a situation of marginality, powerlessness and exploitation.

A very different critique of the !Kung paradigm came out of the work of ethnographers such as George Silberbauer and Alan Barnard, who have studied other Kalahari Bushmen groups. They described the different adaptations which Bushmen or San communities made to local ecological circumstances. They also drew attention to the variety of cultural traditions represented in the area, which are evidenced most obviously by the wide range of linguistic variation. Where Wilmsen would ignore the cultural particularity of various San groups, representing all San as an underclass in a Marxist sense, the exponents of regional comparison stress that the !Kung Bushmen are not typical even of the Kalahari Bushmen. And once other Kalahari peoples are drawn into the comparison, it is evident that there are a variety of distinctive cultural traditions in the region.[12] The Kgalagari themselves were sometimes forced to resort to hunting and gathering in the last century, just as a few San groups managed to establish themselves as pastoralists. Nevertheless, even in the second half of the twentieth century most of the San remained culturally distinct from even the most impoverished Kgalagari. This reflects a series of choices that it would be foolish to discount.

On the great issue – the existence of some universal forager way of life, of which the !Kung might be an exemplar – I remain agnostic. Two possibilities at least deserve further investigation. Jiro Tanaka remarks: 'The longer I have spent with the San, the more I have become convinced that their unique "egalitarianism" is not an illusion. Even if historical evidence confirms that close links have long existed with the outside world, it does not lessen the importance of describing this cultural uniqueness.'[13] But is it unique? Nurit Bird, who has studied foragers in India, argues that despite their universal encapsulation in broader social and economic relations, there is a forager world view, based on a model of nature as exchange partner, one facet of a deep ideology of generalised exchange.[14]

There is a second issue of great significance. As Wilmsen correctly pointed out, foraging bands do not live in isolation. Indeed, it seems that they never did. Even hunters in a world of hunters found themselves in a differentiated environment. Archaeologists have shown that even in the remote Kalahari, and even before the spread of agriculture and pastoralism to Southern Africa (in the third and fourth centuries CE), small communities of hunter-gatherers were exchanging locally variable resources over large distances. The same is true of most stone age hunter-gatherers. This is hardly surprising. Local foraging traditions were based upon the local mix of food resources and the raw materials conveniently available. These differ from place to place. Variation, in turn, leads ineluctably to borrowing and exchange. The !Kung are therefore perhaps most representative of hunter-gatherers in general precisely because they are different from their neighbours, and yet engaged in complex relations of exchange with them. Any model of early human sociability must leave room for this open trading life, which was crucial for the survival of each community. There cannot have been a single, fixed type of Palaeolithic hunter-gatherer community, but for precisely that reason one can discern a broader system of exchange relationships that made possible the particular adaptation of local communities. Ecological and technological variation, and the communication and exchange it imposed, underlay the earliest human adaptations.

Leaving aside the substantive issues in play in the Great Kalahari Debate, the nature of the debate has implications for the issues I am addressing in this paper. The Great Kalahari Debate does not revolve around the reliability of ethnographic observations, but has to do rather with their interpretation, and their salience for larger debates. Wilmsen and Lee argue heatedly about some facts – in the main about detailed historical questions concerning contacts between particular Bushman populations and other groups. However, in general their ethnographic observations confirm or extend the record. It is also worth remarking that Wilmsen began his research with precisely the same theoretical orientation as Lee. He has remarked that he was surprised when his archaeological findings began to push him away from the idea that the !Kung were exemplars of late Palaeolithic foraging strategies.

VII

As it turned out, my Kgalagari study was a sideshow compared to the extremely influential work of the Bushmen specialists. It did not resonate within, or with, a large thesis about human behaviour. But the contextualisation of my field study soon led me in a new direction, which is relevant to my argument here. Where the !Kung debate was about the historical significance of the !Kung way of life, I became involved rather in debates about a large culture area, to which my Kgalagari study gave me no more than an entry ticket. From the first, I had referred to the extensive published ethnography on the related Tswana groups to the east, and my thesis had been examined by Isaac Schapera himself, the doyen of Tswana studies. Gradually, I began to attempt more systematic and ambitious comparisons within the culture area, between what had once been a relatively homogeneous set of agrarian communities, drawing on other ethnographic reports on the Southern Bantu culture area.[15] The exercise convinced me that the Southern African ethnographies contain information that transcends particular theoretical or political discourses. The data can be evaluated, compared and reanalysed. To be sure, each ethnography requires careful source criticism, as historians have always insisted, but sources can also be weighed against each other. One is seldom helplessly dependent on a particular author. For many communities, a variety of sources is available, and often their authors are not anthropologists at all. The very range of sources makes it easier to assess any particular report. Systematic comparison of related communities also puts particular ethnographies to the test. In some instances I was able to correspond with the ethnographers, and to debate with them alternative interpretations of their own data.

Were Lee and I, as authors, any different from our predecessors in the field, 'not primarily concerned with factual truth', as Leach would have it; more concerned, perhaps with ideological causes? We would not have got away with it! Lee soon had reading over his shoulder a growing international community of experts with first-hand knowledge of Bushmen groups, and often with fieldwork experience among the !Kung themselves. As his reputation grew, he became more vulnerable to critics. Tripping up Richard Lee might make a person's reputation . . . . There were fewer people hanging on to my words, but once I began to undertake regional comparative studies I stung a number of local specialists into paying close and critical attention.

The essential fact is that both Lee and I were working within a living tradition of local scholarship. What we had to say was assessed by experts with considerable

first-hand experience. They were not likely to be intoxi-
cated by our rhetoric. Like virtually any modern ethnographers, we were both participants in a lengthy process of
collaborative and interactive research. Our studies emerged
in the course of extended public dialogues with colleagues
and with local specialists. This is now the normal context of
ethnographic research. There are no more isolated pioneers,
no Malinowskian monarchs of all they once surveyed.

<h1 style="text-align:center">VIII</h1>

I suggest that Lee and I were operating in many ways
like conventional scientists. We had explicit – more or
less systematic – theoretical ideas. We collected bodies of
objective data. We formulated our findings for the benefit
of various groups of experts, and we engaged in debate with
them and with local authorities of all kinds. The question
that dominated these debates was, to put it crudely, were we
right? Was the description accurate? Had we left out some
crucial facts? Was the analysis logical, appropriate, adequate?
We had no doubt that we were contributing to a collective
enterprise, governed by shared standards of argument and
evidence. The measure of our work was the extent to which
it recast, developed, upset, illuminated the work of other
ethnographers. Both of us also had quite explicit political
interests, but these never seemed to us to conflict in principle
with our scientific commitments.

   This is not to deny that we were caught up in particular anthropological discourses, with their own rules and
claims. Lee was working within the rather aggressively scientific, ecological, evolutionary tradition of North American
anthropology, while I operated with the European social
science tradition of anthropology, one that is still a minority
interest in North America. But while Lee and I argued,
we took it for granted that we were both engaged in
legitimate and broadly scientific exercises. Practically all
the ethnographers who did fieldwork in the Kalahari –
from a variety of anthropological perspectives – shared

the belief that their research would stand or fall by the objective quality of their observations, and the success they had in making sense – for others – of our jealously checked information. Even the critical reanalysis of Lee's findings by the 'revisionists' demonstrates once more that data can be shared, and reordered in alternative frameworks. In short, one should distinguish the true claim that ethnographies can be analysed to say something about their authors, or about the rhetorical procedures of particular genres, from another valid claim, which the first does not contradict, namely that ethnographies can also be assessed to establish whether they provide reliable accounts of human behaviour in particular times and places. To put it another way, source criticism is a preliminary to the critical use of sources, not an alternative.

The political use of ethnographic studies is a distinct issue. Certainly, nobody working in Southern Africa could have been naive about this question. One of the curious features of the Wilmsen-Lee debate is that they compete to demonstrate that their studies are politically more helpful to the !Kung, and even that their opponents are a danger to the very survival of their ethnographic subjects. They also both claim to provide the true Marxist account of the !Kung, which they seem to think proves just how politically correct their analysis is. They are right to be aware that their studies will have effects. An interesting study could be written on the consequences that theories about the Bushmen have had for their lives in the past century. But it is hard to predict the uses that will be made of academic studies, and in the end we must in any case distinguish the political effects of a theory from its validity.

Some post-modernists have argued that a scientific stance is always politically suspect, since it excludes the actors' voices and imposes an imperialist authorial perspective. The notion that the author's voice should be muted in order to allow other – indigenous – voices to be heard strikes me as paternalistic, since it suggests that the ethnographer has been elected to be the representative of

a community. Is the ethnographer supposed to serve as
a medium? In that case, the medium will very quickly
become the message. Sometimes the argument seems to be
that the actors themselves could produce, barely mediated,
the most acceptable ethnographic account of themselves;
or at least that they should be the final arbiters of the
ethnography (perhaps even its censors). But an ethnography
is a contribution to an academic debate, and it is necessarily
phrased in terms that will be largely unintelligible except to
the initiated.

What, then, are we make of Leach's claim that ethnographies are no more 'scientific' than historical novels?
When I interviewed him for *Current Anthropology* in 1985 he
said, speaking of theoretical vogues in anthropology:

> the sequence is always dialectical. There was a point in
> my anthropological development when Malinowski could
> do no wrong. In the next phase Malinowski could do no
> right. But with maturity I came to see that there was
> merit on both sides. I see this as a Hegelian process,
> a very fundamental element in the way that thinking
> in the humanities develops over time. But when this
> sequence leads you round in a circle, you are not just
> back where you started. You have moved on a bit, or
> you have moved somewhere else. But always the process
> involves the initial rejection of your immediate ancestors,
> the teachers to whom you are most directly indebted.[16]

Leach is not in fact my immediate ancestor (if only because
I chose to become an Africanist), but I repudiate his final
statement on ethnography, albeit with a certain sadness. I
am emboldened to disagree because of what I have learnt
in the course of the ethnographic process. Leach's version, which is the strong version of the post-modernist
position, is untenable. But there is something to be said
for Leach's cyclical image of theoretical development in
anthropology, and I therefore predict that we are in for
a phase of neo-positivism. The prospect does not dismay
me.

Notes

1 Edmund Leach (1989) 'Writing Anthropology', *American Ethnologist*, 16: 137-41 (p. 141).
2 Michael Carrithers (1990) 'Is Anthropology Art or Science?' *Current Anthropology*, 31: 263-82 (p. 263).
3 Clifford Geertz, Comment on M. Carrithers (1990) 'Is Anthropology Art or Science', *Current Anthropology* 31: 274.
4 Paul A. Roth (1989) 'Ethnography Without Tears', *Current Anthropology* 30: 555-69 (p. 561).
5 Richard Lee (1979) *The !Kung San: Men, Women, and Work in a Foraging Society*, Cambridge: Cambridge University Press, p. 9.
6 Richard Lee and Irven DeVore (eds) (1968) *Man the Hunter*, New York: Aldine.
7 Adam Kuper (1970) *Kalahari Village Politics: An African Democracy*, Cambridge: Cambridge University Press.
8 Lee, *The !Kung San*, p. 17.
9 Jiro Tanaka (1980) *The San: Hunter-Gatherers of the Kalahari*, Tokyo: Tokyo University Press.
10 See the volume edited by Lee and DeVore (1976) *Kalahari Hunter-Gatherers: Studies of the !Kung San and Their Neighbours*, Cambridge MA: Harvard University Press.
11 Edwin N. Wilmsen (1989) *Land Filled With Flies: A Political Economy of the Kalahari*, Chicago: University of Chicago Press, p. 271.
12 See Alan Barnard (1992) *Hunters and Herders of Southern Africa: A Comparative Ethnography of the Khoisan Peoples*, Cambridge: Cambridge University Press.
13 Jiro Tanaka, Comment on E. Wilmsen and J. Denbow (1990) 'Paradigmatic History of San-Speaking Peoples and Current Attempts at Revision', *Current Anthropology* 31: 515-16 (p. 515).
14 Nurit Bird-David (1992) 'Beyond "The Original Affluent Society": A Culturalist Reformulation', *Current Anthropology* 33: 25-47.
15 Adam Kuper (1982) *Wives for Cattle: Bridewealth and Marriage in Southern Africa* (London: Routledge.
16 Adam Kuper (1986) 'Interview with Edmund Leach', *Current Anthropology* 27: 375-82 (p. 380).

3
Culture, Identity and the Project of a Cosmopolitan Anthropology

I

In the 1960s and 1970s we argued about theory. However, these were turbulent times, and the theoretical debates all had a political edge. The European empires had recently fallen apart, the Americans had picked up the sword of the French in Indochina, and many sane people thought that we were heading for nuclear catastrophe.

Among anthropologists certain truths were very generally accepted, except by the naive (the favoured epithet of the day), and, of course, the old and out-of-touch. World historical processes shaped local histories, the imperial factor was dominant (though disguised, perhaps, as multi-national companies took over from the colonial administrators). Structuralism and functionalism were equated with conservatism, their proponents suspected of indifference to the events in Vietnam. Social science should become at one with history (not, to be sure, the discipline of history, but the Hegelian movement of history). Too many old-style anthropologists had, if unwittingly, promoted colonial interests. Anthropologists who worked in any capacity in the Third World should rather serve revolutionary nationalist or socialist forces. Neutrality was the refuge of fools and scoundrels.

I exaggerate, but not very much. One of the questions put then with some seriousness – I cite it just to give the flavour of the time – was whether Lévi-Strauss was really, deep down, or at least implicitly, a Marxist. (Asked this question recently, Lévi-Strauss replied, 'Only a few lessons from Marx's teaching have stayed with me – above all, that consciousness lies to itself'.)[1] There was a slogan in those days, 'Structures do not go out in the streets'. This was regarded as a devastating critique of academic anthropology. A Marxisante evolutionism and a commitment to 'development' were thought to be at once morally preferable and intellectually more fruitful than the theories of anthropologists, blind to the course of history, tainted by their association with colonialism.

Then very suddenly – perhaps just as the last Americans were winched into helicopters hovering above the Saigon embassy – the New Left tide turned in the USA. In Europe, more and more people concluded that Marxism represented an unlikely source of freedom and progress. By the late 1970s, and increasingly in the 1980s, intellectual debate concerned itself less with a global politics of clashing empires than with a more personal politics, a politics of identity and representation. The ground contested in this new politics was often defined as 'culture'.

Within anthropology we found ourselves arguing about ethnography and the representation of cultures. Ethnography was bound up with the problems of identity, of the 'self' and the 'other'. 'These days', Renato Rosaldo announced in the very first sentence of his *Culture and Truth*, 'questions of culture seem to touch a nerve because they quite quickly become anguished questions of identity.' And this identity was at once personal, cultural and political. 'For me as a Chicano,' Rosaldo affirms, 'questions of culture emerge not only from my discipline, but also from a more personal politics of identity and community.'[2]

As much as ethnic identity, gender became a key to self-definition. The feminists, who became the most influential cultural activists within anthropology, insisted that the hitherto muted voices of women should be granted a privileged hearing, not only to promote a sort of ethnographic balance, redressing the wrongs of the past, but in order to introduce a fresh and vital perspective on other cultures. For some, feminist ethnography was at once a theoretical enterprise, a contribution to female emancipation, and an exercise in self-definition.

II

The recent debates have been dominated by American scholars, and it is necessary to make explicit something they take
for granted. The project of anthropology that is in dispute in
their work is the American project of cultural anthropology,
one quite distinct in the second half of the twentieth century
from the dominantly European project of social anthropology. Moreover, the political spirit that often informs it
has, again, a distinctively American character. This is very
evident in the rhetoric of Marcus and Fischer's *Anthropology
as Cultural Critique*, which was published in 1986.[3] Rosaldo
collapses into a single movement the Geertzian denial of
social theory and his advocacy of interpretative ethnography,
the New Left's adoption of a rainbow coalition of minority
causes, and the much-trumpeted 'experimental moment' in
ethnography (a moment that seems to have lasted a very long
time and produced only one kind of experiment).

We must contextualise these texts if we are to interpret
them. One approach would be to set them in the context
of a long-running debate about the nature of culture and
cultural history. Two contrasting perspectives recur, again
and again. One is sympathetic to the traditional Western
equation of 'culture' with 'high culture', high culture being
derived in an unbroken line from classical antiquity. This
orthodox idea was long confronted by a contrary perspective,
favoured by nationalist and also by socialist writers, who
argued that authentic culture was not cosmopolitan, not an
élite monopoly, but rather the achievement of the people
– whether Black Forest peasants or workers in Wigan Pier.
This authentic culture was a shield against the corruption
emanating from the mass media, and it could become a
resource in battles for political emancipation.

There was a comparable division among anthropologists.
For proponents of an evolutionary view, all human cultures
were more or less developed variants of a single type, one
in origin and in destiny. This view came naturally to the
classically educated generation of anthropologists, to men
like Robertson Smith and Frazer, for what it did, in effect, was

simply to extend back in time the Enlightenment account of intellectual progress, by which was meant the development of reason and of high culture. An alternative view derived from the German romantic tradition. This was always more relativist, and antagonistic to the notion of progress, and in due course to ideas of cultural evolution. Human populations were differentiated not according to the degree of cultural achievement they exhibited but by the election of distinct and incommensurate ways of being. Every people expressed through its culture a distinctive *Volksgeist.*

A critical discourse on culture developed in the ethnology of the Berlin school in the 1870s and 1880s, and it was diffused by Franz Boas to Columbia University at the turn of the century. Through his influence it became institutionalised in American cultural anthropology, the dominant school in twentieth century anthropology. The Boasian scholars identified 'culture' as a distinct historical agency, the cause of variation between populations, and the main determinant of consciousness, knowledge and understanding. In contradiction to the evolutionists, they insisted that cultural history did not follow any set course. A culture was formed by contacts, exchanges, population movements. Each culture was a historically and geographically specific accretion of traits. And if there was no necessary course of cultural development, cultures could not be rated as higher or lower. The Boasians favoured a relativist position. Values were culturally variable, and so there could be no objective evaluation of cultural traits.

Although a 'culture' was an accidental, historical growth, some of Boas's outstanding students (notably Kroeber, Sapir and Benedict) argued that it nevertheless constituted a complete way of life. Each culture had its particular configuration of values, to be grasped intuitively, guided by art and mythology. Moreover, this culture shaped the being of actors in particular communities. It created distinct modes of experiencing the world. A coherent, holistic culture shapes action by informing consciousness and, in the formulations of the culture and personality writers, by moulding personality.

In mid-century, leading cultural anthropologists were

drawn into broader enterprises in the social sciences. Some of the leading neo-Boasians, notably Kluckhohn, were associated particularly with Talcott Parsons, who created an interdisciplinary school that incorporated anthropology at the Social Relations department at Harvard. Parsonian social science had a significant philosophical rationale. As Darnell has noted, 'Pragmatic philosophy produced a new view of science in this period, stressing "multiple independent causation" in which causes at different levels of structure could not be reduced to one another.'[4] In the spirit of the time, Parsons endeavoured to define different structural levels at which human behaviour could be analysed. There was a hierarchy of what he called 'ontological' concepts: physical, biological, sociological and cultural. Each was to be treated in the first instance autonomously, by a distinct discipline. The cultural level was assigned to the anthropologists. (Parsons himself would eventually provide a grand synthesis.)

The two leaders of neo-Boasian cultural anthropology in the second half of the twentieth century – Clifford Geertz and David Schneider – began their careers with Parsons. They generated a cultural anthropology in which the Boasian project was recast within a Parsonian framework, becoming a more specialised operation. Geertz's famous, first collection of essays, *The Interpretation of Cultures*, set out the programme most fully. First, culture is one of several possible abstractions from the observation of human behaviour. Prefacing a long citation from Parsons' *The Social System* (New York: Free Press, 1951), he wrote: 'Culture is the fabric of meaning in terms of which human beings interpret their experience and guide their action; social structure is the form that action takes, the actually existing network of social relations. Culture and social structure are then but different abstractions from the same phenomena.'[5] And social structure should be left to the sociologists. Anthropologists were to concern themselves only with culture.

Moreover, the notion of culture was now refined, or, at least, redefined. It was a system of symbols, located in the mind of the actor. This conception was also derived from Parsons. ('Parsons, following not only Weber but a line of thought stretching back at least to Vico, has elaborated a concept of culture as a system of symbols by which man confers significance on his own experience.')[6] Here was a narrower, more mentalistic understanding of 'culture' than that of the Boasians, for whom 'culture' meant something closer to 'tradition'.

Particular programmes trading under the names of 'symbolic anthropology', 'the new ethnography' and Geertz's own 'thick description' were attempts to operationalise this view of culture. All were hostile, or at best indifferent, to sociological considerations. Schneider, in his *American Kinship: A Cultural Account*, which appeared in 1968, refused to consider social factors – class, divorce rates, regional variation – because he posited the existence of a universal symbolic system, which, like the American language, could be treated at one level at least without dragging in dialect, pragmatics, or sociolinguistics.[7]

Treated as a system of symbols, a culture had to be approached in a phenomenological spirit. The messages of a 'culture' had to be grasped and rendered, in Geertz's phrase. 'Doing ethnography is like trying to read (in the sense of "construct a reading of") a manuscript . . . written not in conventionalized graphs of sound but in transient examples of shaped behavior'. [8] The product of such a reading was an interpretation, not an explanation. The new cultural anthropology did not aspire to compare and explain. 'Believing, with Max Weber, that man is an animal suspended in webs of significance he himself has spun, I take culture to be these webs, and the analysis of it to be therefore not an experimental science in search of law, but an interpretive one in search of meaning. It is explication I am after. . . . '[9] This was a project in the hermeneutic tradition, and, indeed, Ricoeur was much cited by the interpretive anthropologists; but Geertz was also influenced by literary theorists of the day, notably Kenneth Burke.

The post-modernist movement in American anthropology is, in essence, a radical repositioning of this programme. Its founding statement, the symposium entitled *Writing Culture*,[10] takes off from Geertz. Geertz had argued that the anthropologist both reads and writes a text, he '"inscribes" social discourse; he writes it down. . . . 'What does the ethnographer do?' – he writes'.[11] What the contributors to *Writing Culture* argue – strongly influenced by Geertz, and reacting directly to him – is that this writing down does not constitute an authoritative interpretation, different in kind from the cultural text it pretends to 'inscribe'. Rather, it constitutes another cultural text, its author equally trapped in a web of significance that he or she has constructed but cannot escape. Instead of Kenneth Burke, the new generation – some of whom held joint appointments in departments of literature – favoured the critical literary theorists of the 1980s. Geertz's response, *Works and Lives: The Anthropologist as Author*, published in 1988, very largely accepts this reconstitution of his platform.[12]

III

It is not surprising that Europeans are sometimes confused as to what American anthropologists mean by post-modernism, and in particular by its political affinities. In France, where it all began, the deconstructionists and the post-modernists were on the whole antagonistic to the established left, and sometimes adopted a quietist political position. They rejected global narratives and prescriptive judgements 'in favour of recounting the *petits récits* of localizable collectivities'.[13] They preached only against preachers. Initially it seemed as though the post-modernist movement, as it gained ground, must therefore undermine the traditional political programmes of the left.

And, indeed, when a version of post-modernism became current in American anthropology, this appeared to be its effect. Some early post-modernist ethnographies seemed to herald a retreat to a world of privacy, to the examination of the self. The true purpose of ethnographic research in other cultures was really to gain self-knowledge. We learn about ourselves, Rabinow suggested, quoting Ricoeur in what seems to have been a rather unidiomatic translation, by way of a 'detour of the comprehension of the other'.[14] The first wave of post-modernist ethnographies was largely about the ethnographer's own experience of cultural dislocation, inspiring the joke (for which Marshall Sahlins claims authorship) in which the native pleads with the ethnographer, Can't we talk about *me* for a change!

For others – Clifford, for instance, or Taussig – cultural texts and performances were like works of art. In recreating and representing these acts, the ethnographer worked like a critic of literature or art. The rhetorical performances of actor and ethnographer became the subject-matter of anthropology. Ethnographies mattered not because they recorded what in more innocent days had been thought of as ethnographic data, but because they were themselves cultural acts. Ethnographers learnt, some to their surprise and delight, that they had not only been writing, but had indeed been writing poetry, or at least poetics, all along.

There could be no single true account of a cultural event or a social process. No objective summary was possible. The post-modernists preferred the image of a cacophony of voices, commenting upon each other and as they say, somewhat mysteriously, ironicising. The ethnographic object is multi-faceted, it can only be partially and fleetingly glimpsed from any one perspective, and cannot be analysed. The assertion of objectivity in traditional ethnography had been in reality a display, promoting a claim to authority, political as well as intellectual. The rhetorical performance of the ethnographer was a trick, an exercise in persuasion, and the critic's job was to unmask it.

Yet a paradoxical condition was attached to this new praxis. Though lacking independent authority, and without making claims to objective insight, there was a kind of truth to which the ethnographer was nevertheless obliged to bear witness: the natives had to be given their unedited say. This prescription was justified by a political argument against domination, and in favour of democratic expression. (Most explicitly, perhaps, in Marcus and Fischer's *Anthropology as Cultural Critique*.) The ethnographer therefore had the duty to bear witness for the natives, but without imposing an editorial voice. There was increasingly a vogue for ethnographies in which the ethnographer simply acts as a facilitator for a native autobiographer, or for oral histories. The ethnographer is a medium, translating and publishing texts (an enterprise which, interestingly enough, can be traced back to Boas).

This view of the ethnographer as a spokesperson – or medium – for the demos permitted some to reincorporate the post-modernist programme with a Marxist view, or, in other cases, a feminist programme (or indeed both) that had been inherited from the 1960s and 1970s. This line of argument feeds readily into a current political discourse that links identity, culture and politics. That is perhaps hardly surprising, since the tradition of thought can be traced directly to Herder and the *Volk* romanticism of the nineteenth century.

However, the ethnographer need not end up as a spokesman, or medium, only for a particular ethnic interest. Everywhere the oppressed share a common cause. While there is no objective truth, there is an Hegelian movement in history. The privileged lie and mislead, but the oppressed come gradually to appreciate their objective circumstances and formulate a new consciousness that will ultimately liberate them. It is the voices struggling to articulate a message of liberation that the ethnographer must strain to hear. The ethnographer should therefore convey the messages of progressive forces to sympathizers abroad. Rosaldo, for instance, advises us to pay particular attention to 'social criticism made from socially subordinate positions, where one can work more toward mobilizing resistance than persuading the powerful', and he cites approvingly as one example of what he has in mind 'Fanon's uncompromising rage'.[15]

It is tempting – though no doubt politically suspect – to suggest that the politically correct post-modernist ethnographer is an academic theorist for the rainbow coalition that Jesse Jackson was trying to build in American politics. This was precisely the moment that Marcus and Fischer were writing *Anthropology as Cultural Critique* and Rosaldo was preparing his *Culture and Truth*. The perhaps surprising elective affinity between post-modernism in American scholarship and political correctness is also abundantly illustrated in many recent ethnographies. There are difficulties, methodological complications. Lila Abu-Lughod has a sophisticated and sometimes anguished discussion of the problems of representation and advocacy in the introduction to her *Writing Women's Worlds: Bedouin Stories*.[16] Crapanzano, allowing white South Africans to speak in *Waiting*, is obliged to editorialise, lest their voices should be granted too much credence.[17] Feldman, whose *Formations of Violence* is based on interviews with republican activists in Northern Ireland, many of them engaged in terrorism, 'found that the cultural dynamics of secrecy, of editing, became the precondition for the interpersonal construction of meaning'.[18] Nevertheless, in the cacophony of voices, the best lines are always given to the oppressed.

IV

Something of a *bien-pensant* consensus clearly dominates current American anthropology. The intellectual contradictions within this consensus are nonetheless evident enough; and it also lays itself open to charges that are formulated in its own terms. If the focus is upon the experience of the ethnographer, the native may enquire why ethnography should serve as an exotic accompaniment to the psychotherapy of the Western self. The foreign ethnographer is, however, also at an evident disadvantage if the purpose of ethnography is to bear witness to the muted voices of the oppressed.

To be sure, a native protest against metropolitan ethnographers had been articulated long before post-modernism swept into anthropological discourse. African intellectuals – and others – were making a nationalist case against foreign ethnographers, and sometimes against ethnography altogether from the 1960s onwards. However, today the nativist ethnographer can and does deploy the rhetoric that became current in the 1970s and the 1980s.

To begin with, to be the subject of foreign, metropolitan, exoticising ethnography is equated with the experience of colonialism. Certainly, the two did often go together. Where the ethnographers were not, literally, from the former colonial country – as in Greece, for instance – nevertheless they are associated with the dominant 'West'. The thrust of Michael Herzfeld's *Anthropology Through the Looking Glass* is that Greece is in a sense the intellectual colony of every Western intellectual, which they mine not for copper, gold and precious stones but for fragments of sculptures, temples and lost inscriptions. Everywhere the dominant Westerners do the ethnography, marginalizing the natives, packaging their way of life for exploitation (if only in the economically rather unprofitable business of academic life).[19]

Moreover – and here the nativist borrows the rhetoric of the eighties – the foreign ethnographer, imprisoned in a culturally-constructed mind-set, cannot truly understand the native, master the inwardness of the native language. American intellectuals had been told for some time that white people could never appreciate what it meant to be black, that men could not understand women, and that only the ill or disabled could understand those similarly afflicted. Some believed it. Few argued publicly to the contrary. These American gospels penetrated anthropology, and some were led to the conclusion that only the native can understand the native, only the native has the right to study the native. Who needs a white American male to give a voice to an Inuit shaman, who elected some donnish European to speak for a Melanesian big-man?

The nativist can also appropriate the premise – mysteriously taken for granted in much of the recent literature – that the only reliable knowledge is self-knowledge. The native ethnographer can claim an intuitive understanding of the native. This may be taken to confer a natural and exclusive right to be the spokesperson of all natives. Some would go further, and argue not only that the native should speak for the native, but that the native ethnographer should address himself or herself not to the foreign scholar but to a native audience; and should, indeed, write up the ethnography in the native language. This would avoid the distorting compromises that result from translation into one of the colonizing, metropolitan languages; and, moreover, would protect the confidences of the family from prying eyes. (There is, though, another danger: that this mode of ethnography exposes the secrets of families and communities to their own neighbours.)

These debates have had consequences for access to the field. The seventies spawned a whole library of books about the ways in which anthropology inspired and legitimated colonialism. I am sceptical about some of these historical claims. Nevertheless, this radical critique of colonialist anthropology certainly did have an impact on post-colonial policy – if most particularly upon policies concerning anthropological research. Increasingly in the past three decades, anthropologists in many parts of the formerly colonial world were obliged to do research that would be useful: that would improve the economic development of particular groups. (They often did this research, though the impact on economic development was on the whole disappointing.) In the eighties, the requirement was commonly that this applied research should pay particular attention to women, who, it was argued, had been neglected by the earlier wave of development experts. Quite often it was an anthropologist – at times a foreign anthropologist – who actually applied these new guidelines that restricted ethnographic research, answering for native interests against the interests of their professional colleagues. In principle, however, the subjects of study were also now given a voice in deciding whether an ethnographer should be granted access; though who asked, and, indeed, who answered these questions (and precisely what question was put) was commonly specified only in the vaguest way.

V

The view that only natives should study natives is a logical step from the orthodoxies of the previous decades. It is the *reductio ad absurdum* of a whole movement of academic anthropology.

This premise has potentially dangerous implications for the practice of anthropology today. In the nineties, we will find ourselves increasingly preoccupied with ethnicity. We must beware lest the question of who we should study, who should make the study, and how it should be conducted is answered with reference to the ethnic identity of the investigator.

There is a precedent, in the neglected history of our discipline. This is the form of ethnography that European ethnologists once called *Volkskunde*, the romantic celebration of an ethnic identity by nationalist scholars. Disgraced for half a century in most centres of the discipline after its apotheosis in Nazi ethnology, *Volkskunde* nonetheless survived in parts of Eastern Europe, and it flourishes in some universities in contemporary Spain. It may be due for a more general revival.

When, very recently, a Greek association of social anthropologists was formed, the most emotive issue was 'whether foreign anthropologists working and writing on Greece could become regular members of the Association and also whether folklorists who were originally trained in Greece but studied ethnology or anthropology abroad could also become members.' [20] The decision was taken that only 'pure' Greeks might become members.

The reasons behind this decision are familiar enough: they could be duplicated in many other places. Gefou-Madianou gives a clear account of the sources of this nativism in Greek anthropology, which are ironically, but hardly surprisingly, the hegemonic discourse fashionable in American academia.

> Taking their cue from the seminal work of Said's *Orientalism*, and the post-modern reflexive anthropological discourse . . . they seek to create an anthropology at home. Pointing out western biases and generalizations they criticize western anthropological discourse on Greece for exoticizing and misrepresenting Greece and for 'concealing Greek self-knowledge' altogether. It is implicit in their writings that native Greek anthropologists have

greater reflexivity and ability to 'truly' understand Greek culture and indigenous categories.[21]

The nativist argument can become rather complicated, since it turns out that there are natives and natives. Although it is assumed to be given, primordial even, native identity is represented as liable to corruption, demanding an effort of self-realisation. The politics of culture require the discovery of the true, the authentic identity, and the study of culture becomes an act of personal politics. (By implication, an immigrant or convert cannot achieve an authentic identity through a process of assimilation.)

Kwame Anthony Appiah, who has brilliantly and crushingly reviewed the new Afrocentric discourse in America, tells a possibly too-good-to-be-true anecdote: 'I am reliably informed that, on one occasion not so long ago, a distinguished Zairian intellectual was told by an African-American interlocutor that "We do not need you educated Africans coming here to tell us about African culture"'. [22] The point is that one cannot trust every native. Only an authoritative native can say what is truly native: and authority is not necessarily bestowed by academic qualifications – on the contrary, these may be the stigmata of the sell-out. Others grant special authority to the avant-garde native, who understands what the native will think and feel tomorrow, whose role is to crystallise their emergent consciousness.

The nativist also usually insists that the native must be the proper judge of ethnography, even its censor. Citing a nativist Greek scholar, Gefou-Madianou reports that some Greek nativists have taken to 'reading excerpts from a westerner's ethnography to the local people studied "asking the people of the community to comment on both the quality of the foreign anthropologist's data as well as his interpretations"'.[23] Gefou-Madianou is critical, pointing out the value of a debate with involved, knowledgeable outsiders, with their particular perspectives. She argues for the power of foreign, international sociological models and theories in the interpretation of local social and cultural processes, even if these are unintelligible to many natives.

There have been other interesting critiques written by native ethnographers – and also by the 'halfies' (a term that Abu-Lughod and Narayan use of themselves)[24]. They have expressed reservations about the privileged insight ascribed to insiders, pointing out the difficulties that may confront the anthropologist working in his or her home country (though, almost always, among people to whom he or she is an élite outsider), and protesting against the chauvinistic rejection of foreign expertise. There is indeed an ironic counterpoint between these sophisticated 'native' reflections about the complexities of doing ethnography at home and the patronising self-denial preached by some metropolitan scholars.

There are foreign ethnographers who have been bold enough to make comparable arguments, and I share this sceptical view of nativist ethnography, with its nationalist – occasionally even racist – overtones. Yet I do not believe that it will be enough to criticise and situate these nativist anthropologies by way of ethnographic studies by outsiders (so long, indeed, as they are permitted to undertake them). What is required is a reconsideration of the whole project of which nativism is simply the culmination. We must ask fundamental questions about the nature of ethnography and its uses. We must remember that there are alternative definitions of our project available. What does the process of ethnographic work really involve? Is the ethnographer analysing and composing 'texts' that are on a par with literary texts? And who reads the ethnographies, and for what purpose?

VI

It has become a cliché of American cultural anthropology that culture is a text, and an ethnography a second-order text. However, the metaphor is too simple. Even if we limit ourselves to the elements of ethnography that are most text-like – the descriptions and exegeses of expert informants, recorded by ethnographers – it is apparent that

these are not generally treated by ethnographers in the way
that classicists or orientalists, for example, handle their texts;
and they are constituted in a very different fashion.

Boas systematically employed local experts who were bilin-
gual, literate, often bicultural and of mixed ancestry; most
notably George Hunt. They were under the control of Boas,
collecting information he might have collected. There is no
record that they helped him to interpret the material, but
then Boas deliberately did little by way of interpreting. The
ethnographer, he believed, should recover what Malinowski
was to call 'documents of native mentality', but these should
be presented in an undigested form, so that other scholars
and later generations could use them. Boas saw his business
as the creation of texts that would serve the same purpose
as the texts that formed the main resource of the classicists
and orientalists, which would be pored over and annotated
by generations of scholars.

At the other extreme from the austere Boasian is the
creative text-maker, exemplified powerfully by the French
Africanist Marcel Griaule, who virtually created together with
the remarkable Dogon seer Ogotemmeli a new cosmology.
Van Beek has subjected the Griaule-Ogotemmeli dialogue
to a thorough critique and has come to the conclusion that
the books that resulted were original works of creative art, in
which both interlocutors played a part. No Dogon would ever
replicate these cosmological ideas because they resulted from
the interaction between a highly individual Dogon mystic
and a European with a particular and time-bound agenda
of his own.[25]

Between these extremes there remain, of course, many
other possibilities. The neo-Malinowskian, Victor Turner,
for instance, collected texts from informants, but he also
prepared his own sources, based on direct observation,
participation, counting, measuring and the compilation of
censuses and genealogies. In Turner's view, the ethnographer assesses and compares informants, paying particular
but critical attention to experts (and carefully negotiating
the Ogotemmeli trap – the trap of the creative informant).
Texts are related always to contexts of performance. He

compares what is said to what is done, records patterns
of interaction, follows through micro social processes. He
then redeploys these very different sources of information,
confronting them with each other in a critical fashion. The
social process – which Turner constitutes from his own
observations – provides the context for the explication of the
texts. The conclusions he draws will therefore necessarily be
different from those drawn by any informant, and they serve
a different purpose. Turner's aim was to explain Ndembu
divination and symbolism to his colleagues. If an educated
person (including an educated Ndembu) wants, for whatever reason, a thorough, careful, sophisticated account of
Ndembu ritual behaviour as it was in the mid twentieth
century, he or she will read Turner. And Turner wrote for
precisely such scholarly readers.

It is the approach represented so brilliantly by Turner that
was dominant for a generation. The challenge of the post-
modernists is that Turner has no justification for his selection
of voices; or for his claim to be standing at some point
outside the system – above the system, perhaps. The nativist
advances a rather different objection. There *is* an authentic
native view, but it is inaccessible to the outsider. At its most
prized and most profound, this deep native understanding
is presented only in symbolic form, and is kept secret except
from the initiated (which, some Afrocentrists suggest, is why
Griaule's findings have not been duplicated by later ethnographers). Certainly Turner's confidence must seem today a
little overdone, aware as we are of the discrepancies between
accounts of similar situations given by able ethnographers.
A richer account of fieldwork practice, and in particular
of interactions between ethnographers and local experts, is
Gudeman and Rivera's *Conversations in Colombia.*[26]

Gudeman is an American, trained at Harvard and Cambridge. Rivera is a Colombian trained (partly by Gudeman
himself) at the University of Minnesota and professionally
employed as an anthropologist in Colombia. They worked
in the field as a partnership, travelling about together, interviewing peasant farmers about their economic arrangments
and the conceptions that underlie them. As the research

progressed, they discussed their findings. The fieldwork was increasingly accompanied by, interwoven with, a conversation between the two ethnographers. But as their understanding deepened, they found that they were not so much interviewing the farmers, as engaging them too in their conversations, soliciting critiques of their own ideas.

At some stage they began to recognise parallels between the largely implicit economic ideas of the farmers, which they were piecing together, and the theories of the French Physiocrats, pioneer economists of the 1760s and 1770s. It is possible that the Colombian farmers have been indirectly influenced by Physiocratic ideas, which were widely diffused in Europe. But they also suggest that the Physiocrats (like other classical schools of economic theory) were really crystallising contemporary European folk ideas about economics, ideas that would have been shared by Spanish peasant immigrants to Colombia. In short, the conversation – Gudeman and Rivera's image of the fieldwork process – stretches beyond the ethnographers to include their more articulate informants, and then further again, to encompass echoes of earlier conversations, elsewhere, which nevertheless (in different ways) feed the thinking both of the ethnographers and their peasant interlocutors.

This is a model of fieldwork more flexible and modest than that of Turner, in which local expertise is granted a position of greater equality, although the ethnographers (a local-foreign partnership) add something – an analytical, historical and comparative perspective - which no native expert could provide. They end with an analytical model that encompasses and analyses the variety of explicit and implicit folk models they encounter. Folk models serve as ways of thinking and as guides to action, but they do not address the comparative and more abstract project of the ethnographers.

I would add another level of conversation or debate to the Gudeman-Rivera model of ethnography. This is the intercourse between social scientists with local expertise. The ethnography – before and after publication – is subjected to critical, collegial examination by other ethnographers, and also by geographers, historians, economists and so on, themselves engaged in local research and equipped with overlapping and complementary expertise. This is a conversation that today decisively shapes ethnographic production, and, of course, it may often include both local scientists and a variety of foreigners, representing distinct intellectual traditions as well as different disciplinary backgrounds. There are, in consequence, increasingly rich and distinctive local debates into which every ethnographer is drawn.

At this level, a more sophisticated debate is possible between native and foreign *ethnographers*, and indeed between different traditions of ethnographic study. Pina-Cabral's critique of the anthropological treatment of the Mediterranean as a culture area is a good example. He accepts the widely diffused view that the 'Mediterranean culture area' was constituted very largely to meet the needs of Anglo-Saxon anthropological departments, but he notes that this point has also been made by foreign ethnographers who had written about the motives for the exoticizing of Mediterranean ways of life. Pina-Cabral agrees that:

> It is time . . . for a rethinking of the notion of the Mediterranean – one that sees anthropologists as strategists, wheeler-dealers, and manipulators of power like Italian, Greek, and Spanish peasants. In this case it is academic power that is in question, but one should not forget that this is also political, also has central economic importance for the participants, and, finally, is also clearly subject to patron-client relations.

But Pina-Cabral moves on from this by now conventional critique. 'I want to make it quite clear', he insists, 'that I do not consider this fact sufficient to deny the scientific validity of social anthropology. The subjection of scientific knowledge to constant critical and reflexive scrutiny is not to my mind an argument against its validity but the primary condition of its privileged status.'[27] Pina-Cabral's claim is that the process of critical mutual evaluation by specialists raises the quality of ethnography beyond that of other sorts of cultural reportage.

Such debates between regional specialists surely provide good tests of ethnographic research, and allow for the production of increasingly rich and sophisticated ethnographic accounts. The regional debates are, however, not without their own dangers. Local debates develop their own momentum, and may become partly insulated from broader disciplinary debates. One finds local traditions of research and argument, even where scholars from a variety of different backgrounds are involved.[28] A form of ethnographic provincialism may easily evolve. Does the conversation peter out as one crosses the boundaries between regional traditions of study?

VII

But ethnographers do not only converse, or only write. They read, and are read. The point of ethnography, and its methods, must therefore be understood also with reference to its users. Who buys it?

There are four possibilities. One – attributed to the most corrupted of ethnographers – is to write for curious foreigners, armchair voyeurs, who want only the safe pleasures of vicarious travel. A second is to write for the natives. This is a plausible enterprise in Greece or Spain, for instance, less so in many other places, perhaps. (There is only a very small indigenous market for Bushman ethnography.) I shall not criticise it further, but simply accept it as a possibility, though not one that excludes all others. A third option is to write for a locally-based though not exclusively native community of experts – social scientists, planners, intellectuals. This is not, of course, the same as writing for natives, and it is again a perfectly acceptable choice, though with obvious limitations. The final option, however, is the one that I want to emphasise. This is that ethnographers should write for anthropologists. We must in that case be prepared to go back to the seventies (at least), to a time when it was assumed that ethnographies had to fit somehow into broader theoretical and comparative projects.

This involves taking a further step along the path I have indicated. Ethnography is a conversation, as Gudeman and Rivera have shown, implicating ethnographers, informants, and the ancestral voices they invoke in their conversations. Regional debate is another element in the production and use of ethnographies, a debate between experts with first-hand knowledge, shared preoccupations and overlapping expertise. Anthropological debates draw in colleagues studying other regions, who invoke cases from a range of sites, reinterpreting them, mining them for information. And these debates address long-running questions about social and cultural processes in general, so ultimately contributing to the larger conversation of the human or social sciences. If social and cultural anthropology are to escape from the current impasse, we must generate debates that have a resonance beyond our immediate fields of ethnographic study, and avoid theoretical involution. Our contemporary concern with ethnicity, for example, should stimulate fresh thinking in political anthropology and kinship studies, but we seem to have succumbed instead to all the culturological talk about 'imagined communities', and to interest ourselves only in the ways in which ethnic identities are culturally constructed.

In short, I do not believe that we need to take our agenda from the inward-looking, self-referential writers who have captured the Boasian tradition in American anthropology. Our discussions need not be restricted to the interpretation of symbol systems, while we wait for Parsons to come back and put it all together again. The cultural anthropology of the neo-Boasians is a project in the humanities, its object the interpretation of cultural texts. Social anthropology is a social science, closely allied to sociology and social history. We must be clear as to what conversations we wish to enter. To the extent that the discourse of *social* anthropology can be reinvigorated, it will provide an alternative answer to the question: for whom is the ethnography written? We should once again address social scientists; and aspire to contribute a comparative dimension to the enlightenment project of a science of human variation in time and space. Our object

must be to confront the models current in the social sciencs
with the experiences and models of our subjects, while insisting that this should be a two-way process. This is, inevitably,
a cosmopolitan project, and one that cannot be bound in the
service of any political programme.

Notes

1 D. Eribon (1991) *Conversations with Lévi-Strauss*, Chicago: University of Chicago Press, p. 108.
2 Renato Rosaldo (1989) *Culture and Truth: The Remaking of
Social Analysis*, Boston: Beacon Press, pp. ix and xi.
3 G. Marcus and M. Fischer (1986) *Anthropology as Cultural
Critique*, Chicago: University of Chicago Press.
4 Regna Darnell (1990) *Edward Sapir: Linguist, Anthropologist,
Humanist*, Berkeley: University of California Press, p. 383.
5 Clifford Geertz (1973) *The Interpretation of Cultures*, New York:
Basic Books, p. 145.
6 Loc.cit., p. 250.
7 David Schneider (1968) *American Kinship: A Cultural Account*,
Englewood Cliffs: Prentice-Hall.
8 Loc. cit., p. 10.
9 Loc.cit., p. 5.
10 J. Clifford and G. Marcus (eds) (1986) *Writing Culture*, Berkeley:
University of California Press.
11 Loc. cit., p. 19.
12 Clifford Geertz (1988) *Works and Lives: The Anthropologist as
Author*, Stanford: Stanford University Press.
13 D. Ingram (1992) 'The Postmodern Kantianism of Arendt
and Lyotard' in A. Benjamin (ed.) *Judging Leotard*, London:
Routledge, p. 139.
14 Paul Rabinow (1977) *Reflections on Fieldwork in Morocco*,
Berkeley: University of California Press, p. 5.
15 Rosaldo, *Culture and Truth*, p. 195.
16 L. Abu-Lughod (1993) *Writing Women's Worlds: Bedouin Stories*,
Berkeley: University of California Press.
17 V. Crapanzano (1985) *Waiting: The Whites of South Africa*, New
York: Random House.
18 A. Feldman (1991) *Formations of Violence: The Narrative of the
Body and Political Terror in Northern Ireland*, Chicago: University
of Chicago Press, p. 12.

19   M. Herzfeld (1987) *Anthropology Through the Looking-Glass: Critical Ethnography in the Margins of Europe*, Cambridge: Cambridge University Press.

20   Dimitra Gefou-Madianou (1993) 'Mirroring Ourselves Through Western Texts: The Limits of an Indigenous Anthropology' in H. Driessen (ed.) *The Politics of Ethnographic Reading and Writing: Confrontations of Western and Indigenous Views*, The Netherlands: Breitenbach, p. 172 note 7.

21   Loc. cit. pp. 172-3.

22   K.A. Appiah (1993) 'Europe Upside Down: Fallacies of the New Afrocentricism', *Times Literary Supplement*, 12 February.

23   Gefou-Madianou, loc. cit., p. 173.

24   L. Abu-Lughod (1991) 'Writing Against Culture' in R.G. Fox (ed.) *Recapturing Anthropology*, Santa Fe, New Mexico: School of American Research Press; K. Narayan (1993) 'How Native is a "Native" Anthropologist?', *American Anthropologist*, 95: 671-86.

25   W.E.A. van Beek (1991) 'Dogon Restudied: A Field Evaluation of the Work of Marcel Griaule', *Current Anthropology* 32: 139-67.

26   S. Gudeman and A. Rivera (1990) *Conversatons in Colombia: The Domestic Economy in Life and Text*, Cambridge: Cambridge University Press.

27   J. Pina-Cabral (1989) 'The Mediterranean as a Category of Regional Comparison: A Critical View', *Current Anthropology* 30: 399-406 (p. 400).

28   See Richard Fardon (ed.) (1990) *Localizing Strategies: Regional Traditions of Ethnographic Writing*, Edinburgh: University of Edinburgh Press.

4
Darwin and the Anthropologists

'Origin of man now proved. – Metaphysic must flourish. – He who understands baboon would do more towards metaphysic than Locke.'[1] Darwin wrote that famous note in 1838. In the event, however, metaphysics continued to flourish without reference to primatology. More surprisingly, even the scientific anthropology that emerged in the 1860s was not entirely Darwinian in its orientation.

In the two decades following the publication of *The Origin of Species* in 1859, a series of monographs appeared that dealt in a fresh and urgent manner with primitive society, the evolution of marriage and the family, and the rise of magic, religion and science. The authors of these books (who included Maine, Fustel de Coulanges, Lubbock, McLennan, Morgan and Tylor) quickly developed a coherent new discourse. Referring to each other's work, and despite differences on many issues that seemed to them to be of critical importance, they generally agreed upon a crucial organizing premise: that a direct progression could be established from primitive society through various intermediate stages to modern society.

When anthropology became established in universities in the twentieth century, and histories of the discipline began to be written, these pioneer anthropologists were conventionally grouped together as 'evolutionists'. In 1966, however, J. W. Burrow protested in his *Evolution and Society* against the ritual invocation of Darwin's name to explain the emergence of a new anthropology in the second half of the century. 'Darwin was undoubtedly important', he concluded, 'but it is a type of importance impossible to estimate at all precisely. He was certainly not the father of evolutionary anthropology, but possibly he was its wealthy uncle.'[2] By profession, the pioneer anthropologists were lawyers, classicists and theologians. It is therefore not altogether surprising that they were more susceptible to the influence of historians and philosophers than to that of natural scientists. But Burrow also showed that in so far as they did take account of scientific advances, they were more impressed by the lessons of uniformitarian geology and comparative philology than by evolutionary biology.

Reacting, in part, to Burrow, George Stocking in his *Victorian Anthropology* emphasised the ways in which the Darwinian revolution obliged intellectuals to reconsider the place of human beings in nature and in time. The myth of divine election was challenged by a natural history of the human species. Yet the new ideas about human origins did not necessarily undermine the established rationalist ideas about cultural progress. 'Indeed, in a sense it might even be said that while Darwinism gave man a new place in nature, classical sociocultural evolutionism reasserted a traditional one; for if in origin man was part of nature, and controlled by it, the progress of civilization removed him from nature and won him control over it.'[3] Moreover, this older tradition offered a welcome alternative to the disturbing Darwinian view that the course of change might have no obvious direction, that natural selection was the law of higgledy piggledy. As Bowler remarks, 'there is little evidence that [Darwin] was able to disturb his contemporaries' faith in teleology'.[4]

To be sure, a wealthy uncle is not to be despised, and Darwin was a major influence on the nascent anthropology. However, Darwinian theory offered a number of distinct leads, and it was possible to pick and choose among them. Furthermore, some of the most important Darwinian principles had only doubtful relevance to social and cultural history. Burrow identified 'three specific implications of Darwinian theory which were relevant to evolutionary anthropology':

The first was that man, by his kinship with animals, is part of nature, not outside it. . . . Secondly, Darwinism seemed to justify social theorists in accounting for racial differences in terms of environmental differences over a long period, rather than regarding them as ultimate and unaccountable data. . . . Finally, there is the question of natural selection. . . .[5]

The first principle, common descent, was generally accepted by British biologists and anthropologists, at least after 1871. Its acceptance raised the question of how (by what uniform processes) human civilization had developed from a common primate starting-point. But the acceptance of common descent did not explain these processes of development. Secondly, even if monogenesis was accepted some anthropologists were inclined to the view that racial differences had evolved over a long period, and that the races had become highly differentiated. There was much disagreement on that question even in Darwin's inner circle, and Darwin himself became more favourable to racialist views. Finally, Darwin's theory of natural selection was much disputed by biologists, even Huxley remaining a sceptic. The anthropologists found it of little interest. 'Neither Maine, nor Tylor, nor McLennan made much use of the theory of natural selection and Spencer used it only as a garnish for a theory he had already developed', according to Burrow.[6]

Lubbock, Darwin's country neighbour, and Galton, Darwin's cousin, were among the orthodox Darwinians in the human sciences. Lubbock's main contribution was to introduce and adapt Scandinavian models of archaeological 'stages' into the argument on historical development. Galton's central concern was the selection of intelligence – 'genius' – and its role in competition between 'races'. Other leading figures in the emerging community of anthropologists were more remote from Darwinian preoccupations. Maine came late and briefly to Darwin, in the 1880s, invoking Darwin's critique (in the second edition of *The Descent of Man*) of his old rivals, McLennan and Morgan. However, his writings were firmly in the Germanic tradition of philology and legal history, and he was hostile to the emerging consensus (represented especially by Lubbock and Tylor) that all human populations passed through the same stages of historical development. Perhaps no anthropologist of his generation was less touched by Darwinian theory.

Even the self-confessed Darwinians among the anthropologists treated Darwinian theory as an *à la carte* menu. McLennan's vision of primitive foragers engaged in a perpetual gang-war had obvious affinities with a Darwinian approach, yet as late as 1876 he felt he could afford to ignore Darwin's views on mating. His writings on primitive marriage by capture and female infanticide reflect rather the direct influence of Malthusian thinking.[7] In his biography of E. B. Tylor (the father-figure of British anthropology) whom he knew well, Marett insisted that while Tylor was an orthodox Darwinian 'whenever he has to pronounce on the physical problems relating to human descent', his Darwinism did not otherwise run deep:

> Though he occasionally used . . . the rather high-sounding phrase 'evolution' which Darwin had taken over from Herbert Spencer, perhaps without paying much heed to its philosophical implications, Tylor decidedly prefers to speak simply of the 'development' of culture. Probably he realizes, though subconsciously, that the growth of culture is a distinct, if analogous, process as compared with that involved in biological evolution in the sense of such race-propagation as makes for an increasing complexity.[8]

Robertson Smith and Frazer were also apparently indifferent to Darwinian ideas. A recent, authoritative biography of Frazer includes only three glancing references to Darwin in the index. In his textbook *Anthropology*, written in 1911, Marett insisted that 'Anthropology is the child of Darwin', but like Tylor he emphasised the theory of common descent and had next to nothing to say about natural selection. 'What is the truth that Darwinism supposes? Simply that all the forms of life in the world are related together; and that the relations manifested in time and space between the different lives are sufficiently uniform to be described under a general formula, or law of evolution.'[9] Marett's Cambridge counterpart, Alfred Haddon, who began his career as a biologist, made just two brief references to Darwin in his *History of*

Anthropology (London: Watts and Co., 1934), and, like Marett, he concluded that Darwin's main contribution had been to establish the natural origin of the human species. For Tylor, Frazer and Marett, the essential message of evolution was in practice virtually identical to the familiar Whig principle that progress was inevitable.

Burrow was surely right: the direct influence of Darwinian theory on the theoretical thinking of the first two generations of anthropologists was diffuse and often superficial. And there was good reason for this. Formidable difficulties confronted an aspiring Darwinian historian of social and cultural institutions. This is apparent if one considers Darwin's own interventions in the debates of the social and cultural evolutionists – an aspect of his intellectual history that has been relatively neglected. I shall therefore consider three episodes in the development of Darwin's anthropology: his ethnography of the Fuegians; his views on race, selection, and mental progress, as they developed during the Years of the American Civil War, and in the local context of an institutional split in the anthropological community; and his intervention in the debate about primitive marriage. The exercise will help to make clear why Darwin's ideas did not revolutionise the understanding of social and cultural history, for even Darwin found that he could be a Darwinian only intermittently when he reflected on the course of human history.

II

Darwin's commander on the *Beagle*, Robert FitzRoy, had encountered the Fuegians on an earlier voyage (1826-30). Bothered by thieving, he took hostages, but this strategy back-fired. The miscreants kept his goods, and he was left with three Fuegians on his hands. A fourth was purchased for a pearl button and named Jeremy (Jemmy) Button. FitzRoy decided to take the Fuegians back to England with him, where they would be exposed to civilization and Christianity. One of the party (Fitzroy's favourite) died from smallpox, but under the guidance of the rector of Walthamstow the survivors were instructed in the Christian religion and in English language and customs. (The young woman in the party, Fuegia Basket, also picked up some Spanish and Portuguese on voyage.) They were presented by FitzRoy to the King and Queen. A fund was launched to finance missionary activity among the Fuegians, and a missionary joined the *Beagle's* second voyage, during which the three Fuegians would be returned to their homes.

Darwin's first direct encounter with what he called 'untamed savage' Fuegians came on the morning of December 1832, and as he remarked in his diary and in letters home, it impressed him profoundly. Writing to his sister Caroline from the *Beagle* in 1835, Darwin listed 'the three most interesting spectacles I have beheld since leaving England – a Fuegian savage. – Tropical Vegetation – & the ruins of Concepcion'.[10] When he returned to the islands a year later he wrote: 'Viewing such men, one can hardly make oneself believe that they are fellow creatures placed in the same world'.[11] Fuegian homes were rudimentary; they slept 'on the wet ground, coiled up like animals'; their food was miserable and scarce; they were at war with their neighbours over means of subsistence. 'Captain FitzRoy could never ascertain that the Fuegians have any distinct belief in a future life.' Their feelings for home and hearth were stunted. Their imaginations were not stimulated, their skills 'like the instinct of animals' were not 'improved by experience.'[12] 'Although essentially the same creature, how little must the mind of one of these beings resemble that of an educated man.' And yet: 'There can be no reason for supposing the race of Fuegians are decreasing, we may therefore be sure that he enjoys a sufficient share of happiness (whatever its kind may be) to render life worth having. Nature, by making habit omnipotent, has fitted the Fuegian to the climate and productions of his country.'[13]

There was little to distinguish Darwin's reflections from those of Captain FitzRoy, a more representative, if anything a rather conservative man of his time. To be sure, there were signs of Cambridge deism, and of the liberalism of the Darwins. The evocation of Nature's purpose is consistent with Paley's deism, in which Darwin had steeped himself while at Cambridge. His curious harping on the question of happiness must be a response to Utilitarian discourse. But FitzRoy, for example, was willing to consider the Fuegians as the equivalent of the ancient Britons:

> Disagreeable, indeed painful, as is even the mental con-templation of a savage, and unwilling as we may be to consider ourselves even remotely descended from human beings in such a state, the reflection that Caesar found the Britons painted and clothed in skins, like these Fuegians, cannot fail to augment an interest excited by their childish ignorance of matters familiar to civilized man, and by their healthy, independent state of existence.[14]

This anticipates Darwin's most famous reflection on the Fuegians: 'The astonishment which I felt on first seeing a party of Fuegians on a wild and broken shore will never be forgotten by me, for the reflection at once rushed into my mind – such were our ancestors.'[15]

Darwin and FitzRoy also agreed that while savages were very different indeed from Victorian Englishmen, they were capable of rapid improvement. FitzRoy's party of Fuegians had quickly absorbed English culture. When the Fuegians were set ashore with the missionary, Matthews, in February 1833, Darwin reflected that 'in contradiction of what has often been stated, 3 years has been sufficient to change savages into, as far as habits go, complete & voluntary Euro-peans'.[16] Indeed, Darwin worried rather that the Fuegians in the *Beagle* party would not be able to adapt again to their former way of life, and he was pleasantly surprised by what transpired. When, in March 1834, the *Beagle* returned to the Fuegian camp, Fitzroy found Jemmy Button much thinner, but he assured the captain that he was 'hearty, sir, never better', and that he was contented and had no desire to alter his present way of life. And it seemed that civilization was catching. It was generally agreed, the captain noted, that Jemmy's family 'were become considerably more humanized than any savages we had seen in Tierra del Fuego'. Perhaps one day a shipwrecked seaman might be saved by Jemmy's

children 'prompted, as they can hardly fail to be, by the
traditions they will have heard of men of other lands; and
by an idea, however faint of their duty to God as well as their
neighbour'.[17] Equally, it seemed that a civilized person could
also revert happily to a state of savagery. Darwin himself
wrote in his diary, noting the farewell signal fire that Jemmy
lit as they sailed away, 'I hope & have little doubt he will be
as happy as if he had never left his country; which is much
more than I formerly thought.'[18]

Darwin and FitzRoy were agreed that the Fuegians stood
low on the scale of civilization – on the lowest rung, Darwin
believed. Nevertheless, there was no intrinsic reason why
individual Fuegians should not very quickly be 'civilized'.
'These Indians appear to have a facility for learning languages' Darwin noted, 'which will greatly contribute to
civilization or demoralization: as these two steps seem to
go hand in hand.'[19] Lack of intelligence did not seem to
be the explanation for their apparent backwardness:

> Although the Australian may be superior in acquirements
> [to the Fuegian], it by no means follows that he is likewise
> superior in mental capacity: indeed, from what I saw of
> the Fuegians when on board, and from what I have read
> of the Australians, I should think the case was exactly the
> reverse.[20]

It is remarkable that the one speculation Darwin made on
the cause of the backwardness of these people was purely
sociological in nature. The Fuegians bartered freely and
shared everything – 'even a piece of cloth given to one
is torn into shreds and distributed; and no one individual
becomes richer than another'.[21] This insistence on exchange
(which so tormented their English visitors) was based on the
assumption of equality. And it was precisely this equality that
held them back, in Darwin's view.

> The perfect equality among the individuals composing the
> Fuegian tribes, must for a long time retard their civiliza-
> tion. As we see those animals, whose instinct compels them

to live in society and obey a chief, are most capable of
improvement, so is it with the races of mankind . . .
On the other hand, it is difficult to understand how a
chief can arise till there is property of some sort by
which he might manifest his superiority and increase his
power.[22]

Conversely, Darwin attributed the relative sophistication of
the Tahitians to their hierarchical social order.

It is clear that Darwin's account of the 'untamed savages'
took for granted current ideas about human development,
which he conceived as the consequence of reasoned choices,
expressed institutionally in civil order and private property.
All humans possess reason, and the development of this
faculty depends on the stimulus provided by the environment, on exposure to sources of enlightenment, and upon
the existence of an ordered social hierarchy.

III

The theme that pervades Darwin's 'Notebook on Man',
which he opened in 1838, is that all mental activities are
reducible to states of the brain. Even love of the deity
was a function of the organization of the brain – 'oh,
you Materialist!'[23] The evolution from apes to humans was
itself a result of the growth of the brain. Huxley contributed
a special note that was published as an appendix to chapter
7 of the second edition of *The Descent of Man* in which he
compared the brain of humans and those of other primates, and established their structural similarity. The main
difference was one of size and, presumably, complexity. 'As
the various mental faculties gradually developed the brain
would almost certainly become larger', Darwin concluded.
'No one, I presume, doubts that the large proportion which
the size of man's brain bears to his body, compared to the
same proportion in the gorilla or orang, is closely connected
with his higher mental powers.'[24]

The specialization of the brain was a consequence of

natural selection, but Darwin allowed for a feedback between nature and culture. The individuals best suited to use language and tools would be those with the most active brains, and their cultural success would bring them gains in the procreative stakes.

> We can see, that in the rudest state of society, the individuals who were the most sagacious, who invented and used the best weapons or traps, and who were best able to defend themselves, would rear the greatest number of offspring. The tribes, which included the largest number of men thus endowed, would increase in number and supplant other tribes.

Like intelligence, the moral and social qualities (which Darwin reckoned of greater importance than the purely intellectual) were to be found among other animals. Their high development among human beings was the result of natural selection 'aided by inherited habit'. Populations in which these qualities were most developed would be successful in competition with their rivals. 'Thus the social and moral qualities would tend slowly to advance and be diffused throughout the world.[25]

It has often been remarked that the conception of natural selection shifts subtly but significantly in this argument. The classical Darwinian view is that natural selection operates on individuals. Each individual has unique features, and these features may help it or handicap it in competition with other individuals, of their own species and of other species. The better adapted are relatively more successful in terms of procreation. Consequently their particular features spread in the population. This held true, Darwin thought, so long as civilization remained undeveloped.

> Savages are known to suffer severely from recurrent famines; they do not increase their food by artificial means; they rarely refrain from marriage, and generally marry whilst young. Consequently they must be subjected to occasional hard struggles for existence, and the favoured individuals will alone survive.[26]

However, when writing about more civilized human populations, and sometimes more generally about other gregarious species, Darwin allowed an element of group selection. When treating what he termed the 'moral qualities' which distinguish human beings, he argued that their yield was social rather than individual. Being a good citizen might have a high cost for the individual, but it benefits the community.

> It must not be forgotten that although a high standard of morality gives but a slight or no advantage to each individual man and his children over the other men of the same tribe, yet that an increase in the number of well-endowed men and an advancement in the standard of morality will certainly give an immense advantage to one tribe over another. A tribe including many members who, from possessing in a high degree the spirit of patriotism, fidelity, obedience, courage, and sympathy, were always ready to aid one another, and to sacrifice themselves for the common good, would be victorious over most other tribes: and this would be natural selection.[27]

In this argument, it is the tribe that adapts, as a community, rather than the tribespeople as individuals. Societies, perhaps even 'races', compete, sometimes to the death.

Why did Darwin flirt with group selection? Most obviously, it suggested one answer to the puzzle as to how selfless and risky modes of behaviour were transmitted to later generations. A community benefited if moral individuals 'sacrifice themselves for the common good'. But why should individuals put community interest before their own, and how was a tendency to such self-destructive behaviour passed on to the next generations? Darwin argued that the community rewarded people for behaving in ways that served the public interest. Apparently selfless conduct had its selfish rewards, although Darwin did not suggest that these included procreative success.

Acceptance of the principle of group selection – at least for civilized human populations – shifted the emphasis from the evolution of the brain itself to the effects of education:

from nature to nurture. Moreover, as societies became more civilized, so they were better able to inculcate moral, unselfish values through education. 'The more efficient causes of progress seem to consist of a good education during youth whilst the brain is impressible, and of a high standard of excellence, inculcated by the ablest and best men, embodied in the laws, customs and traditions of the nation, and enforced by public opinion.'[28] But if technological inventions, social institutions, values, education were decisive in human evolution, this implied a lesser role for biological adaptations. Darwin approvingly cited Wallace's views on this question:

> Mr Wallace . . . argues that man, after he had partially acquired those intellectual and moral faculties which distinguish him from the lower animals, would have been but little liable to bodily modifications through natural selection or any other means . . . He invents weapons, tools, and various stratagems to procure food and to defend himself. When he migrates into a colder climate he uses clothes, builds sheds, and makes fires; and by the aid of fire cooks food otherwise indigestible. He aids his fellow-men in many ways, and anticipates future events. Even at a remote time period he practised some division of labour.[29]

Cultural developments might even work against natural selection. As human beings became essentially a domesticated species they would shield their weaker relatives from the effects of natural selection. This could bring about a deterioration of the stock, particularly since, Darwin complained, men chose their wives on frivolous grounds. In any case, the thrust of the argument was clear. After the initial phase of human evolution, any advantage that one population enjoyed over another was by and large the consequence of what we would now call cultural factors. And as natural selection, classically conceived, became less decisive, so group selection assumed increasing importance.

Darwin sometimes rhetorically set 'races' in competition

with one another, although he did not necessarily suppose that this competition would be settled by the biological qualities of each race. There was, however, room in this conception of human history for a more forthright racism. Darwin himself came to argue that brain capacity varied between racial groups. Yet he wavered on the question of race. It was one of the most sensitive political issues of the 1860s, and the debate on the unity of the human species split the nascent anthropological community. The members of the Anthropological Society largely supported the race-determinism of Knox, propagated by their leader, the Tory pro-slavery publicist John Hunt. The Darwinians allied themselves with the rival Ethnological Society, dominated by Whigs and faithful to its roots in the Aborigines Protection Society. The central issue that divided the parties was that of the single or multiple origin of human beings. The Ethnologicals, for Darwinian reasons or, in some cases, theological reasons, favoured monogenesis, but even some who believed in the single origin of the human species nevertheless argued that racial differences were very ancient, and that they implied differences in mentality and behaviour. Perhaps a majority of Darwin's contemporaries conceived of competition in terms of a struggle between races, and assumed that racial differences (particularly differences in the capacity of the brain, which were supposedly signalled by differences in skull shape) explained differential cultural development.

In his long and balanced chapter on the question of race in *The Descent of Man*, Darwin argued that racial differences were not caused by environmental pressures and natural selection. Rather, they were the consequences of sexual selection. There was no apparent survival value in being bearded rather than beardless, red-haired rather than blond, thick-lipped rather than thin-lipped. These variations – which in the long run produced 'racial' differences – were produced by local aesthetic preferences that guided men and women in choosing their mates. Some of his colleagues rejected this argument. Wallace, who might have claimed priority in the statement of the theory of natural selection, was dismissive:

everything Darwin attributed to sexual selection was better explained in terms of natural selection. In any case, at this stage Darwin took the view that there were no substantial intellectual differences between the races.

> The American aborigines, Negroes and Europeans are as different from each other in mind as any three races that can be named; yet I was incessantly struck, whilst living with the Fuegians on board the 'Beagle', with the many little traits of character, showing how similar their minds were to ours; and so it was with a full-blooded negro with whom I happened once to be intimate.

Ethnography suggested the same conclusion. 'He who will read Mr Tylor's and Sir J. Lubbock's interesting works can hardly fail to be deeply impressed with the close similarity between the men of all races in tastes, dispositions and habits.'[30]

To sum up, while Darwin's theory of the origins of human beings was revolutionary, his writings on human evolution did not challenge the well-established ideas current among social and cultural evolutionists. Far from unequivocally 'naturalizing' reason and history, he sometimes endorsed the traditional dichotomy between biological forces and moral, intellectual, what we might call cultural forces. The cultures of the different 'races' might represent stages in a single process of evolutionary advance from magic through religion to science, from promiscuity to monogamy, from stone tools to factories.

IV

Darwinian theory focussed attention on reproduction. Nevertheless, Darwin had very little impact on the great debate among anthropologists on the original forms of human marriage. This first great anthropological controversy was initiated by the publication of Henry Maine's *Ancient Law* in 1861 (London: John Murray) (two years after *The Origin of Species*) and reached a climax with the publication of Lewis Henry Morgan's *Systems of Consanguinity and Affinity of the Human Family* in 1871 (Washington, DC: Smithsonian Institute), the year in thich *The Descent of Man* appeared. Yet although the subject of the debate was marriage, this was not for Darwinian reasons. The protagonists had nothing to say about heredity or sexual selection, and seldom referred back to primate analogies. Lawyers rather than natural scientists, they were concerned with the origins of moral principles and social institutions.

In *Ancient Law,* Maine began with the conventional idea that the original human institution was the patriarchal family (as described in the Old Testament and by Homer). He represented this aboriginal political system as a primitive tyranny, in which all power lay with the father. According to Rousseau, our natural condition was one of freedom and equality. This heritage had been betrayed by our rulers. Maine insisted that on the contrary we were born in chains and had been freed through the development of law, private property and the state. The various Indo-European speaking peoples had all originally been subject of patriarchal despotism, but some had advanced beyond the rest, and introduced individual liberties, private property, and the right to enter into contracts.

A radical Scottish lawyer, J. F. McLennan, set out to counter what he regarded as a conservative myth of origin. His main strategy was to deny that the original human institution was the patriarchal family. On the contrary, human beings would have lived at first like animals, mating promiscuously. The small wandering bands of hunters were in competition with each other (as Darwin and Spencer insisted). In order to fight more effectively, some groups would jettison their women-folk. They might even practise female infanticide (as Malthus had speculated). When they needed women, they would capture them from their enemies. Given these conditions, nobody could know who his father was. In consequence, only the tie between a child and its mother was recognised. Only after great technological changes led to the development of private property did men began to claim a monopoly of sexual access to their wives, and to establish relationships with their sons, who would inherit from them.

McLennan's ingenious thesis was illustrated with a striking variety of ethnographic instances, in the style of the Scottish speculative historians. But what counted as evidence? McLennan argued that modern savages tended still to be promiscuous and to trace descent in the female line, but he had to concede that there were probably no peoples who now lived the rugged woman-stealing, child-killing lives of the original warrior bands. However, he argued that the memory of these practices was preserved in the rituals and ceremonies of contemporary 'savages'. If a bride ritually protested against being moved from her parent's home, for example, this was a throwback to the institution of marriage by capture.

McLennan did not cite Darwin as his inspiration, but his thesis might have appealed to Darwinians since it stressed competition and mating. They would also have appreciated the parallel he drew between morphological and cultural fossils. However, an American anthropologist, Lewis Henry Morgan, who was more directly influenced by Darwin, attacked McLennan's thesis precisely on methodological grounds. Morgan agreed that ancient institutions were preserved in fossilised practices, but these were to be found not in ceremonies but in linguistic usages. Kinship terms especially preserved the outlines of ancient forms of family organization. And applying this approach, Morgan reached very different conclusions to those of McLennan. All primitive social systems were based on collective marriages, first between a group of brothers and their own sisters, later, as morality advanced, between a group of brothers and a set of women to whom they were not related. Finally, with the introduction of private property, human beings progressed to monogamy.

Competition played no part in Morgan's argument, but when Tylor (the dean of English anthropology) reviewed the debate between McLennan and Morgan he invoked competition to explain the evolution of marriage forms. 'Again and again in the world's history, savage tribes must have had plainly before their minds the simple practical alternative between marrying-out and being killed out.'[31] However, he rejected McLennan's thesis that primitive mating was dependent on the capture of foreign women. According to Tylor, peaceful exchanges of women between groups provided the normal basis for alliances. But if marriage alliances were instituted for diplomatic reasons, the further evolution of marriage occurred as the consequence of moral advances, and the development of private property.

Darwin's friend and neighbour, Lubbock, took an interest in this debate, but his main concern was to endorse the view that the first human populations had lived promiscuously.[32] In the second edition of *The Descent of Man* Darwin himself at last reviewed the debate. The context was his discussion of the relative effect of sexual selection and natural selection on early or primitive human populations. Among 'the causes which prevent or check the action of sexual selection with savages' he listed 'so-called communal marriages or promiscuous intercourse; secondly, the consequences of female infanticide; thirdly, early betrothals; and lastly, the low estimation in which women are held, as mere slaves'.[33] To the extent that promiscuity was general, the effect of sexual selection would be reduced, but Darwin doubted that something very near promiscuity did reign originally in human communities. Sir Andrew Smith, a respected scientist who had written about the native peoples of Southern Africa, 'expressed to me the strongest opinion that no race exists in which woman is considered as the property of the community'.[34] Among other animals, including the apes, adult males were extremely jealous, and the strongest males tended to accumulate mates, whom they monopolised. Darwin concluded that it was therefore unlikely that early human males tolerated free access to their women.

At a very early period [Darwin concluded], before man attained to his present rank in the scale, many of his conditions would be different from what now obtains amongst savages. Judging from the analogy of the lower animals, he would then either live with a single female, or be a polygamist. The most powerful and able males would succeed best in obtaining attractive females. They would also succeed best in the general struggle for life, and in defending their females, as well as their offspring, from enemies of all kinds.[35]

Anything that Darwin had to say was taken seriously by the loose community of anthropologists in the last three decades of the nineteenth century, but even on the crucial question of human mating his theory offered little direct illumination. Darwin's most important contribution to the debate on primitive marriage was to suggest that primate forms of mating might have been carried over to the earliest forms of human marriage, and that therefore the first humans would not have been promiscuous. The one pioneer anthropologist to develop this speculation was the Finnish scholar Edward Westermarck, whose *The History of Human Marriage* was published only in 1891, although Freud was later to seize upon Darwin's image of young males in gorilla bands being driven off by the father-leader when they reached maturity, an arrangement that limited inbreeding but might, Freud speculated, provoke resentment and rebellious plans to kill and supplant the father.[36]

* * *

The founding generation of British anthropologists and ethnologists established itself just at the moment when Darwinism became a major intellectual force in Britain, and yet the influence of Darwinism on their thinking was diffuse and often superficial. As the 'wealthy uncle' of British evolutionism, Darwin helped to legitimate their projects, but his theories of common descent, natural selection and sexual selection did not obviously resolve the problems of cultural development. The first anthropologists continued to draw upon a well-established tradition of sociocultural evolutionism. Darwin himself was prepared to adopt a Whig, progressive thesis on human history that was quite foreign to his theory of biological evolution. Most strikingly, he was prepared to compromise his materialism, shifting the emphasis from the growth of the brain (which was, he came to believe, the most significant single factor in the emergence of the human species) to the development of forms of knowledge and moral principles (which explained the subsequent progress of humanity); and knowledge and morality, he argued, were learnt rather than inherited. He insisted upon the primate origin of human beings, but allowed them thereafter to enjoy a good Whig destiny, fighting their way up a ladder of moral improvement using the weapons of hierarchy, order and education. When it came to human history, in short, even Darwin wrote quite often as a traditional evolutionist, rather than as a Darwinian.

Notes

1 Howard E. Gruber (1974) *Darwin on Man: A Psychological Study of Scientific Creativity*, New York: Dutton, p. 281.
2 J.W. Burrow (1966) *Evolution and Society: A Study in Victorian Social Theory*, Cambridge: Cambridge University Press, p. 114.
3 George W. Stocking (1987) *Victorian Anthropology*, New York: Free Press, p. 325.
4 Peter J. Bowler (1988) *The Non-Darwinian Revolution: Reinterpreting a Historical Myth*, Baltimore: The Johns Hopkins University Press, pp. 150-1.
5 Burrow, *Evolution and Society*, pp. 114-15
6 Burrow, *Evolution and Society*, p. 115.
7 J.F. McLennan (1865) *Primitive Marriage: An Inquiry into the Origin of the Form of Capture in Marriage Ceremonies*, Edinburgh: Black; and (1876) *Studies in Ancient History*, London: Quaritch.
8 R.R. Marett (1936) *Tylor*, London: Chapman and Hall, p. 19.
9 R.R. Marett (1911) *Anthropology*, London: Williams and Norgate, pp. 8-9.
10 F. Burckhardt and S. Smith (eds) (1984) *The Correspondence of Charles Darwin* Volume 1 (1821-1836), Cambridge: Cambridge University Press, p. 434.
11 R.D. Keynes (ed.) (1979) *The Beagle Record*, Cambridge: Cambridge University Press, pp. 222-3.
12 Charles Darwin (1839) *Journal of Researches into the Geology and*

Natural History of the Various Countries visited by H.M.S. 'Beagle', London: Henry Colburn, chapter X.

13 Keynes, *Beagle Record* pp. 222-4.
14 Robert FitzRoy (ed.) (1839) *Narrative of the Surveying Voyages of H.M.S. Adventure and Beagle Between the Years 1826 and 1836*, London: Henry Colburn, pp. 120-2.
15 Charles Darwin (1871) *The Descent of Man, and Selection in Relation to Sex*, London: John Murray. Second, revised edition, 1874 pp. 919-20.
16 Keynes, *Beagle Record*, pp. 141-2.
17 FitzRoy, *Narrative*, pp. 323-7.
18 Keynes, *Beagle Record*, p. 221.
19 Loc.cit.
20 Janet Browne (1995) *Charles Darwin: Voyaging*, London: Jonathan Cape, Part two.
21 Darwin, *Journal of Researches*, chapter X.
22 Loc.cit.
23 Adrian Desmond and James Moore (1991) *Darwin*, London: Penguin Books, p. 250.
24 Darwin, *Descent of Man*, p. 81.
25 Loc.cit., pp. 196-200.
26 Loc. cit., p. 906.
27 Loc.cit., p. 203.
28 Loc.cit., p. 220.
29 Loc. cit., pp. 195-6.
30 Loc.cit., p. 276.
31 E.B. Tylor (1889) 'On a Method of Investigating the Development of Institutions: Applied to Laws of Marriage and Descent', *Journal of the Anthropological Institute*, 18:245-72 p. 267.
32 John Lubbock (1870) *The Origin of Civilization and the Primitive Condition of Man*, London: Longman.
33 Darwin, *The Descent of Man*, pp. 889-90.
34 Loc.cit., p. 897.
35 Loc.cit., p. 906.
36 Sigmund Freud (1918) *Totem and Taboo*, London, Hogarth Press. (First published in German, 1913.)

5
Psychology and Anthropology: The British Experience

I

Like many social anthropologists of my generation, I was from an early stage given to understand that psychology was taboo. Between about 1940 and 1970, a firmly anti-psychological approach characterised mainstream British anthropology. This was the more remarkable because from the 1920s cultural anthropology in the USA had moved in the opposite direction, embracing a developmental psychology of Freudian inspiration. The British, however, would have nothing to do with the 'culture and personality' school associated with Mead, Benedict, Kardiner, Linton and the Whitings. Nor were they interested in the alternatives on offer. As Evans-Pritchard explained, with lordly certainly:

> Psychology and social anthropology study different kinds of phenomena and what the one studies cannot therefore be understood in terms of conclusions reached by the other. Psychology is the study of individual life. Social anthropology is the study of social life. Psychology studies psychical systems. Social anthropology studies social systems. The psychologist and the social anthropologist may observe the same acts of raw behaviour but they study them at different levels of abstraction.[1]

The taboo was conventionally formulated in provisional terms. Psychology and sociology might ultimately prove to be complimentary – like physics and chemistry, it was suggested. Perhaps one day sociological explanations would be reformulated in psychological terms. In the meantime, however, anthropologists should practise sociology and steer clear of psychological reductionism. Evans-Pritchard himself took a more extreme position. Fashions in psychology changed, but the new theories were no better than the discredited speculations of the past. 'This attempt to construct social anthropology on the foundations of psychology has to be, then and since, an attempt to build a house on shifting sands.'[2] In 1960 Rodney Needham asserted that 'in not one case or respect that I have been able to discover has psychology afforded in itself a satisfying or acceptable answer to a sociological problem'.[3]

An American historian of British social anthropology, George Stocking, has suggested that the aversion of the British anthropologists to 'culture and personality' studies might have had something to do with the national character. 'It is tempting to suggest that this resistance is very deeply rooted: for the British, who stood so long at civilization's pinnacle, "culture" never completely lost its hierarchical and absolutist resonance; so also, "character", which had won them their place, was always to be preferred to "personality"'. And he went on to speculate that 'in the long run social structure was to provide an approach to human differentiation that was culturally and characterologically more congenial'.[4]

This particular example of culture and personality analysis was perhaps not intended altogether seriously. In any case, it does not work. To begin with, these stereotypes about the British character could hardly account for the prejudices of so-called 'British' anthropologists in the twenties and thirties, since these scholars were in fact drawn from the dominions and colonies and from Central Europe as well as Britain, and few came from the British upper-middle class whose stereotyped qualities inspired Stocking's generalisations. It is true that an earlier generation of British social anthropologists were more typically British (or as they say 'very English'), but in direct contradiction to Stockings's rule they were generally very interested in psychology. They came to anthropology from psychology and neurology or from anatomy, and they were among the first British scientists to take Freudian theory on board. When the discipline first began to establish itself in the universities, at the turn of the century, psychology provided its foster home. In fact the introduction of the taboo on psychology in mid century marked a radical shift of direction in British social anthropology.

II

Tylor, Frazer and Marett, the first academic anthropologists in Britain, were theorists and synthesisers, drawing their inspiration from classical scholarship. Their successors were natural historians and field workers. Instead of the specualtive world histories of the first generation, Rivers concentrated on a historical ethnography of Melanesia, based very largely on his own field surveys. In time he became the leading British anthropologist of his generation, and an influential commentator on current theoretical issues. He was also the major influence on the next generation. Radcliffe-Brown was his student and close associate. Malinowski saw himself as a rivalry to Rivers for the title of the Great Melanesianist. And yet, despite his crucial role in the development of the discipline in Britain, Rivers's career as an anthropologist was an episode in his career as a psychologist.

Born in 1864, Rivers took a medical degree at St Bartholomew's Hospital in 1886. In 1891 he began do research in neurology under the direction of Sherrington, and to collaborate with Henry Head, who had returned from studies in Germany with Hering. In 1892 Rivers himself spent several months studying with leading psychologists in Jena, in Germany. Returning to London, he taught experimental psychology at University College London. In 1893 he went to Cambridge to lecture on the physiology of the sense organs, offering what Myers described as 'one of the earliest systmatic practical courses in experimental psychology in the world, certainly the first in this country.'[5] Between 1893 and 1901 he wrote a number of important papers on vision.

In Cambridge, Rivers worked closely with A.C. Haddon, who had started his career as a zoologist and who taught physiology at Cambridge. Haddon became interested in ethnology after a natural history expedition to the Torres Strait, and in 1898 he managed to raise funds for what became the first British academic ethnological expedition, the Cambridge University Anthropological Expedition to the Torres Strait. He decided to take a party of six investigators, one of whom was to be an experimental psychologist. Rivers declined the appointment, but after Haddon had recruited two of his students, C.S. Myers and William McDougall, he changed his mind.

> When Rivers found that his two best students were going he asked whether after all he might come too [Haddon recalled]. Naturally I was very much pleased at this though I own that I felt that the psychological side was rather over-weighted. I put the direction of the psychological department entirely into the hands of Rivers and for the first time psychological observations were made on a back-ward people in their own country by trained psychologists with adequate equipment.[6]

The psychological research conducted by Rivers was concerned mainly with the vision of the islanders. He investigated acuteness of vision, colour perception, and susceptibility to geometric illusions. The results were matched with studies made of subjects in the United Kingdom, and Rivers concluded from these studies and subsequent investigations of a similar nature in Egypt and in India that although there were differences in perception (related, for example, to the shapes encountered in the built environment), basic psychological and physiological capacities varied little across cultures. As he commented in a late essay:

> Summing up my own experience – and I believe this will be confirmed by anyone who has used the methods of modern ethnology – I may say that in intellectual concentration, as well as in many other psychological processes, I have been able to detect no essential differences between Melanesian or Toda and those with whom I have been accustomed to mix in the life of our own society.[7]

And in *The Todas*, published in 1906, he remarked:

> It is very difficult to estimate general intelligence, and to compare definitely the intelligence of different individuals, still more people of different races. I can only record my impression, after several months' close intercourse with the Todas, that they were just as intelligent as one would have found in any average body of educated Europeans.[8]

(He did add, however, that the women 'were distinctly less intelligent than the men'!)

Rivers also rejected Lévy-Bruhl's idea that primitive peoples operated by a different logic from ourselves. Examining ideas about the dead in Melanesia, he concluded:

> that many of the instances brought forward by Lévy-Bruhl as examples of prelogical mentality betray no real contradiction at all, and no failure of logic in our sense. They are merely cases in which the facts of the universe have been classified and arranged in categories different from our own.[9]

This point of view was well-established in German ethnology and psychology. Waitz had published the first volume of a comparative ethnology in the same year as *The Origin of Species*, and concluded 'that there are no specific differences among mankind with regard to their psychical life. The great difference in civilization amongst peoples of the same stock, testifies that the degree of civilization does not chiefly depend on organization or mental endowment.'[10] In the next generation, Wundt adhered to the notion of the 'psychic unity of mankind', as did Bastian in the following decades, and Bastian's student Franz Boas brought this thesis into American anthropology at the turn of the century. The alternative point of view, that there were indeed psychological differences in kind between peoples of different race, could be reconciled with a Darwinian model of evolution (on the premiss that races represented stages in a single evolutionary

process, or that local variations amounted to species differentiation). However, by the twentieth century no major British
psychologist or anthropologist propagated such a view, with
the notable exception of McDougall, and then only later in
his career.

In 1901 Rivers was one of the ten people who attended
the foundation meeting of the British Psychological Society.
In 1903 he began his celebrated collaboration with Henry
Head. Nerves were cut on Head's arm, and Rivers measured
the gradual return of cutaneous sensibiity. In the following
year he and James Ward founded and began to edit the
British Journal of Psychology. He also investigated the effect
of drugs on fatigue, which he took as his subject when he
was invited to deliver the Croonian lectures at the Royal
College of Physicians in 1906. It was only in 1907 that he
gave up his university teaching in experimental psychology.
For the following seven years he was inactive in psychological
research. This was the period in which he devoted himself
entirely to ethnology, and in particular to the preparation of
his *History of Melanesian Society*, which appeared in 1914, and
which he considered to be his masterpiece.

In 1915 Rivers was plucked from the field in Melanesia
and recruited into the army psychiatric service. He served
at a military hospital for mental patients at Maghull, near
Liverpool, and later at the Craiglockhart War Hospital in
Edinburgh, where his patients included Siegfried Sassoon
and Wilfred Owen. Among his colleagues were several of his
early associates, and indeed a high proportion of the British
ethnologists, notably McDougall, Myers, Seligman, and the
anatomist and diffusionist Elliot Smith.

'This period not merely marks a new phase in Rivers's
work', Myers observed, 'but is also characterised by a distinct
change in his personality and writings.'

In entering the Army and in investigating the psycho-
neuroses he was fulfilling the desires of his youth. Whether
through the realisation of such long-discarded or sup-
pressed wishes, or through other causes, *e.g.* the gratified
desire of an opportunity for more sympathetic insight into

the mental life of his fellows – he became another and a far happier man. Diffidence gave place to confidence, hesitation to certainty, reticence to outspokenness, a somewhat laboured literary style to one remarkable for its ease and charm. Over forty publications can be traced to these years, between 1916 and the date of his death.[11]

Influenced by his experiences as a psychotherapist, Rivers took up Freudian theory, writing two major neo-Freudian monographs, *Instinct and the Unconscious*, published in 1920, and *Conflict and Dream*, which appeared posthumously in 1923. Characteristically, he became chairman of a committee designed to spread Freudian ideas in medical circles. (According to Ernest Jones, the leading British Freudian, the British Psychological Society set up a special medical section to promote the discussion of psychoanalytic ideas among medical men. 'To heighten its prestige we got W.H.R. Rivers, the distinguished anthropologist, to act as its first President.')[12] In 1922, in the middle of all this activity, Rivers was nominated to fight an election for the London University parliamentary seat in the interest of the Labour Party. He died suddenly in the middle of the campaign.

In short, Rivers made his career largely as a psychologist. This is not to underrate the importance of his ethnological work, and at one stage he regarded ethnology as his true vocation. However, he was active as an anthropologist only between 1898 and 1914, and this was to the exclusion of research in psychology only between 1907 and 1914. Other veterans of the Torres Strait Expedition also continued to play a role in anthropology. Myers always retained contact with the anthropological world, and he served a term as President of the Royal Anthropological Institute. Seligman, a medical man, took up a post in ethnology at the London School of Economics, while retaining a strong interest in psychology, and like Rivers he was an early advocate of Freud, and in his case also of Jung. McDougall actually went on from the Torres Strait to Borneo, where he collaborated with an administrator, Charles Hose, on an extensive field study that led in 1912 to a two-volume monograph entitled *The Pagan Tribes of Borneo*. Reminiscing in old age, McDougall wrote:

> I was tempted to make field-anthropology my main line: for I greatly enjoyed wandering in wild places among primitive peoples and I had found it easy to make sympathetic contacts with such people. Looking back, I cannot now understand why I rejected this alluring prospect. I remember that my conscious ground of rejection was characteristically arrogant. I said to myself, 'That field is too easy for me'; and turned back to my original scheme of direct attack on the secrets of human nature.[13]

T.H. Pear remarked that Myers and Rivers had believed 'that 1912 to 1922 was a period in which ethnology and psychology were coming close together'.[14] Some of the students who came to Rivers after the Torres Strait Expedition also combined an interest in psychology and ethnology. Frederic Bartlett actually chose to study with Rivers because he was particularly interested in anthropology, and although he made a distinguished career in academic psychology he published a book in 1923 entitled *Psychology and Primitive Culture*.[15]

All this is by way of leading up to a question. Since Rivers and his students formed the most influential group of anthropologists in Britain until the early 1920s, and since several of them – most notably Rivers himself – were also amongst the leading psychologists of the day, what relationship developed between anthropology (or 'ethnology') and psychology? The answer is rather surprising.

III

Writing many years later about the Torres Strait expedition, Seligman emphasised the contribution Rivers had made to ethnological methods, particularly his development of the genealogical method, but, he went on:

On the psychological side the results of the expedition were less stimulating, because, though important in themselves in settling matters in doubt or dispute, they raised no fresh questions of first-class importance for subsequent solution. The psychological work of the expedition was almost entirely limited to the experimental psychology of the sense organs and to reaction time. It was determined that the sense perceptions of the lower races differ in no marked manner from those of Europeans, differences where they exist being in the main personal, not racial. . . . Thus it was that the psychological work done on the expedition scarcely concerned the social anthropologist, whose interests it in no way served.[16]

Seligman here takes for granted a necesary dichotomy between ethnology or sociology on the one side and psychology on the other. The two fields had crystallised as distinct academic disciplines in Britain by the turn of the century. When organising the Torres Strait expedition Haddon had sharply demarcated research in 'psychology' from work in 'sociology' or 'ethnology'. In any case, it was evident enough that Rivers's psychological experiments in the Torres Strait was quite distinct from the sociological research he began to undertake there. Rivers was effectively entering a different field. Indeed, Haddon later claimed that he had converted Rivers from psychology in the Torres Strait. 'One of the things of which I am most proud in a somewhat long life is that I was the means of seducing Rivers from the path of virtue . . . (for Psychology was then a chaste science) . . . into that of Anthropology.'[17] Between 1898 and 1907, Rivers pursued his ethnological research in parallel with his psychological work, but they never overlapped. On the contrary, psychological considerations were effectively blocked out of his ethnology and sociology.

Rivers's ethnological research was very much in the mainstream of contemporary anthropology. He investigated the classic questions of kinship organisation and totemism, initially using the methods and theories of Lewis Henry Morgan. Later he came under the influence of the German diffusionists. He was also aware of Durkheim's work, and like his student A.R. Radcliffe-Brown he accepted Durkheim's argument that individual psychology could not explain social facts. This point of view was most explicitly stated in his critique of the American anthropologist Alfred Kroeber, in a course of lectures delivered at the London School of Economics in 1912.

The issue was the interpretation of kinship terms. In the tradition of Morgan, Rivers insisted that kinship terms were social fossils, bearing witness to former modes of kinship organisation. Kroeber argued that they were 'psychologically' determined and that they had no necessary sociological significance. They were mental constructs, which drew upon universal discriminations (of sex, generation, marital status, etc.). Rivers assumed that if Kroeber was invoking psychological explanations, he meant that the classication of kin reflected emotional attitudes. For example, if 'mother's brother' and 'father-in-law' were designated by a single term, then a psychological hypothesis might be that the individual had the same feelings towards these two relatives. Rivers argued that this could only be the result of a social process. A person would have the same feelings for two different classes of relative only if they were situated in the same social relationship to him. For instance, if there was a rule that a man should marry his mother's brother's daughter, then a mother's brother would be a potential father-in-law. Summing up, Rivers said: 'These lectures have largely been devoted the the demonstration of the failure to explain features of the terminology of relationship on psychological grounds.' He went on to say that even though psychology might prove to be of assistance to ethnology, there was no call for 'the interpolation of psychological facts as links in the chain of causation connecting social antecedents with social consequences.'[18]

A.R. Radcliffe-Brown (the first student of Rivers to specialise in ethnology as an undergraduate at Cambridge) became an ardent Durkheimian, and shortly after these LSE lectures he corresponded with Rivers about the place of psychological explanations in anthropology. The immediate issue was the understanding of totemism. Rivers took the orthodox view that totemism was a form of social organisation. A totemic society was organised into clans, each of which was associated with a natural species. Radcliffe-Brown argued that the nature of the social units was irrelevant. Totemism was a system of belief, according to which social groups, however constituted, were associated with natural species. 'By my definition of totemism', he wrote to Rivers, 'I have tried to include under one term a number of different phenomena which are so far similar to each other that we may suppose that they have a common psychological basis.' He expanded this argument in a subsequent letter, writing that the search for social conditions:

> can give us empirical generalisations, but will never give explanations. I hold that the nature of social institutions is dependent on fundamental laws which are laws of psychology, i.e., laws as to how the human mind works, so that the ultimate explanation of social phenomena depends on the discovery of those laws.

To make the case properly he would have to 'write out and publish my general hypothesis as to the nature of society and of social institutions. I don't want to do this just yet, for many reasons, and after all there is a good deal of it in Durkheim.' Like Durkheim, as he emphasised in a later letter, what he had in mind was 'a general theory of social psychology'. 'I never make appeal to individual (as opposed to collective) mental processes'.[19]

Rivers set out his own views in a paper entitled 'Sociology and Psychology' in 1916. He made the conventional analogy with a scientist who might draw from both physics and chemistry, but remarked that while one can be confident of the conclusions drawn from these sciences, 'the psychological assumptions of the sociologist are largely or wholly hypothetical'. Rivers belonged to the generation of British psychologists who had turned away from the tradition of associationist psychology that had informed the theories of Tylor and of Frazer. He was also initially sceptical of theories that dealt with instinct and emotion, partly on the grounds that they were not fully established, and partly because he believed that 'sentiments and opinions' were shaped by their 'social setting'. He noted that Westermarck had tried to explain the blood-feud in terms in vengeful feelings, but the social processes described as blood-feuds vary across cultures, and their variations must be accounted for before the associated emotions could be understood. 'How can you explain the workings of the human mind without a knowledge of the social setting which must have played so great a part in determining the sentiments and opinions of mankind?' His conclusion was that sociology and psychology should each pursue its own specific programme of research, at least for the time being. 'Those who follow one path will devote themselves to the study of the body of customs and institutions which make up social behaviour, while those who follow the other path will inquire into the instincts, sentiments, emotions, ideas, and beliefs of mankind.' [20] Radcliffe-Brown responded that 'the only difference between us is at what stage in the progress of sociology we should take up the fundamental psychological problems. I wish to take them up at once, whereas you wish to postpone them. After all it is perhaps a matter of personal feeling or idiosyncracy.'[21]

IV

Rivers did not have time to bring his late interest in Freudian theory to bear on anthropological questions, but another veteran of the Torres Strait expedition, C.G. Seligman, did attempt to introduce ideas drawn from Freud and Jung into social anthropology. Seligman sent out questionnaires on dreams together with psychoanalytical materials to ethnologists in the field, among others to a young colleague from the London School of Economics, Bronislaw Malinowski, who was engaged in ethnographic research in New Guinea. On his return to Europe, in the early 1920s, Malinowski read up on Freud, and in 1923 he wrote the first of a series of essays that criticised Freud's theory of the Oedipus complex on the basis of evidence drawn from Trobriand ethnography.

Freud posited a universal Oedipus complex. In all societies boys secretly hated and feared their fathers and desired their mothers. According to Malinowski, this was not true of the Trobriand Islanders. The Trobrianders were apparently ignorant of the facts of physiological paternity, believing that conception was caused by matrilineal spirits. A man inherited from his mother's brother, who had authority over him. He resented this dependence, and secretly desired his uncle's death. His father, on the other hand, was an indulgent and much-loved counterweight to the authoritarian and powerful uncle. Malinowski also denied that boys were troubled by incestuous desires for their mothers. In a matrilineal society the brother-sister relationship is more awkward, since a woman's children are under the control of her brother and will succeed him. Brothers and sisters cannot openly express affection, and brother-sister incest is particularly abhorred. The Trobriand case therefore proved that the Oedipus complex was not universal. However, Malinowski suggested that the Trobriand evidence supported what he took to be Freud's most general premiss – 'Psycho-analytic doctrine is essentially a theory of the influence of family life on the human mind'.[22]

In a celebrated counter-attack Ernest Jones (the leader of the British Freudians) argued that the Trobrianders suffered very severely indeed from the Oedipus complex, to the point that they desperately denied the father's role in reproduction and invented institutionalised ways of circumventing his authority. Malinowski responded:

to Dr Jones and other psychoanalysts the Oedipus complex is something absolute, the primordial source . . . of everything. To me on the other hand the nuclear family complex is a functional formation dependent upon the structure and upon the culture of a society. It is necessarily determined by the manner in which sexual restrictions are moulded in a community and by the manner in which authority is apportioned.[23]

The structure of Malinowski's argument recalls that of
Rivers. Emotional complexes are shaped by social institutions. This was essentially Durkheim's position, but Radcliffe-
Brown and Malinowski were drawn to an alternative psychological theory, which seemed to offer an account of instinct
and emotion while still allowing a role for social forces and so
for cross-cultural variation. This was a theory of 'sentiments'
associated with A.F. Shand, whom Malinowski referred to as
'one of the greatest psychologists of our time'.[24] Shand's
theory was also endorsed by Radcliffe-Brown, and it was
taken up by Westermarck.

The gist of Shand's theory was that all human beings have
the same fundamental instincts or drives, but that particular
sentiments associated with these instincts crystallised in specific social contexts. For example, all human beings had a
similar sexual drive, but only in some societies did this lead
to an enduring love between a husband and a wife. Although
the anthropologists cited Shand in particular, British social
psychology between about 1910 and 1930 was characterised
by a series of rather similar theories, all of which assumed
that social institutions satisfied, controlled or channelled
the basic human needs, drives, or instincts. McDougall's
Introduction to Social Psychology drew on both Shand and
on Durkheim. Other notable and influential books in this
tradition include Graham Wallas's *Human Nature in Politics*,
published in 1908, which was praised by Rivers, Morris
Ginsberg's *The Psychology of Society*, which appeared in 1921,
and F.C. Bartlett's *Psychology and Primitive Culture*, published
in 1923.

Malinowski and Radcliffe-Brown were part of the same
broad school of thought, if they later moved on in different
directions. Radcliffe-Brown wrote mainly about the role of
conventionalised sentiment in kinship systems. 'Sentiments'
developed within the family were 'extended' to more distant
relatives.[25] Malinowski was more ambitious, developing a
full-blown theory of culture and instinct. Culture was a
second, artificial environment that satisfied 'basic needs',
but in doing so created new needs that it then also had to
satisfy.[26] There is an obvious kinship between this theory and

that of Rivers's student, F.C. Bartlett, one of the founding fathers of Cambridge psychology, and also with the views of his LSE collegues Morris Ginsberg and Emile Westermarck. I would therefore dispute the judgment of Talcott Parsons that: 'Essentially Malinowski's social psychology turns out to be a modification of the instinct theory of McDougall'.[27] Rather, both were particular formulations of a point of view that was shared by many psychologists and ethnologists in Britain in the 1920s and 1930s.

V

So how and why did the taboo on psychology enter British social anthropology? National character will not help as a source of explanation, and in the best traditions of British anthropology I shall rely rather on tribal sociology, though I shall grant some autonomy to the scientific discourse itself.

Let me restate the puzzle. Rivers began to do research in ethnology at the end of its first, so-called evolutionist phase. Tylor and Frazer drew on associationist psychology. The first generation of professional British psychologists regarded associationism as completely discredited. They were influenced by the new German psychology, which had been established by Wilhelm Wundt, and in particular by the experimental study of individual perception and cognition that he was developing. But Wundt's legacy had two aspects. The other side of it, largely ignored in Britain, was his *Volkerpsychologie*, the study of collective psychic phenomena. This became one of the sources of social psychology, and directly influenced both Durkheim and Malinowski (who had studied with Wundt).

Rivers was committed to the scientific study of perception, but he saw no way of applying it to the problems of ethnology or sociology. He discouraged Radcliffe-Brown's interest in social psychology, and notwithstanding his later endorsement of Wallas he never explored its possibilities. Nor did Rivers take an interest in the psychology of emotion until he took up Freudian ideas (not uncritically) as a consequence of his experience as a war-time psychiatrist.

The issue that faced Rivers, Radcliffe-Brown and Malinowski was how to reconcile the central propositions of ethnology and psychology. Ethnology documented the fact that social institutions varied across cultures. Scientific psychology (from Wundt to Rivers) was committed to the view that the mental and emotional make-up of human beings was pretty much the same everywhere. Rivers effectively kept these two projects in separate compartments. There was, however, a third option. This was social psychology, assicated with Wundt's folk psychology and Durkheim's theory of the collective conscience. Malinowski and Radcliffe-Brown were attracted for a time to the psychology of Shand, which allowed for a feed-back from social institutions to instincts or basic needs, by way of socially inculcated sentiments. This tradition of social psychology was, however, soon to be banished from the mainstream of British psychology. In Britain, therefore the two disciplines became increasingly estranged from each other.

This is an intellectualist account of the relationship between ethnology and psychology. It can be combined with a more sociological view, which would emphasise two distinct processes. A crucial development within the small world of British social anthropology in the late 1930s was the migration of Malinowski to Yale, and the reverse migration of Radcliffe-Brown from Chicago to Oxford. Malinowski came to embrace the behaviorism that he discovered at Yale. Radcliffe-Brown, however, had reacted strongly against the dominance of psychology in the social sciences at Chicago, and he had delivered a famous seminar series attacking psychological reductionism.[28] Within American anthropology there was a turn towards Freudian theory, and 'culture and personality' theory became fashionable. In America Radcliffe-Brown had been a rival of Margaret Mead and Ralph Linton, and a competitor for American funds. Returning to Britain, he assumed the leadership of the new school of social anthropology vacated by Malinowksi, and he led it away from psychological theories, and away from American cultural anthropology, reasserting the Durkheimian dogma that social facts could be explained only in terms of other social facts. According to Radcliffe-Brown, social anthropology was comparative sociology.

A parallel but opposite process was occurring within British psychology. As Hearnshaw has remarked, after the lively promise of the 1920s social psychology became 'a backward area in British psychology, inadequately supported by the universities, starved of research funds and relatively neglected by psychologists themselves'.[29] During the same period academic psychologists turned away from the psychology of the emotions and psychotherapy. A variety of factors led to this reorientation. Hearnshaw himself even adduced the fact that anthropologists had become disillusioned with psychology, so reducing the support for social psychology. But essentially what happened was that the leading academic psychologists came to define psychology as strictly as possible as a natural science. British psychology was still a small subject, like anthropology, which could make a concerted and decisive change of direction. (As late as 1939 there were only six psychology chairs in the United Kingdom, and only thirty lecturers in psychology.)[30]

When the anthropological taboo on psychology crumbled, with so many others, in the 1970s, a few anthropological Freudians came out of the cupboard, but the Freudian revival, such as it was, was shortlived. Other attempts to stimulate psychological interest in British anthropology were few and far between, and none succeeded, though recently there is some interest in cognitive theory. For their part, psychologists – again, perhaps, particularly British psychologists – have seldom ventured forth from behind their own disciplinary ramparts. In an excellent study, a psychologist, Gustav Jahoda, has reviewed anthropology, urging his colleagues to draws upon anthropological ideas and findings and to collaborate with anthropologists.[31] Nevertheless, it must be said that there are few signs that in Britain at least the boundaries between the disciplines are breaking down.

Tribal loyalties may come to be terribly important in small, embattled disciplines.

Notes

1   E.E. Evans-Pritchard (1951) *Social Anthropology*, London: Cohen and West, p. 45.
2   Evans-Pritchard, *Social Anthropology*, p. 44.
3   Rodney Needham (1960) *Structure and Sentiment*, Chicago: University of Chicago Press, p.126.
4   George Stocking (1986) Introduction to Stocking (ed.) *Malinowski, Rivers, Benedict and Others*, Madison: University of Wisconsin Press, p. 8.
5   C.S. Myers (1923) 'The Influence of the Late W.H.R. Rivers on the Development of Psychology in Great Britain', introduction to W.H.R. Rivers, *Psychology and Politics and Other Essays*, London: Kegan Paul.
6   Cited in H.A. Quiggin (1942) *Haddon the Head Hunter*, Cambridge: Cambridge University Press, p. 97.
7   W.H.R. Rivers (1926) *Psychology and Ethnology*, London: Kegan Paul, p. 53.
8   W.H.R. Rivers (1906) *The Todas*, London: Macmillan, pp. 20-1.
9   Rivers, *Psychology and Ethnology*, pp. 43-4.
10 T. Waitz (1863) *Introduction to Anthropology*, London: Longman Green. (First published in German, 1859) p. 327.
11 Myers, 'The Influence of the Late W.H.R. Rivers', pp. 167-8.
12 Ernest Jones (1964) *The Life and Work of Sigmund Freud*, Harmondsworth: Penguin Books, p. 487.
13 W. McDougall (1961) 'William McDougall' in C. Murchison (ed.) *A History of Psychology in Autobiography*, Vol. 1, New York: Russell & Russell, pp. 202-3.
14 T.H. Pear (1960) 'Some Early Relations Between English Ethnologists and Psychologists', *Journal of the Royal Anthropological Institute*, vol. 90: 236.
15 F. Bartlett (1961) 'Frederic Bartlett' in C. Murchison (ed.) *A History of Psychology in Autobiography*, Vol. III, New York: Russell & Russell, pp. 39-52.
16 C.G. Seligman (1932) 'Anthropological Perspectives and Psychological Theory', *Journal of the Royal Anthropological Institute*, vol. 62: p. 196.

17 Cited in Quiggin, *Haddon the Head Hunter*, p. 97n.
18 W.H.R. Rivers (1914) *Kinship and Social Organisation*, London: Athlone Press. (First published 1914) citation p. 94.
19 Adam Kuper (1989) 'Radcliffe-Brown and Rivers: A Correspondence', *Canberra Anthropology*, 11: 79-80.
20 The essay was republished in a posthumous collection of Rivers's articles (1926) *Psychology and Ethnology*, London: Kegan Paul. Citations from this edition, pp. 15, 11 and 6.
21 Kuper, 'Radcliffe-Brown and Rivers: A Correspondence', p. 79.
22 Bronislaw Malinowski (1927) *Sex and Repression in Savage Society*, London: Kegan Paul, p. 17.
23 Malinowski, *Sex and Repression*, pp. 142-3.
24 Malinowski, *Sex and Repression*, p. 240.
25 See for example A.R. Radcliffe-Brown (1924) 'The Mother's Brother in South Africa', *South African Journal of Science*, vol. 20: 542-55).
26 See B. Malinowski (1931) 'Culture', *International Encyclopaedia of the Social Sciences*, vol. 4: pp. 620-45.
27 Talcott Parsons (1957) 'Malinowski and the Theory of Social Systems' in Raymond Firth (ed.) *Man and Culture*, London: Routledge and Kegan Paul.
28 These lectures were published posthumously, A. R. Radcliffe-Brown (1957) *A Natural Science of Society*, Chicago: Free Press.
29 L.S. Hearnshaw (1964) *A Short History of British Psychology 1840-1940*, London: Methuen, p. 237.
30 Loc. cit., p. 208.
31 Gustav Jahoda (1982) *Pyschology and Anthropology: A Psychological Perspective*, London: Academic Press.

6
Lévi-Strauss and Freud: Symbols in Myths and Dreams

I

Structuralism and psychoanalysis offer quite distinct modes of interpretation, yet they have accepted, even sought, a more or less uneasy coexistence. In *Tristes Tropiques*, Lévi-Strauss named the three great intellectual influences during his formative student years as Freud, Marx and geology. (All three, he suggests, are united in their insistence that surface appearances are a poor guide to underlying realities.)[1] Yet he generally maintained a distant and often sceptical relationship with the Freudian tradition. His theory of myth and of symbolism is very different from Freud's. Indeed, it has come to constitute the main challenge to the entrenched Freudian and Jungian traditions in this field. However, it was only with the publication in 1985 of *La potière jalouse* that Lévi-Strauss directly confronted the Freudian alternative to his own approach to the analysis of a mythology.

It is common ground between Freud and Lévi-Strauss that dreams and myths should yield to the same form of analysis, although in practice Freud was particularly concerned with dreams, as Lévi-Strauss has been with myth. In the context of a comparison of their approaches there is therefore a special interest in an otherwise little-known work of Freud's, *Dreams in Folklore*, which was written in 1911 but not published until 1958.[2]

Freud's essay dealt with German folk-tales that incorporate dreams. He was particularly intrigued by the fact that these stories not only retail dreams, but also offer an interpretation of them. To be sure, the folk-tales are quite light-hearted. They offer interpretations of dreams in order to make fun of girlish innocence, peasant greed, and so forth. Yet although he fully appreciated – even enjoyed – their lack of serious-ness, Freud came to the remarkable conclusion that 'folklore interprets dream symbols in the same way as psychoanalysis'. At one point he went even further, suggesting that:

> It is very much more convenient to study dream symbolism in folklore than in actual dreams. Dreams are obliged to conceal things and only surrender their secrets to interpretation; these comic anecdotes, however, which are disguised as dreams, are intended as communications, meant to give pleasure to the person who tells them as well as to the listener, and therefore the interpretation is added quite unashamedly to the symbol. These stories delight in stripping off the veiling symbols.[3]

The main body of folk-tales considered by Freud and D. E. Oppenheim revolve around a symbolic association of gold and faeces. For example:

> My neighbour once dreamt that the Devil had led him to a field to dig for gold; but he found none. Then the Devil said: 'It is there for sure, only you cannot dig it up now; but take note of the place so that you may recognise it again by yourself.'
> When the man asked that the place should be made recognisable by some sign, the Devil suggested: 'Just shit on it, then it will not occur to anybody that there is gold lying hidden here and you will be able to recognise the exact place.' The man did so and then immediately awoke and felt that he had done a great heap in his bed.

It is, of course, a familiar psychoanalytical thesis that there is a deep association between faeces and treasure, particularly gold. As Freud explained it, 'All the interest which the child has had in faeces is transferred in the adult on to another material which he learns in life to set above almost everything else – gold.' The folk-tale makes the association explicit, just as an analyst might do in interpreting the dream of a patient. 'In dreams in folklore,' Freud concluded, 'gold is seen in the most unambiguous way to be a symbol of faeces. If the sleeper feels a need to defecate, he dreams of gold, of treasure.'[4] In short, Freud was enchanted to find unexpected support for his theory of dream symbolism in the ancient peasant wisdom of Central Europe.

II

Lévi-Strauss suggests that Freud oscillated throughout his career between a realist and a relativist conception of symbolism. Freud the realist assumes that each symbol should have a set meaning, and that in principle it should be possible to compile something like a dictionary of symbolism. When operating as a relativist, however, Freud emphasises that symbols can have different meanings in different contexts, and that a particular use of a symbol can be interpreted only by a process of free association which takes into account the personal history of an individual. Freud the relativist wins the approval of Lévi-Strauss – indeed, he goes so far as to say that when operating as a relativist Freud is attempting 'to understand an individual in the way an ethnographer seeks to understand a society.'[5] There can be no higher praise. Freud the realist, however, is making the vulgar error of the amateur ethnographer: he assumes that symbolic meanings are independent of context.

In *The Interpretation of Dreams* (1900), Freud suggests that a balance should be struck between the realist and relativist positions. 'We are thus obliged', he wrote, 'in dealing with these elements of the dream-content which must be recognized as symbolic, to adopt a combined technique, which on the one hand rests on the dreams' associations and on the other hand fills the gaps from the interpreter's knowledge of symbols.' He does offer a check-list of fixed definitions – a King and Queen represent parents, a Prince or Princess the dreamer, and so on; and he notes recurrent symbols that symbolise the genitals – hats, weapons, stairs, shafts, and so forth. And yet he admits that symbols may have several meanings, and even suggests at one point that 'as with Chinese script, the correct interpretation can only be arrived at on each occasion from the context'. But it is difficult to strike a balance in practice, and Freud generally opts for the realist alternative, putting aside, as he says, these 'qualifications and reservations'.[6]

The radically realist position is superficially attractive because it promises – like Mr Casaubon in *Middlemarch* – a Key to all Mythologies. Unfortunately, it can get one into all sorts of difficulties. Indeed, only a few pages after his confident statement that 'In dreams in folklore gold is seen in the most unambiguous way to be a symbol of faeces', Freud introduces a set of tales in which a peasant dreams that he is climbing up to heaven, or down to earth from heaven. He constructs a rope or thread from various materials which come to hand, but it is just too short. The angels suggest that he defecate and lengthen the rope with turds. He wakes up and finds he has defecated on his wife. In this instance, apparently, faeces are not associated with treasure at all. Freud comments, moreover, that in this folk-tale 'we encounter spun thread as a new symbol for evacuated faeces, although psychoanalysis furnishes us with no counterpart to this symbolization but on the contrary attributes another symbolic meaning to thread'. In the Freudian lexicon, thread is a symbol of semen. Clearly, there is a problem here. If gold always stands for faeces, and thread always symbolises semen, then a thread of faeces is not easy to interpret. To be sure, just because gold symbolises faeces, it does not follow that faeces must stand for gold and that it could not, for example, stand for semen; but it must be admitted that the conventional Freudian lexicon does not offer these associations.

In interpreting this dream, however, Freud abandons the lexicon and suggests that the peasant is sexually rejecting his wife and insulting her. He concludes that 'his wife, who lies by him, does not attract him; he exerts himself in vain to get an erection for her . . . But the disappointed sexual libido finds release along the path of regression in the excremental wishful impulse, which abuses and soils the unserviceable sexual object.'[7] In short, the thread symbolises semen, but the faeces stand for – excrement. How does one know what is and what is not a symbol? Evidently, symbols refer to body parts and bodily functions. Therefore if a bodily function occurs in a dream then it must stand for itself. This essentialist view of symbolism is anathema to Lévi-Strauss.

III

Lévi-Strauss rejects any decontextualised interpretations of symbols. Nor do the elements of a myth have a meaning in themselves. Their significance can be gleaned only from a quite elaborate process of contextualisation. This implies that the elements of a myth must first be analysed in relation to each other, not taken out of context and related directly to some point of reference in the outside world. Myths must also be studied in all available versions, and related to other myths in a larger corpus. Lévi-Strauss also denies that any one version of a myth has special authority. In the absence of a written text, myths are constantly in flux. Quite commonly a myth will change with each telling. And it is precisely these variations – or, more formally, transformations – which permit the analyst to come to grips with a mythology.

In *The Jealous Potter*, Lévi-Strauss takes as his point of departure the myths of the Jivaro Indians of the western foothills of the Andes in Peru and Ecuador. One of their favourite mythical characters is a bird, the nightjar or 'goatsucker' (the name favoured by the translator, who tells us that the bird belongs to the same family as the nighthawk and whippoorwill). The goatsucker figures prominently in the mythology of many South American Indian peoples. Rather as Punch is famous for his large nose (in the childrens' version at any rate), so the goatsucker is notable for its huge beak and for its jealousy. These are both aspects of its greed, its oral incontinence. Indeed, this bird is supposed to eat much more than it is able to digest, and is much given to belching and breaking wind.

In South American mythology the goatsucker is opposed to the sloth, which is represented as eating hardly anything at all, and very rarely defecating. This is not the only contrast between them. The goatsucker eats hugely and is chronically troubled with intestinal gas; it flies; and it is associated with the creation of pottery clay, creepers and gourds. In stark contrast to the goatsucker, the sloth eats little, seldom excretes, and then only on the ground; and it is associated with the creation of grain and with the invention of weaving which is, with pottery, the main Jivaro craft.[8]

The two characters are clearly conceived of as polar opposites, or perhaps as two extremes within a triangle, for there is clearly room for a creature that both eats and defecates excessively, a role played in much of South American mythology by the howler monkey, that eats all the time and constantly and shamelessly defecates and urinates. While the goatsucker flies and the sloth descends to the ground to defecate, the howler monkey does its business in the trees. And while the sloth hangs on to a tree trunk with his forepaws, the howler monkey often hangs upside down – because, the Indians explain, he suffers from chronic diarrhoea. In some areas – for instance, where one of these animals is unknown – other creatures are pressed into one or other role. The ant-bear often takes the place of the sloth as a creature which eats only small insects and defecates seldom, if at all. Sometimes purely imaginary animals are introduced into this set, for instance animals that have no anus and must eat and defecate through the mouth.

It would be quite mistaken to imagine that the Indians observe, say, the sloth, agree upon its characteristic traits and then weave stories around it. They certainly know a great deal about the creatures of the forest, but once introduced into a myth they become mythical creatures. In the context of the myth their critical attributes are defined in opposition to those of other mythical creatures. They come to embody particular values within a structure of oppositions that is established by the myth. The goatsucker, the sloth and the howler monkey are defined most starkly in terms of simple oral and anal characteristics. They are orally or anally incontinent or grotesquely retentive. However, they are also contrasted along other dimensions. There is an opposition between ground-based, flying, and arboreal creatures; and in some myths between silent and noisy creatures, and so on.

These dimensions of contrast have to do with what Lévi-Strauss calls mythical codes. If a myth draws images and incidents from geography, then it is operating a geographical code. It may also operate a cosmological code, a physiological code, a colour code, a botanical code, or whatever. Each code creates a set of oppositions and embodies the polar values in specific characters and objects. All myths employ several codes at once, and it is an egregious error to assume that one has priority. There is no privileged set of images that will unlock all the other codes in a myth. No myth can be solved by translating it into a master code that controls all the others. One of Lévi-Strauss's recurrent criticisms of Freud is that he gives priority to the physiological code, which becomes the ultimate point of reference for all the other codes in a myth or a dream.

The cardinal rule, then, is that the elements of a myth take their meaning from their place in a code, which defines specific oppositions and relationships. But these codes in mythology are not like security codes that take a vital message and disguise it in order to smuggle it past the enemy, as Freud imagined. No code simply translates a literal message into another, secret language. Rather, each code has its own preoccupations and images, and combines with others, like instruments in an orchestra, to yield the myth. Consequently, the codes must be interpreted with reference to other codes. An entire myth is, moreover, just one of a sequence of myths, and each myth takes its meaning at least in part, from its relationship to other myths.

The relationship between episodes within a myth and between one myth and another is typically one of 'trans-formation'. By transformation Lévi-Strauss means a formal change in the organisation of an argument or of a story, which affects every element and every relationship in a consequential manner. If a story-teller were to take a well-known tale (say Red Riding-Hood) and simply alter a few details, or even tack on a new conclusion (the little girl's discovery of a treasure during her escape, for instance), this would not amount to a transformation. But if the little girl were to be accompanied by a brother, then a fundamental change would have been introduced, and a structuralist would expect this to be matched by other changes, perhaps leading to a complete reversal of the outcome.[9]

There have been a number of attempts to formulate transformation rules. One procedure that is frequently used by story-tellers transforms the plot by changing one character and inverting the outcome of an incident. A good example can be found in a folk-tale discussed by Freud and Oppenheim, and already referred to. A peasant dreams that he defecates on some treasure in order to hide it, and awakes to find that he has soiled his conjugal bed. Freud notes that the dream has a conclusion: 'As he was fleeing from the house, he put on a cap in which a cat had done its business during the same night. . . . '[10] This is a straightforward inversion of the main plot (especially if the cat and the wife are substitutable for each other, and a cat is indeed commonly associated with females in European folk culture).

Transformations in mythology are commonly more elaborate. *The Jealous Potter* begins, for example, with a myth of the Jivaro. The sun and moon were formerly human beings, and lived on earth. They shared a home and a wife, who was named goatsucker, like the bird. She welcomed the warm embrace of the sun, but recoiled from the cold body of the moon. Moon became angry and climbed up a creeper into the sky. He also blew out the sun's fire. Both her husbands having disappeared, goatsucker felt herself abandoned. She tried to follow the moon into the sky, carrying a basket filled with the special clay used by women to make pottery. Moon, however, cut the creeper that joined the two worlds, and the woman fell to earth with her basket. The clay scattered over the earth and can now be gathered here and there. The woman changed into a bird and at the time of the new moon she cries plaintively to the husband who deserted her. Later, the sun climbed up to the sky on another creeper, but the moon continues to pursue him and they are therefore never seen together.

A Finnish ethnographer, R. Karsten, who recorded this tale, collected other versions of the story. In one, goatsucker is married to the moon alone, and when she is rejected by her husband and falls to earth it is with a basket of gourds. The seeds of the gourd that were scattered by her fall provide the main plants cultivated by the Indians today. Neighbours of the Jivaro provide further variants. In one tribe, instead of a woman with two husbands there is a story about moon who has two wives. One day he sends the first wife to collect ripe gourds for him. She makes a soup and drinks it herself, and brings back just three green gourds for moon. Furious, he climbs into the sky on a cord. The woman follows, he cuts the cord, and she falls and is shattered into pottery clay. In an alternative version, the terrified wife defecates clay. Another Jivaro myth represents the goatsucker as a male, wooing the female moon. The moon is also being courted by the sun. Fed up with both suitors, she escapes into the sky. The goatsucker tries to follow her, but the moon cuts the creeper up which he is climbing and it falls to the ground and becomes the creeper of the forest, on which gourds grow. Moon makes itself a baby of clay, but the jealous goatsucker causes it to fall and break into pieces. It becomes the earth on which we live. The sun reaches the sky and marries the moon.[11]

According to Lévi-Strauss, there is no point in giving priority to any one of these versions. However, considered as a group these tales are obviously transformations of each other. The same set of elements, more or less, are arranged in a series of alternative relationships – the woman with two husbands becomes the husband with two wives, and so on; the characters are interchangeably male or female, suitor or pursued; and the outcome changes as the transformation is effected, so that one myth explains the origin of pottery clay while a transformation may end with the creation of gourds.

Clearly, Lévi-Strauss's approach is very different from Freud's. Freud in general treated each dream – or myth or legend – individually and as a coded expression of a censored wish. The wish is real, typically sexual in origin, and it supplies the meaning of the dream. Similarly, the symbols in which it is encoded usually stand directly or indirectly for genital organs or physiological functions. He delighted in the German folk-tales about dreams because they made explicit the link between various symbols and the physiological organs and processes for which they stood.

From the point of view of Lévi-Strauss, Freud is making a fundamental error when he tries 'to decipher myths by means of a single and exclusive code, while a myth will always put several codes in play, and it is from this layering of codes, one on top of another, that rules of interpretation derive'. More specifically, he reproaches Freud for assuming that the deepest meaning of a myth will always find expression in a physiological code.[12]

Lévi-Strauss has, of course, deliberately selected American myths that deploy an oral-anal code in order to make his point, which is that the physiological code does not have a special status. It does not necessarily stand for itself; nor does it have any other straightforward, universal meaning or point of reference; nor, finally, is it the ultimate point of reference of the other codes in the myths.

IV

I am particularly interested in the ethnography of southern Africa. Reading Lévi-Strauss on the Jivaro made me recognise that southern Bantu folk-tales make very different use of oral-anal imagery. Many southern African stories contrast normal animals with cannibals. Normal animals (in Southern Bantu folk-tales, at any rate) may be killed by stopping up the anus. The cannibal, by contrast, is killed by closing its mouth. Its victims are then released by cutting open the cannibal's anus, or by opening up his stomach.

Cannibals are also contrasted with human beings along other dimensions, one being their household arrangements. A human house has a single entrance. If someone dies, a hole is cut in the rear and the body is taken out through the hole. A cannibal cave has two entries. Victims are locked in by closing the front entrance. If the front entry is blocked from outside, the cannibal dies and the victim escapes alive through the back. These contrasts between the entries and exits to the human and cannibal huts obviously recall the contrasts between the cannibal's mouth and anus and those of an animal. Other contrasts are in play as well. For example, people escape from cannibals by flying or by burrowing under the earth, while cannibals are powerless if they fall into pits or climb above the ground. This code has to do with the idea that ancestor spirits, who protect human beings, live above or below the earth.[13]

V

Obviously it would be a pity if, confronted with these stories, one were to allow the oral-anal code a privileged status, or assume that oral and anal symbolism must refer to infantile obsessions. But perhaps I have loaded the dice against Freud by concentrating on myths, for he was more particularly interested in dreams, although he certainly had a good deal to say about myths and stories. Accordingly, let me turn back to dreams again, and to a dream that Freud dreamt himself, in which the oral-anal code is very important. This is the famous 'specimen dream' in *The Interpretation of Dreams*, the dream of Irma's injection. It has been reanalysed dozens of times in neo-Freudian terms, but I shall summarise a structuralist account of this text, published by Alan A. Stone and myself.[14]

Freud dreamed that a patient, whom he called 'Irma', came up to him at a party and complained that she was still suffering choking pains in her throat, stomach and abdomen. Freud was alarmed. His first impulse was to blame her for not having accepted his 'solution'. He tried to examine her, but she was reluctant to open her mouth. When she did so at last, he saw scabs in her throat. Colleagues joined in the examination, discovered chest occlusions and finally diagnosed an abdominal infection. The senior member of the team predicted that dysentery would supervene. This would rid the patient of the poison. Finally, Freud became aware of the source of the infection. His friend Dr Otto had injected Irma with a dangerous preparation, probably using a dirty syringe.

Freud's own analysis of the dream supported his view that dreams were wish-fulfilments. On the previous evening, Dr Otto had suggested that 'Irma' had not been helped by Freud's treatment. The dream-solution was to blame Dr Otto for her sickness, and so to exculpate Freud himself. A number of commentators have remarked that in this case at least Freud was reluctant to identify an underlying sexual theme at the heart of the dream, and several of them have attempted to put this right. It is certainly remarkable that the oral-anal code is treated so perfunctorily.

Our specific interest, however, was in the kind of logic exhibited in the dream. First of all, we pointed out that the dream recapitulated the stages of routine medical examinations, in which doctors investigate first the throat, then the chest, and finally the lower body. Secondly, as the examination proceeded, so more profound symptoms were uncovered. There was, then, a double progression in the dream, down the body, and from the superficial to the hidden, inner, and more significant. Thirdly, the solution – the expulsion of the toxin in dysentery – inverted the initial problem, the choking and the difficulty in opening the mouth. Moreover, choking and the resistance to opening the mouth were physical metaphors for the rejection of Freud's 'solution'. Freud believed that 'Irma' was not physically sick but rather psychologically disturbed. Her symptoms were the physical expression of a psychological illness. The cure was to have a 'catharsis' – to talk out the problem. In his dream, 'Irma' is physically ill and the catharsis is a physical purge of the poison through the anus. The mouth which will not open voluntarily for a speech catharsis is replaced by the anus which purges a physical poison in an uncontrollable fit of dysentery. The conclusion inverts the beginning. The dream's conclusion is a formal transformation of its opening scene.

The dream makes elaborate play with Freud's theory that psychological illness may present itself as physical illness,

and effects a highly structured transformation. Freud had
treated 'Irma' for hysteria. Dr Otto believed that 'Irma' was
physically ill, and that Freud's treatment had been at fault.
Freud's dream brilliantly resolved this troubling question.
A more detailed reading of the dream, including an analysis
of what the hapless Dr Otto injected into Irma, revealed that
the apparently physical cause of Irma's condition was itself
capable of psychological interpretation: for Dr Otto injected
a sexual metabolism, trimethylanlin.

Our analysis showed, moreover, that the dream does not
simply rush to a happy ending: it works its way there. The
resolution is achieved in an ordered fashion, by a series of
quasi-logical steps. It represents not only an investigation,
and a diagnosis, but also an argument, all progressing
together. The issue at stake in the argument is the relationship between physical and psychological causation of
illness, the crucial question for Freud's theories. And it
is these theories that give the oral-anal code its special
function in the dream. The two ends of the digestive
tract come to stand for two opposed kinds of theory and
of cure: the psychodynamic and the physical. Far from
reducing the dream to a physiological code, we argued
that the physiological references were symbols that stood
for abstract, scientific ideas.

VI

To a structuralist, the physiological code is a language that
can convey many messages. Yet even the most extreme
relativist would have to concede that the body is a very special
source of symbols: everywhere the same, in a sense, and
everywhere endowed with powerful psychological properties.
The Freudian would probably go further and say that not
only the body but also certain complexes of sexual desire and
repression are virtually universal. Myths and dreams might
then be expected to convey rather standardised messages in
a repetitive set of images. The structuralist, however, would
be inclined to take a relativist position here as well. The

meaning of the body, the form of family relationships, all are variable; and even where the external reality is, by chance, perceived in a similar fashion in two cultures, it need not generate the same myths and dreams. The outside world provides only a jumping-off point for dreams and myths.

In *The Jealous Potter*, Lévi-Strauss makes this point with reference to Freud's *Totem and Taboo* (1913). Freud's monograph was subtitled: 'Resemblances between the psychic lives of savages and neurotics.' This notorious identification of so-called savages and neurotics was based upon two ideas current at the time. One was the now discredited view that the development of the organism in its lifetime recapitulates the evolution of the species. The second was the belief that contemporary so-called 'savages' were survivals of ancient types of man. Given these assumptions, savages were perhaps like children, and like neurotics. All this is anathema to a modern anthropologist, and Lévi-Strauss ridicules the notion that savages are like neurotics in our own society. Nevertheless he is ready to concede that 'there are points on which the mental lives of savages and psychoanalysts coincide', which he pretends is by way of complimenting psychoanalysts. In support of this coat-trailing, he remarks that Jivaro myths use 'perfectly explicit notions and categories – such as oral character and anal character – that psychoanalysts will no longer be able to claim they have discovered. All they have done is to rediscover them.'

What is more, the Jivaro have a myth of incest and parricide that has uncanny resemblances to the myth of origin which Freud made the centre-piece of his *Totem and Taboo*. The myth in question is a continuation of the creation story I introduced earlier. The sun and moon eventually marry each other and have four children, the first being the sloth. The sloth marries the pottery-jar, Mika. In time, they have a child, Ahimba, the serpent. In the absence of the sloth, the serpent sleeps with his mother, the pottery-jar. The sloth finds out and turns his anger not against the guilty pair but against his own mother, whom he accuses of having condoned their crime – perhaps blaming her, Lévi-Strauss suggests, for his own incestuous desire to make love to her.

The sloth's murder of their grandmother turns his wife's incestuous children against him, and they kill him. Mika, the pottery-jar, then kills the children for committing parricide. Thenceforth the three camps – of the father, the mother and the son – wage a relentless battle. This is the origin of society.[15]

As Lévi-Strauss insists, this myth is very like the myth of incest and parricide in *Totem and Taboo*, though with some intriguing variations. (It is not for nothing, he suggests, that the Jivaro were famous in the Andes region for hunting heads and shrinking them. They are obviously exotic 'shrinks'.) But that does not mean that either Freud or the Jivaro have cracked the primal code, or that both vaguely remember some primal crime. Rather, if human societies prohibit incest with the mother and endow the father with authority, then in myths and stories people will experiment with the relationships between these elements – indulging in the intellectual pleasure of generating transformations. Even a universal set of concerns will trigger a series of creative experiments in myths and dreams, not a predictable if coded rehearsal of some standard response.

It will be evident that I take Lévi-Strauss's side in this argument. Nevertheless, it must be admitted that Lévi-Strauss does not make things easy for his supporters. First of all, his various methodological pronouncements cannot always be reconciled with each other. A degree of divergence is only to be expected, perhaps, for he has written about myths for many years now; but it is in fact quite possible to construct very different methodologies from his various prescriptions. As a sympathetic commentator, Jarich Oosten, admits, 'no generally accepted method of structural analysis exists in cultural anthropology and this has been the cause of much confusion and misunderstanding among anthropologists'.[16] Lévi-Strauss himself quite often seems to follow his intuitions even when they conflict with his methodology. He can even at times make remarkably blunt realist statements. To take one example, when the serpent sleeps with his mother, the pottery-jar, he comments that they symbolise respectively the male and female organs, 'naturally destined to unite, notwithstanding the social rules that would restrain their freedom'.[17] This is a very unstructuralist interpretation!

A more fundamental problem is posed by Lévi-Strauss's insistence, particularly in his earlier writings, that myths are always engaged with problems posed by real life. Such reductionism implies that a myth does have a relatively simple meaning. It must refer directly to some real event or person or idea. This is not easily reconciled with his later and, I think, more coherent view that myths operate, as it were, in a hall of mirrors, but that they reflect only each other. This implies that myths – and dreams – are not mechanisms for communicating messages in a secret language. They are best understood as modes of thinking, or perhaps more precisely, reflection. One critic, Dan Sperber has even claimed that:

> when we strip the work of Lévi-Strauss of the semiological burden with which he has chosen to encumber it, we will then realise that he was the first to propose the fundamentals of an analysis of symbolism which was finally freed from the absurd idea that symbols mean . . . if Lévi-Strauss thought of myths as a semiological system, the myths thought themselves in him, and without his knowledge, as a cognitive system.[18]

I have presented the differences between the two Masters as a contrast in method, but they also have two very different preoccupations. Freud is concerned with the emotions, Lévi-Strauss with the intellect. Moreover, they operate within very different national, intellectual traditions. Nevertheless, they do represent two powerful, comparable and *competitive* theories of myth and dream. They may well both be wrong, but I have come to doubt that they can possibly both be right.

Notes

1   When I first read Freud his theories seemed to me to represent quite naturally the application to individual human beings of a method of which geology had established the

canon. In both cases the investigator starts with apparently impenetrable phenomena; and in both he needs a fundamental delicacy of perception . . . if he is to detail and assess the complexities of the situation. And yet there is nothing contingent, nothing arbitrary, in the order which he introduces into the incoherent-seeming collection of facts.

Claude Lévi-Strauss (1961) *A World on the Wane*, London: Hutchinson. (First published in French, 1955) p.60.

2   Sigmund Freud (1958) *Dreams in Folklore*, New York: International Universities Press. This essay was written in collaboration with D. E. Oppenheim, a classicist who was briefly associated with the Vienna Psychoanalytical Society. It disappeared from view for a generation before turning up in the possession of Oppenheim's daughter. The work was published in German with a simultaneous English translation.

3   Freud, *Dreams in Folklore*. Citations pp. 63 and 26-7.

4   Loc. cit., pp. 37 and 38.

5   Claude Lévi-Strauss (1988) *The Jealous Potter*, Chicago: University of Chicago Press. (First published in French, 1985) pp. 188-9.

6   Freud (1953) *The Interpretation of Dreams*, London, Hogarth, pp. 388 and 289. For the list of symbols see section E of chapter six.

7   Freud, *Dreams in Folklore*, citations pp. 45 and 50.

8   See Lévi-Strauss, *The Jealous Potter*, pp. 93-6.

9   See the discussion in Jarich Oosten (1985) *The War of the Gods: The Social Code in Indo-European Mythology*, London: Routledge, p. 4.

10 Freud, *Dreams in Folklore*, p. 38.

11 These stories can be found in chapter three of Lévi-Strauss *The Jealous Potter*.

12 Lévi-Strauss, *The Jealous Potter*, pp. 186-7.

13 See the essay 'Cannibals, Beasts and Twins' in my book (1987) *South Africa and the Anthropologist*, London: Routledge.

14 Adam Kuper and Alan A. Stone (1982) 'The Dream of Irma's Injection: A Structural Analysis', *American Journal of Psychiatry*, 139(10): 1225-34.

15 Lévi-Strauss, *The Jealous Potter*, pp. 185-6.

16 Oosten, *The War of the Gods*, p. 8.

17 Loc.cit.

18 Dan Sperber (1975) *Rethinking Symbolism*, Cambridge: Cambridge University Press, p. 84.

7
Audrey Richards:
A Career in Anthropology[1]

I

Unprejudiced, unshockable, in many ways unconventional, Audrey Richards nevertheless operated unselfconsciously by the standards of her parents and their class. Her family belonged to the strikingly endogamous and coherent community Noel Annan called the intellectual aristocracy, a very English intelligentsia, 'wedded to gradual reform of accepted institutions and able to move between the worlds of speculation and government'. Its charter was the reform of the Indian and English civil services on meritocratic principles in the mid nineteenth century. 'No formal obstacle then remained to prevent the man of brains from becoming a gentleman'. Influenced by the Utilitarians, fascinated by the new social sciences, these public-spirited intellectuals 'were agreed on one characteristic doctrine; that the world could be improved by analysing the needs of society and calculating the possible course of its development.'[2] Their theoretical work addressed practical concerns, and their official reports – perhaps their most characteristic genre – sometimes made pioneering intellectual contributions.

Born in London on 8th July, 1899, Audrey was the second of four daughters of Henry Erle (later Sir Erle) Richards and Isabel, the daughter of Spencer Perceval Butler. The Butler side of the family was prototypical of the intellectual aristocracy – Annan took them for one of his case-studies.[3] Spencer Perceval Butler, a double first in classics and mathematics, was a barrister and public servant. Two brothers were headmasters, respectively of Haileybury and Harrow. Among his children were Sir Spencer Harcourt

Butler, a Governor of Burma, and Sir Montagu Butler, Governor of Central Provinces, India, and later Master of Pembroke College, Cambridge, and the father of R.A.Butler, Chancellor of the Exchequer and Master of Trinity College, Cambridge.

H.E. Richards, younger son of a Welsh lawyer who married a local heiress and became Lord Chief Baron, was educated at Eton and qualified as a barrister. He served as legal member of the Indian vice-regal council from 1904 to 1909, and returned to England in 1911 as Chichele Professor of International Law at Oxford University and fellow of All Souls. Audrey once told me that this had been a difficult choice – her father could have expected a glittering career in India – and that it was her mother who insisted that the girls should not be sent alone to England, to boarding school, while the parents remained in India, as was customary. (She also said her father regretted that his four children were all daughters.)

Audrey later recalled that in her younger days her mother 'did much entertaining for the clever, popular, amusing husband. There were large, formal parties at Simla and Calcutta. . . . Those were the days when the children were pulled up and down on rugs by Indian servants to polish the floors; when the father became more and more exuberant; and the mother, the last flower placed, stood at the top of the stairs to receive her guests with that very charming, almost regal, carriage of the head and opened the ball with the Viceroy to the strains of the "Blue Danube".' Her mother she recalled as not only a solicitous and kindly hostess but as a selfless woman and 'one of the sincerest characters I ever met'. And, like Audrey herself, she was very amusing: 'she had all the family's quick sense of the ridiculous, a dry humour and that piercing judgment of character on which so much English fun depends. Her comments on people were a delight.' Her father 'was brilliant, witty, and a born raconteur . . . In his intimate circle he bubbled over with an irresistible flow of pure nonsense and fantasy.'[4]

Audrey attended Downe House School near Newbury, and developed intellectual interests that her parents did not encourage (rebelliously, she read books during meals, holding them below the table). Her parents were against her going up to university, and they insisted that if she did so, she should study science. She attended Newnham College, Cambridge from 1918 to 1921, and read for the Natural Sciences tripos.

Coming down from Cambridge she taught for a year at her old school, then worked as assistant to Gilbert Murray, the classicist, who remained a friend and who was to read and criticise her doctoral thesis. (In a spoof reference in 1924 he wrote, 'As for papers, she will hide them so as no inspector could find them . . . ')[5] For eighteen months she did relief work in Frankfurt, at a Friends' Ambulance Unit Family Welfare Settlement, and began to take a practical interest in problems of nutrition. Between 1924 and 1928 she was secretary to the labour department of the the League of Nations Union in London. ('I was one of the idealists who thought war could be prevented by the League of Nations. We used to speak in its favour on Hampstead Heath, in Methodist chapels, and in schools etc.')[6]

Her two younger sisters married, both to fellows of All Souls, but her elder sister Gwynedd, who also remained unmarried, embarked on a career as a social worker. Audrey was always close to Gwynedd (who spent some months with her in the field among the Bemba), and it must have seemed that she was drifting into a similar career; yet given her background she could hardly have doubted that academic research might contribute to welfare. Certainly neither she nor her relatives had any doubt that she would have to earn a living.

Influenced by the socialist political scientist Graham Wallas, father of a Newnham friend, she decided to begin postgraduate study at the London School of Economics. According to a letter from Wallas to the anthropologist, Bronislaw Malinowski, asking Malinowski to supervise her work, she intended to treat the history of European ideas about 'nature' and 'freedom' 'in relation to the permanent facts of human biology'.[7] Malinowski took her on but persuaded her to change her topic, and between 1928 and 1930 she worked under his supervision on a doctorate, based on published sources, teaching anthropology at the same time at Bedford College.

II

Bronislaw Malinowski, himself a transplanted member of the Polish intelligentsia, dominated social anthropology at the London School of Economics from 1924 (when he took up a position as Reader at the School, shortly after completing his first great Trobriand monograph) to 1939. The LSE was associated with new ideas of social improvement, and was committed to the application of the social sciences. Still somewhat marginal, not yet entirely respectable, it offered an ideal environment for an ambitious and creative outsider, and was more hospitable than the ancient universities to the aspirations of women. Malinowski had developed new methods of intensive ethnographic fieldwork, and was propagating a theory he called 'functionalism'. He 'had no doubt about his greatness', according to Edmund Leach, also one of his students, and saw himself as 'a missionary, a revolutionary innovator in the field of anthropological method and ideas'.[8] Volatile and charismatic, 'a man whose expressions became more extreme with opposition,' as Audrey Richards noted, he gathered around him a brilliant group of mature students, often graduates in other fields, and always including a large proportion of women.

Malinowski demanded what he called loyalty, but he engaged his students in debate and challenged them to apply his theory of culture to ethnographic materials, in particular his own Trobriand data. 'The idea,' as Audrey Richards has explained, was 'that rites, beliefs, and customs, however extraordinary they appear to an observer, actually fill "needs", biological, psychological, and social.' Seminar discussions had 'the fascination of a game for which the *chose donnée* was the necessity of the custom or institution under discussion to the individual, the group or the society. If the Trobriand islanders did it, or had it, it must be assumed to be a necessary thing for them to do or have.' In consequence, 'discussions of the function of aspects or institutions of tribal life led directly into field-work material . . . and we began actually to visualise ourselves "in the field"'.[9]

But before going into the field students were required to write library theses, based on the ethnographic literature. Audrey's background in biology was broadly relevant to the Malinowskian project, which insisted that culture was rooted in biological needs, and she chose a topic in which both biology and culture were implicated: nutrition. Malinowski had dealt with the domestication of sex in his *Sexual Life of Savages*, which appeared in 1929, but in the very first sentence of her book Audrey Richards pronounced: 'Nutrition as a biological process is more fundamental than sex'.[10] Nutrition was also one of the classic subjects of the social surveys favoured by reformers in Britain, and in the 1920s it had become a subject of rapidly growing interest in academic and government circles. Institutes of Nutrition were set up in Aberdeen and Cambridge, and in 1927 with the assistance of the Dietetics Committee of the Economic Advisory Council the Aberdeen Institute collaborated with the Kenya Medical Service on studies of Kikuyu and Masai nutrition.

However, the functionalist approach promised a fresh perspective. First, Audrey Richards insisted, 'nutrition in human society cannot be considered as a biological instinct alone.'[11] Moreover, the study of nutrition could not be restricted to a review of agricultural techniques or an analysis of diets. Drawing on the ethnographic literature on the Southern Bantu peoples, she argued that social institutions are organised essentially to meet this fundamental physiological need, and that a 'whole series of institutions and relationships' constitute 'the *nutritional system.*'[12]

This was an orthodox Malinowskian formula, and Audrey Richards was to remain an orthodox Malinowskian, always passionately loyal to him. It is true that she was sensitive to one of the fundamental difficulties of the approach: that it made comparison very difficult. (Later she experimented with structural methods that facilitated comparison.) However, she never accepted the other conventional criticism of functionalism, 'the charge often made by administrators,' she noted, 'that functional anthropologists were not prepared to allow for any changes in the tribes they were studying.'[13] On the contrary, she was convinced that the type of information and analysis that functionalist ethnography provided would be of great value to policy-makers in the colonies, and that it could indeed illuminate the problems of social change.

III

Audrey Richards and Lucy Mair (step-daughter of Sir William Beveridge, the director of the LSE), another of Malinowski's most loyal students, were among the first anthropologists to carry out applied research in Africa. With Malinowski's blessing, they hoped to bring the insights of function-alist anthropology to bear on the problems of colonial administration.

Audrey's fieldwork proposal, dated July, 1929, begins with a conventional enough Malinowskian statement of intent: 'To make an intensive study of the social institutions, customs and beliefs of the Awemba tribe . . . of N.E. Rhodesia, with special reference to the part played by women in tribal and economic life, the nature and importance of the family system and the marriage contract, and problems connected with the rearing and education of children.' This should not be read as a precociously feminist proposal. Rather, Malinowski was inclined to think that women ethnographers would find it easier to study women. ('As long ago as 1930,' she recalled in a lecture on feminist anthropology in 1974, 'I was sent to study a matrilineal society because it was thought particularly appropriate for a woman anthropologist to study women. When I got there you will not be surprised to hear I found as many men as women!')[14]

In any case, she immediately turned to the potential appli-cation of the study. 'I believe such work to be of immediate importance in view of the proposed extensions of the railway system to the Plateau area, and the further development of the copper resources of the district. Both these factors are likely to raise important administrative problems in native government, and to lead almost inevitably to new sources of conflict between the white and black races.'[15]

From May 1930 to July 1931, and again from January 1933 to July 1934, Audrey did fieldwork in what was then Northern Rhodesia, among the Bemba, who occupy the north-eastern plateau of modern Zambia. In the 1930s the Bemba numbered between 115,000 and 140,000, but lived in small villages dispersed over a very large territory. Their kinship system was indeed matrilineal, they practised shifting cultivation, and they were organised into numerous chiefdoms under a highly ritualised but not very powerful paramount chief. Pacified without much resistance in the last years of the nineteenth century, they had accepted the imposition of British colonial government. In return, they had been allowed to retain their system of chieftainship. Nevertheless, taxation in cash became general from 1905, and from 1914 large numbers of men were engaged in migrant labour in the mines of Katanga and Southern Rhodesia, and from 1920 in the Copperbelt. By 1914 between twenty and thirty per cent of the men were away from their villages as labour migrants, and food production at home began to suffer in consequence. In 1929 the Native Authority and Native Courts Ordinance introduced Indirect Rule.[16] Audrey was intrigued by the rapid social changes, even if she was perhaps unaware that they had been in train for a generation before her arrival. 'I really think they are an interesting people,' she wrote to Malinowski from Chilonga in September, 1930, in another letter preserved in the Malinowski archive at the LSE, 'the queer mix up of a conquering people who had only been installed for 50 years in this country when the first white people came, and are now being transformed by the mining industry 500 miles off.'

Malinowski's students were expected to learn the vernacular and to live in close association with the people they were studying. Audrey made long forays into the villages, but she used the estate of the colonial grandee, Stewart Gore-Browne, as her base, and never pretended that she had 'gone native': 'in an area where the only white people consist of three main classes – Government officials, missionaries, and traders – and where the tribe itself is organized on an autocratic basis . . . the anthropologist will find it impossible to be treated as an equal by the natives.' She was accorded the status of Chieftainess, and learnt to use the appropriate Bemba royal speech conventions. 'This position of prestige prevented my attaining any real position of equality with the people but was an advantage in carrying out village censuses when it was helpful to be able to exert a certain amount of authority.'[17]

She lived in a tent, spending between three and six weeks in each village. On the move, she must have made a striking impression:

> Off the main road you must travel from village to village by footpaths, the white man or woman ahead on a bicycle or on foot, and the most motley procession of carriers behind. A native can carry a 60 or 70lb load on his head, and seems to have an infinite capacity for hanging incongruous objects together with strands of bark. . . . Behind this will follow your tent, and a clatter of cooking equipment, while the kitchen boy brings up the rear with a live chicken strung by its feet round the barrel of your rifle, and a couple of flat-irons in a basin on their heads.[18]

Lorna Gore-Browne, who accompanied her on some expeditions, reported in a letter in 1933, 'Audrey never fusses . . . and is able to laugh and laugh when things go just a little wrong.'[19] She was one of the outstanding ethnographers of her generation, her gregariousness, her stamina, her acuteness of social observation and above all her ability to laugh and make people laugh with her carrying her triumphantly through the inevitable crises and periods of fatigue and discouragement. The difficulties were always reported as farce:

> There is the difficulty of taking photographs and simultaneously writing notes during rites that take place in bush and village and on the road between the two. There is

also the factor of exhaustion. Songs and dances often went on until two and three in the morning. On such occasions the company is usually elated by beer and accustomed to the heat of a small hut about eight feet in diameter filled with twenty or thirty people and an enormous fire. The observer is dead sober, nearly stifled, with eyes running from the smoke, and straining all the time to catch the words from the songs screeched around her, and to transcribe them by the firelight that penetrates occasionally through the mass of human limbs.[20]

A sober Bemba testimonial is available from an occasional field assistant, the evangelist Paul Bwembya Mushindo. 'I was very much impressed by the character of Dr A.I. Richards who was a European and purely English lady, who treated me, who was a pure African and her servant, very kindly. She had very good will to all African people. She was like a sister to me . . . Dr Richards thought I was helping her in her duties . . . I felt I was in a university for study. In this way Dr Richards learned less, but I felt I had learned much more without my teacher, Dr Richards, realising it.'[21]

The first generation of Malinowski's students were encouraged to make a rounded study of a culture, rather than to concentrate on a particular facet of social life. It was only on her return to London that Audrey Richards decided that the focus of her first Bemba monograph should be, once again, nutrition. This had not been her original plan, and she had not organised her fieldwork systematically to collect material on the production and use of foods. Rather, very characteristically, the topic emerged as part of an interdisciplinary project with a strong 'applied' cast to which Audrey decided to subordinate her choice of subject-matter.

In 1935 she had taken the chair of the Diet Committee of the International Institute of African Languages and Cultures, a 'small group of anthropologists, medical and nutritional experts', and she persuaded them that social and cultural information should be included in the nutritional surveys being planned. 'It was therefore suggested that it would be instructive if I wrote a short book describing, in

the case of one particular tribe . . . the variety of different
factors, whether economic, political, legal, or religious which
actually affected the people's diet. The result is in effect a
description of the whole economic life of the tribe.'[22] It
is more, being virtually a complete ethnography of the
Bemba with an emphasis on the economy. In her first
book she had 'tried to prove that hunger was the chief
determinant of human relationships'. Her aim in the second
was rather 'to show how the biological facts of appetite and
diet are themselves shaped by the . . . cultural mechanisms
for producing, preparing and dividing food.'[23] This is an
intriguing shift of emphasis, but the book was still a characteristic Malinowskian ethnography. Its specific model was
the first volume of Malinowski's masterpiece, *Coral Gardens
and Their Magic*, his account of Trobriand husbandry that had
appeared in 1935. There was, however, one major difference:
unlike Malinowski, she situated her ethnography firmly in
the current, colonial context.

In 1940 Audrey Richards published another monograph
that was aimed primarily at a readership of colonial administrators: *Bemba Marriage and Present Economic Conditions*,
which was published by the Rhodes-Livingstone Institute
in Northern Rhodesia. Because of the time and place of
the publication it never became widely known, yet it is
one of the most sociologically sophisticated accounts of the
effects of migrant labour on African family life, illustrating
and probing the thesis that while industrial change created
similar problems in many parts of the continent, 'the reac-
tions of the different Native tribes . . . are not identical.'[24]

Her first major theoretical article dates from the same
period, appearing in 1940 in a famous collection, *African
Political Systems*, edited by Meyer Fortes and E.E. Evans-
Pritchard. She tried to place the Bemba political system in
a more general framework of African government, drawing
out the universal features and indicating what was particular
about the Bemba; but what is perhaps most remarkable about
this essay, in contrast to her contemporary 'applied' publications, is that the influence of British colonial government,
and economic and religious change, are noted only in a

concluding section, while the Bemba are presented for the most part in a timeless, 'traditional' mode. It is as if she felt that academic anthropology need not address the impact of colonial overrule, while 'applied' anthropology dealt with with the realities of social and cultural change. Similarly, her contribution to *African Systems of Kinship and Marriage*, in 1950, ignored the urgent problems of family change with which she had been concerned in her essay on Bemba marriage. This essay is, however, of far greater intrinsic interest than her earlier paper on political systems, presenting as it does a comparative (and notably structural) account of the problems common to matrilineal systems in Central Africa. It greatly influenced thinking about matrilineal kinship.

While she was writing up, Audrey Richards taught at the LSE: and now her personal relationship with Malinowski came to a crisis. She had become an intimate friend both of Malinowski himself and of his chronically ill wife, Elsie. After Elsie's death, in 1935, 'Audrey and Bronio came very close to marrying', according to Malinowski's daughter, Helena. However:

> their temperaments were perhaps too much alike; Audrey could not, as my mother had been able to, stand back as it were from his volcanic nature. Audrey tried to intervene for us three children, to see that Bronio fulfilled his fatherly duties, but what he demanded from his friends, especially in the unhappy times right after Elsie's death, was total, uncritical support of all his actions. . . . So their marriage plans came – alas – to nothing. His daughters have always wished that they had married.[25]

It is possible that Audrey would have undertaken the marriage only in the interests of the Malinowski daughters, but Raymond Firth attests (personal communication) that both Audrey and Malinowski had other serious attachments at the time. In the event, Malinowski moved to Yale in 1939 and remarried. He died suddenly in the United States in 1942.

Audrey moved to South Africa, teaching from 1937 to 1940 at the University of the Witwatersrand in Johannesburg.

Characteristically she both began new fieldwork and forged friendships with interesting and powerful people, among them the Prime Minister Jan Smuts, at whose farm, Irene, near Pretoria, she was a regular guest. Intermittent fieldwork among a Tswana group in the Northern Transvaal yielded only one paper, but it is a brilliant piece, analysing the revival of 'tribalism' in an area in which traditional cultures had been destroyed a generation earlier. She argued that the movement had nothing to do with nostalgia for a golden age, or with traditionalism, but was rather to be explained as a manoeuvre in the competition for land rights.[26] Similarly, in a better-known essay on the spread of anti-witchcraft movements in Central Africa, she had argued that they were a response to cultural dislocation and, above all, the social conflicts and uncertainties generated by industrialisation.[27]

IV

'I mean to come back next Xmas,' she wrote from Johannes-burg to Raymond Firth in December, 1938, 'and then if nothing else turns up go back for another two years at least. I don't want to stay here all my life and miss much as you may imagine, but it was good to get away and I want to do one bit of fieldwork and get something done at the university here.' However, the war intervened and she returned to London as a temporary principal at the Colonial Office. Working with Lord Hailey, she participated in the reorientation of research policy in the colonies.

She became special lecturer in Colonial Studies at the LSE from 1944-5, and continued as a Reader from 1946 to 1950, but she also served as a member of the Colonial Social Science Research Council. (The appointment of Raymond Firth as Secretary was largely her initiative.) Various career paths were now open to her, but Audrey felt that at long last British African policy-makers had come to appreciate that they could benefit from expert social science advice, and this presented a great opportunity. 'It is said that youth is the time of enthusiasm,' she wrote later, reflecting on this time, 'but I believe there is no sense of commitment so great as that of middle-aged men and women who suddenly find themselves in a position to do the good they have been trying to do for many years.'[28]

One of the most important initiatives of the CSSRC was the establishment of research institutes in the African colonies. In 1950 she went out to Makerere University in Uganda, as director of the newly-established East African Institute of Social Research. The model for the new institute was the Rhodes-Livingstone Institute in Northern Rhodesia under the direction of Max Gluckman. She later wrote that 'both Gluckman's Institute and mine were really experiments in organising field research'.[29] Both also promoted interdisciplinary research, and both were committed to applied studies of interest to colonial governments. Audrey's gregarious, hospitable style nevertheless gave the Makerere Institute a distinctive tone. 'Talented cuisine, great entertainer on a shoe string, informally without fuss,' notes one of her colleagues, Aidan Southall. 'Shrewd vagueness covering sharp precision . . . Catholic in friendship with Ganda princes, chiefs, clerks, as well as the humble . . . Her close friendship with Sir Andrew Cohen [Governor of Uganda] spilled over on to EAISR and made for a unique period of discourse between high government and intellectuals black and white.'[30]

Audrey divided up the work between anthropologists already in the field (coopting some who were only notionally, if at all, answerable to her) and members of the institute staff, almost regardless of their formal specialisms, and drawing in, as equals, her secretary Jean Robin and locally recruited interpreters and field assistants. She would chivvy her collaborators to write up, in the last resort commandeering their notes and writing them up herself. It was in this way that the major studies of her Uganda period were produced, most notably *Economic Development and Tribal Change: A Study of Immigrant Labour in Buganda* (1954) and *East African Chiefs* (1960). Many years after she had left East Africa she organised a comparable study that resulted in the book, *Subsistence to Commercial Farming in Present Day*

Buganda (1973). These studies mobilised all her talents for administration, teaching, fieldwork and synthesis, however much she complained that they took her away from the 'theoretical' work she hoped to complete, especially when she found herself filling in for colleagues who had not delivered their promised chapters.

While at Makerere she did, nevertheless, find the time to complete her most extensive 'theoretical' study, *Chisungu* (1956). This is an account of female initiation among the Bemba, based largely on observations of a single ceremony through which two girls passed. The account is painstaking and detailed, and the analysis has often been praised, but the 'functionalist' analytic framework already seemed dated. The ritual is very largely presented as it appears to the outside observer, the actors' experience and native exegesis being subordinated to the sociological and psychological interpretations of the anthropologist. Just as the book appeared, Victor Turner was beginning his study of initiation ceremonies and other rituals in another Zambian tribe, the Ndembu. In the early sixties he began to publish richly documented, phenomenological analyses, which were to transform the study of African ritual behaviour, making Audrey Richards's study – which had, after all, been conceived thirty years earlier – seem old-fashioned and inadequate. A telling instance is the contrast between Richards's straightforward and one-dimensional account of the symbolism of the *musuku* tree and Turner's famous exegesis of the symbolism of the same tree.[31] Audrey was uneasily aware of these problems, but she explained that her ethnography was necessarily less specialised than Turner's, since she was working in the Malinowskian tradition of 'multi-purpose' ethnography, in which the fieldworker was expected to cover all the important social institutions.

> I once tried to list the symbolic meanings of the immense variety of trees, bushes and plants used in Bemba magic. I got surface meanings for some thirty-four of these and was beginning to get some of the deeper associations, but I had to give up the attempt since I found it impossible

to combine this with the study of the main outline of the social structure, institutions and beliefs of the people in which I was engaged.[32]

V

In 1956 she returned to a fellowship at Newnham College, Cambridge, where she later served as Vice-Principal. She held the Smuts Readership in Commonwealth Studies in the University from 1961-6, and built up the University's African Studies Centre, lobbying for its formal recognition and becoming its first director. She also supervised ethnographic research, carried out largely by Cambridge students, on the small Essex village, Elmdon, in which she lived for most of this period, introducing aspirant anthropologists to the realities of fieldwork and finally facing up to the fact that if she did not herself arrange for the collation of the material it would never be written up. She also produced a pamphlet for the villagers on the genealogical studies that had been made.

She was, however, a marginal figure in the social anthropology department at the University, perhaps largely because she and the Professor, Meyer Fortes, did not get on. She was, of course, a greatly respected figure, and much loved by most of those who worked with her. Her career had been a distinguished one. Her honours included a CBE for her work in Uganda, election to the British Academy, and the Presidency of the Royal Anthropological Institute. Nevertheless, in these Cambridge years she was not a major intellectual influence in the discipline.

It has been suggested that she was undervalued, even discriminated against, because she was a woman.[33] She herself resisted this suggestion, and any handicap she laboured under as a woman was at least counter-balanced by the advantages of her background and connections. 'Her upperclass background no doubt added to her self-confidence,' wrote her friend Edmund Leach, 'her reputation for modesty was perhaps deceptive. She was quick to make the most of unexpected opportunities but sometimes authoritarian in her treatment of collaborators.'[34] This is broadly accurate, although according to her nephew Dr T. Faber her background was rather 'upper-middle class'. He added that she was 'certainly privileged in being born into a secure, intelligent and comfortably-off clan. . . . But all the Butlers were made to feel that they had to work, and my grandmother and my mother were both, by training and inclination, economical women in a typically bourgeois way.' In a later letter to me he emphasised, however, that 'a lifetime spent in universities' was more important to Audrey than the particular circumstances of her childhood.

Audrey was also a critic of the feminist movement that developed within anthropology in the seventies. She argued against the ethnocentricism and special pleading that she discerned in the feminist critique, and insisted on 'the duty of the field-anthropologist to distinguish very clearly when she considers the position of women between what shocks her and what shocks "them".' Are women generally discriminated against? Societies like the Bemba clearly distinguish between 'the reproductive period of a woman's life and the rest. In a sense it would be true to say that Bemba regarded the individual who was producing and rearing children as a woman and the female persons who were not doing so as men.' A similar distinction might come to be accepted in the West. 'We may see a clearer division between women who want children and those who are willing to give them up for professional or other reasons.'[35] This was the sacrifice she had made herself, but it had freed her to enjoy a rewarding career.

Yet within her chosen career she had made a further choice, which she did believe had a deleterious effect on her reputation. This was her primary commitment to 'applied' as against 'theoretical' research. She was prepared to argue that applied research could yield theoretical dividends. 'I personally learnt more about the political organisation of the Ganda while conducting an immigrant labour survey which could be described as "applied anthropology", than I might have done by a "theoretical" study of the political system because I attended local council meetings at all levels to discuss the project.'[36] However, she felt that her applied work was not properly appreciated by her colleagues, and that it had robbed her of the time she wanted to devote to her pure research. *Chisungu* was finally completed, but not the promised study of Bemba royal ritual, on which she published only a few papers rather than the major monograph she had in mind.

Her theoretical essays were sometimes influential, most notably the classic paper, 'Some Types of Family Structure among the Central Bantu' (1950). Nevertheless, the theoretical framework which she generally retained, rooted in Malinowski's functionalism, was not favoured by the next generation of anthropologists, and she did not sympathise with the very general shift from the study of 'function' to the explication of 'meaning'. As Edmund Leach has remarked, 'She showed little sympathy for post-functionalist developments in social anthropology.'[37] This was perhaps surprising, since she increasingly came to concern herself with the study of ritual; but if Victor Turner neglected her work so did she his, and that of other younger theorists in the field, like Lévi-Strauss and Geertz (although in general she followed closely debates within British social anthropology).

Moreover, while her 'applied' studies were distinguished by their ethnographic realism, and their acute attention to processes of social change, the theoretical papers seemed to shut out the colonial realities. Perhaps it was the legacy of functionalism, or the example of the Trobriand monographs, but when she wrote what she called 'theoretical' studies Audrey Richards adopted the pastoral idiom of the 'ethnographic present'. The richly nuanced accounts of social change in her 'applied' studies were informed by shrewd, pragmatic, if often *ad hoc* sociological analysis, yet they too lacked a crucial dimension, for criticism of the colonial govenments could not be risked, at least in print.

Audrey Richards was nothing if not a realist, and she had an intuitive understanding of the official mind. She was well aware that African colonial administrators might accept expert advice on matters of practical policy, but that they were not open to criticisms on fundamentals. She thought it obvious that the anthropologist was not in the business of criticising colonial governments. 'I tried very hard to follow the precepts then taught by Malinowski as to the complete neutrality that was desirable for a fieldworker. I made it my business not to criticize European or African officials or to express strong views on policy.'[38] In any case, however successful in their own terms, the interest of the applied studies was ultimately both short-term and local. They were addressed to 'social problems' defined by the preoccupations of government officials, and they were largely forgotten with the end of the British Empire in Central and Eastern Africa in the early sixties. The new universities and research institutions, and the international aid agencies, put their faith, for a while, in five-year plans, built around large-scale capital projects: exercises in 'planification' that had little room for anthropologists.

Moreover, in the new African states, anthropologists were discredited precisely on account of their association with the colonial regimes. This disconcerted Audrey, and she defended the record of applied anthropology and of the colonial welfare programmes more generally. 'We were all "do gooders"', she wrote, 'trying to organize research which we felt to be helpful for "welfare and development", the term used in the Colonial Development and Welfare Act. Many would deny the validity of our belief . . . especially those who feel that cultural and structural differences between the peoples inhabiting the ex-colonies should be obliterated as soon as possible.'[39]

This suggests that she had limited sympathy with African nationalism and with the African intellectuals' critique of 'tribalism' and of colonial motives. There is little in her writings, or even her correspondence, to suggest that she appreciated the significance of the post-war nationalist movement. Her main political study of this period, *East African Chiefs* (1960), was formulated in classic colonial terms.

Why is the selection of these chiefs described as a problem? Because British administrators have considered themselves to be committed to a policy of raising the standards of living of the people under their rule and of introducing something like Western types of social service.[40]

There is little in the book about the colonial administration as a whole, which her American colleague and friend Tom Fallers had described so acutely in one Uganda region, Busoga.[41] Two years after *East African Chiefs* appeared, Uganda was independent. I taught anthropology at Makerere in the late sixties, and this study longer seemed to be relevant to the political problems of the country.

*   *   *

Ironic, self-mocking, a hilarious companion, famous in Uganda for her party trick of lighting matches with her toes, Audrey was nevertheless a most serious and moral person. 'I have spent most of my life sucked into "do-good" things,' she once wrote to a friend.[42] In her last years, her health fragile, Audrey willingly accepted responsibility for an old friend who was suffering from alcoholism. One evening she tried to carry her upstairs, fell and cracked a bone in her leg. But when I visited her she was buoyant. She knew she was needed, she said. If she thought she could no longer be of use to others, then she would rather die. Only a few days before her death, she told a close friend that she was ready to die because 'there is no one any longer for whom I can do anything'. She lived until 1984.

Notes

1 I am very grateful to Professor Sir Raymond Firth and to Dr T.E. Faber, for allowing me to consult and cite Audrey Richards's letters in the collection of the London School of Economics, and to Dr Angela Raspin, the Keeper of Manuscripts, for her kind help. Unless otherwise indicated the letters cited are to be found in this collection. Professor Firth and Dr Faber also wrote very helpful comments on an earlier draft, as did Professors Jean La Fontaine and Andrew

Roberts. Professor Roberts also directed me to valuable historical sources on the Bemba and corrected some key passages in
the original draft. Walter Elkan and Aidan Southall, former
colleagues of Audrey Richards in East Africa, answered a
number of my questions.

A full bibliography of Audrey Richards's publications by
T. M. Luhrmann appears in Shirley Ardener (ed.) (1992)
Persons and Powers of Women in Diverse Cultures, New York and
Oxford: Berg, pp. 51-7. This bibliography is also published in
a special commemoration number of *Cambridge Anthropology*
(10:1 1985) which includes memoirs of Audrey Richards by
Helena Wayne, Raymond and Rosemary Firth, Sir Richard
Faber, and several of her former students and associates.
Marilyn Strathern wrote a substantial obituary, 'Audrey I.
Richards, 1899-1984', *Proceedings of the British Academy*, 82
(1993): 439-53.

2   N.G. Annan (1955) 'The Intellectual Aristocracy' in J.H.Plumb
    (ed.) *Studies in Social History*, London: Longmans.
3   Loc.cit., pp. 269-73.
4   The citations are from a memoir of her mother written
    by Audrey Richards and kindly put at my disposal by Dr
    T. Faber.
5   Duncan Wilson (1987) *Gilbert Murray OM. 1866-1957*, Oxford:
    Clarendon Press, p.350.
6   Letter to Adam Kuper, 13th June, 1978.
7   Letter (in the LSE collection) from Graham Wallas to Malinow-
    ski, dated 13.11.1926.
8   E.R. Leach (1957) 'The Epistemological Background to Mali-
    nowski's Empiricism' in Raymond Firth (ed.) *Man and Culture:
    An Evaluation of the Work of Bronislaw Malinowski*, London:
    Routledge and Kegan Paul, p. 124.
9   Audrey Richards (1957) 'The Concept of Culture in Malinow-
    ski's Work,' in R. Firth (ed.), *Man and Culture: An Evaluation
    of the Work of Bronislaw Malinowski*, London: Routledge and
    Kegan Paul, pp. 18-19.
10 Audrey I. Richards (1932) *Hunger and Work in a Savage Tribe: A
    Functional Study of Nutrition among the Southern Bantu*, London:
    Routledge and Kegan Paul, p. 1.
11 Loc. cit. p. 211.
12 Loc. cit. p. 213.
13 Richards, 'The Concept of Culture in Malinowski's Work', p.
    19.

14 Audrey Richards (1974) 'The 'Position' of Women – an Anthropological View', *Cambridge Anthropology*, Vol 1, No. 3: 7.

15 The fieldwork proposal is in Audrey Richards's student file in the LSE archive.

16 On the history of the Bemba, see Andrew Roberts (1973) *A History of the Bemba*, London: Longmans. Professor Roberts comments: 'Audrey, of course, may have been unaware of this background when she arrived in 1930. I don't think, indeed, she acknowledges it anywhere; and she doesn't seem to refer at all to the extended study of the N. Rhodesian economy (including labour migration) made in 1932 by Austin Robinson, who was already a Cambridge lecturer in economics (and a member of the Intellectual Aristocracy – his father was Dean of Winchester . . .) I do wonder whether Audrey – at least in the 1930's – regarded even contemporary scholarship of this sort as 'knowledge' – let alone the testimony of 19th century travellers!'

17 Audrey Richards (1939) *Land, Labour and Diet in Northern Rhodesia: An Economic Study of the Bemba Tribe*, London: Oxford University Press for International Institute of African Languages and Cultures, pp. 12-13.

18 Audrey Richards (1949) 'Colonial Future: the Need for Facts,' *Spectator*, 4 February 1949).

19 Cited in Robert I. Rotberg (1977) *Black Heart: Gore-Browne and the Politics of Multiracial Zambia*, Berkeley: California University Press. This book gives a good account of the expeditions the two women made together.

20 Audrey Richards (1939) *Land Labour and Diet in Northern Rhodesia*, pp. 12-13.

21 Paul Bwembya Mushindo (1973) *The Life of a Zambian Evangelist*, Lusaka: University of Zambia Institute of African Studies, Communication no.9., p. 28.

22 Audrey Richards, *Land, Labour and Diet in Northern Rhodesia*, Preface.
        For appreciations of Audrey Richards's contributions in the field of nutrition see Jo Gladstone (1986) 'Significant Sister: Autonomy and Obligation in Audrey Richards' Early Fieldwork', *American Ethnologist*, 13: 338-62; Jo Gladstone (1987) 'Venturing on the Borderline: Audrey Richards' Contribution to the Hungry Thirties Debate in Africa', *Bulletin of the Society for the Social History of Medicine*, no.40; and Jo Gladstone (1992) 'Audrey I. Richards: Africanist and Humanist' in

136

Shirley Ardener (ed.) *Persons and Powers of Women in Diverse Cultures*, New York and Oxford: Berg.

23 Audrey Richards, loc.cit.

24 Audrey Richards (1940) *Bemba Marriage and Present Economic Conditions*, Livingstone: Rhodes-Livingstone Institute (Rhodes-Livingstone Papers, no.4, p. 7.

25 Helena Wayne (1985) 'Bronislaw Malinowski: the Influence of Various Women on His Life and Works', *American Ethnologist*, 13 (3).

26 Audrey Richards (1942) 'Some Causes of a Revival of Tribalism in South African Native Reserves', *Man*, no.41: 89-90.

27 Audrey Richards (1935) 'A Modern Movement of Witch-finders', *Africa*, 8: 448-61.

28 Audrey Richards (1937) 'The Colonial Office and the Organisation of Social Research', *Anthropological Forum*, 4 (2): 168-89 (p. 173).

29 Letter to Firth, 27th May, 1984, in Firth papers, LSE collection.

30 Letter to Adam Kuper, 12th April, 1994.

31 For an early statement see V.W. Turner (1961) *Ndembu Divination: its Symbolism and Techniques*, Manchester: Manchester University Press for the Rhodes-Livingstone Institute.

32 Audrey Richards (1967) 'African Systems of Thought: An Anglo-French Dialogue', *Man*, 2 (2): 286-98 (p. 292). She is making a distinction between what she terms 'British' and 'French' approaches to fieldwork, but is in fact describing the Malinowskian tradition. At a later point in the same paper (p.296) she specifically distances herself from Turner's approach.

33 See, e.g., Jo Gladstone (1992) 'Audrey I. Richards: Africanist and Humanist', in Shirley Ardener (ed.) *Persons and Powers of Women in Diverse Cultures*, New York and Oxford: Berg.

34 E.R. Leach (1990) 'Richards, Audrey Isabel (1899-1984)', in *Dictionary of National Biography, 1981-5*, Oxford: Oxford University Press, p. 338.

35 Audrey Richards (1974) 'The "Position" of Women – an Anthropological View', *Cambridge Anthropology*, 1 (3): 3-10. Citations from pp. 4 and 9.

36 Richards (1977) 'The Colonial Office and the Organisation of Social Research', *Anthropological Forum*, p. 183.

37 Leach, 'Richards, Audrey Isabel (1899-1984)'.

38 Richards, 'The Colonial Office', p. 169.

39 Loc. cit. p. 174.
40 Audrey Richards (ed.) (1960) *East African Chiefs: A Study of Political Development in Some Uganda and Tanganyika Tribes*, London: Faber & Faber, pp. 13-14.
41 Lloyd A. Fallers (1965) *Bantu Bureaucracy: A Study of Integration and Conflict in the Political Institutions of an East African People*, Chicago: University of Chicago Press.
42 Letter to Jean La Fontaine, quoted in Jean La Fontaine (1985) 'Audrey I.Richards, obituary', *Africa*, 55: 64.

8
Ernest Gellner. Two Notes

I

In one of the key passages in his last collection of essays (*Anthropology and Politics: Revolutions in the Sacred Grove* Oxford: Blackwell Publishers, 1995), Ernest Gellner identified three contemporary views of truth. Roughly, the fundamentalists are sure that truth is revealed by God; the relativists believe that truth (which, of course, they refer to as 'truth') is a matter of opinion; while the Enlightenment Puritans reason that armed with reliable observations, and aided by imagination and scepticism, one may chip away at error.

An uncompromising Enlightenment Puritan himself, Gellner's central premise is that all cultures are equal, except for the cosmopolitan and polyglot sub-culture of science. Based on reason and observation, it delivers reliable knowledge and technological gains to which virtually all the people of the modern world aspire. This sub-culture is available to all. Consequently, science and technology are breaking down the old communities, and also the modern states that fail to deliver the goods, most dramatically the former Soviet Union and its colonies.

The fundamentalists are unlikely to become anthropologists, since they have no sympathy with unbelievers. Anthropologists – and philosophers – are, accordingly, either relativists or realists. ('It is well known that every philosophical baby that is born alive is either a little positivist or else a little Hegelian.') Gellner's commitment was to realism and positivism: to science. He was at once a philosopher and an anthropologist, and these essays are wonderfully stimulating excursions on behalf of the positivists. The relativists are shown no quarter: 'Cognitive relativism is nonsense, moral relativism is tragic'.

The good anthropologist, like any good scientist, is a Popperian. A theory should 'be more or less compatible with available facts; or at any rate, it is not blatantly in conflict with them. It explains them better than any available alternative, and it suggests further ethnographic, historical and other enquiries. As a good Popperian, I ask no more of theories.' The facts about social life are most reliably gathered by ethnographers, practicing participant observation in the manner of Malinowski. Gellner quotes Kim Philby's observation that a spy who only collects documents is no use at all. After all, a document may be a ploy in some bureaucratic game, or may languish in a file if some general finds it inconvenient. 'What *is* valuable is to be able to speak informally and at length with the members of the embassy in question, and to get a real feel for the way they habitually and naturally think. Once that is understood, it becomes easy to interpret even minor signs that are not confidential.' And finally, hypothesis and observations are worthless unless they are clearly and unambiguously phrased, and open to refutation. The relativists prefer the false profundities of obfuscation. 'It is not obvious to me that, because the world is a diverse, complex and tortured place, which it is, that only cumbersome and ambiguous sentences can do it justice, and that clarity is some kind of intellectual treason. . . . I can accept neither a murky relativism nor a semiotic mysticism.'

At one level, the essays in this book endorse the direction taken by social anthropology in what Gellner calls the intellectual sterling area, which, for anthropologists, now covers the European Union and the former Soviet Empire. (He gave the opening address, reprinted here, at the foundation meeting of the European Association of Social Anthropologists, which unites the practitioners of social anthropology in the tradition of Malinowski – and of Gellner.) Conversely, Gellner is merciless on the cultural determinism, the romanticism and relativism, and the hermeneutic methods, associated with the modern – and post-modern – American school.

Yet his essential points of reference lie elsewhere, in the Austro-Hungarian Empire of the early twentieth century, in which he grew up, and which nurtured the schools of thought that dominated his lifetime. On the one side were the positivists and universalists, notably Mach and Popper, the liberals, like Hayek, and the satirical writers he admired, like Robert Musil and Karel Capek; on the other side were the relativists, epitomised by Wittgenstein, the prophets of false science, notably Freud, and the romantic nationalists and revolutionaries. There was an elective affininity between the protagonists of these great parties, so that the later Wittgenstein can be shown to have peddled a philosophical version of romantic communalism, while Freud gave comfort to the moral relativists.

His hero, Malinowski, crossed the divide. He was brought up a romantic. His father studied peasant folk-lore in Carpathian villages for nationalistic reasons. But Malinowski wrote his thesis on Mach, preferred the tolerant, multi-ethnic Empire to the dreams of Polish chauvinists, and adapted the tradition of nationalist folk-lore studies to the investigation of exotic others, the Trobriand islanders, whom he represented as driven by the same motives as the most hard-nosed and cynical Viennese man of affairs. One of the most successful essays here is on another cross-over, the Catholic priest Alois Musil, a cousin of the author of *A Man Without Qualities.* The Moravian answer to Laurence of Arabia, he became a sympathiser with Islam, a great ethnographer of the Bedouin, and, like Masaryk (another cross-over), an Enlightenment Puritan at last.

In the preface to this book, dated November, 1994, Gellner insisted that 'Anthropology is inevitably political'. This is because theoretical anthropology must affirm 'what we are, what our society is and can be'. A realist anthropology is therefore the precondition for realistic politics. And he ended the final chapter with a plea to his colleagues:

> Our predicament is – to work out the social options of our affluent and disenchanted condition. We have no choice in this matter. To pretend otherwise, to claim that the problem does not even arise, but has been replaced by the Permanent Carnival, is absurd. The *fin de millénaire*

should have it fireworks, but let it not deprive us of our sense of reality.

Ernest Gellner died in December, 1995, a few weeks after this book appeared. It will serve as a splendid introduction to his characteristic themes, but reading these essays will also reinforce our sense of loss. He will not be there any longer, leading the good fight, indomitable in combat, mocking error, learned, witty, truly worldly-wise.

II

I once described Ernest Gellner as a social anthropologist of the school of Malinowski, and a philosopher in the tradition of Popper. He sent me a note to say that was just about right, but I am tempted now to reverse the formula. He was a Malinowskian philosopher, who was concerned above all with the uses to which ideas were put. And as an anthropologist he was a Popperian, exuberantly inventing models late into the night, but beady-eyed the morning after, a relentless critic, unmoved by reputation.

Like Popper and Malinowski, he was a realist and a positivist. The universe, he remarked, was not there to pander to our self-esteem. Any theory about our behaviour in that stubbornly independent universe should be firmly rooted in observation, open to falsification, and expressed clearly, though not, of course, without wit and style. (He would approvingly cite Popper's fulminations against 'the cult of un-understandibility, the cult of impressive and high-sounding language'.)

Like Gellner himself, Popper and Malinowski found a second spiritual home at the LSE, but intellectually they were all the progeny of Franz-Josef's Vienna, that extraordinary school of all our modernities. (Malinowski's Cracow and his own Prague, as Gellner remarked, were intellectual suburbs of Vienna.) In that milieu, Gellner was of the Enlightenment party. Politically he was liberal: not a raw-meat Hayek liberal, but like Popper and Malinowski, an open-society man. A cultural pluralist, he nevertheless believed that science offered a model for a rational discourse that could cross cultural boundaries.

The opponents against whom he battled throughout his career were also identified with their Viennese prototypes, Freud and Wittgenstein. Freud stood for the pseudo-scientist, the shaman. Wittgenstein spoke for the anti-scientists, the relativists. They were the enemies of rationality and universal values. Fostering irrationalism, Wittgenstein's influence could also have dangerous political consequences. Gellner noted that Heidegger and Merleau-Ponty ended up supporting, respectively, Hitler and Stalin, just as Bertrand Russell had predicted.

The main issue in Popper's philosophy was the nature of science. Popper argued that science was a unique intellectual enterprise. It was first institutionalised in the West, and historians of science spent much of their energy trying to identify the reasons for this unique development, but so far as Gellner was concerned the consequences were more interesting. Science went everywhere, and wherever it went it caused a great rupture in human history. Once science was institutionalised in a society, that society became modern, industrial, secular – and nationalistic.

This was latterly perhaps his best-known thesis: that industrial and secular modern societies would inevitably become nationalistic. Traditional societies were stratified, culturally plural, religious. Their stability was guaranteed by the limited horizons and repetitive experience of local communities. Industrial societies had to foster a complex division of labour, labour mobility, universal literacy, competitive individualism, and cultural homogeneity. Only a nationalist ideology, or perhaps a puritan version of Islam, could motivate the political arrangements necessary to manage these great social changes.

The two types of society were, I think, connected in Gellner's imagination with the still largely agrarian old world of the Austro-Hungarian Empire, and the new rational, scientific, industrial, nationalistic societies that were ushered in by the intellectuals who had occupied the tables of the Viennese coffee-houses before the Great War. Although he was an apostle of science, Gellner rather regretted the passing of that tolerant, rickety old world. Science delivered a progressively more accurate understanding of a discrete natural world, but this triumph of science did not make for a rational society. Science and reason flourish only in carefully bounded enclaves (even, he found, at the LSE). Outside, the forces of unreason rule. Although the machines of Industria liberate most of its inhabitants from want, they do not free us from coercion. Gellner found the political arrangements of advanced industrial societies generally squalid. His optimism about scientific progress was combined with a sceptical and rather pessimistic account of our social and political prospects.

Gellner's Malinowskian philosophy had an impact on many intellectuals. Philosophies had a life of their own in society, which could be grasped ethnographically. He first demonstrated this insight in his corruscating account of the smug conservatism of the Oxford epigoni of Wittgenstein. Later he analysed Islam as a pattern for living. Then he showed how politics shaped scientific thinking, in his accounts of Soviet Marxism. Above all, he found new links between nationalist ideologies and the processes of modernisation.

These exercises in Malinowskian philosophy were very influential. His Popperian anthropology, however, found few takers among his colleagues, even after he had become a paid-up member of the anthropological community, on moving from the LSE to the chair of social anthropology at Cambridge, when he was already almost sixty. The bold models were perhaps a little unnerving, the positivism unfashionable. His devastating critiques of bad theory were too often ignored by those who made a virtue of vague, puddingy relativism, or who felt that good intentions might be a substitute for logic. Immune from the pressures of fashion, or the moral blackmail of political correctness, Gellner nevertheless continued to address epistles to the anthropologists, and as each new variety of Wittgensteinian error made its appearance he took the trouble to point out its true affinities and its philosophical weaknesses.

There are signs that his critique of relativism and idealism is at last reaching the anthropologists, but we have lost not only our most sophisticated critic but our emissary to the intellectuals, our link to the great traditions of modern European thought, our precious Voltaire.

9
South African Anthropology: An Inside Job[1]

I

The historical relationship between social anthropology and African imperial or colonial policy is still poorly understood, but it should be evident that the relationship was neither stable nor uniform, even if too little attention has so far been paid to periodisation, and to local or regional differences. But perhaps less obvious is the fact that the traffic between colony and metropolis was by no means one way. Not only were funds, jobs, even careers sometimes on offer to metropolitan anthropologists from colonial or dominion governments: there was also a two-way traffic in ideas. Indeed, it could be argued that the institutional and intellectual origins of British social anthropology should be traced to Australia and South Africa.

As late as 1920, social anthropology had barely established a foothold in British universities, and it had only fugitive and peripheral connections with African colonial governments. A.R. Radcliffe-Brown,[2] the first British student to have specialised in anthropology as an undergraduate, was the coming man in the field, but in 1920, almost forty years old, he was unemployed, recovering from ill-health, and obliged to live with his brother in Johannesburg. He wrote a letter to his former teacher and patron, Alfred Cort Haddon, to give some idea of his job prospects in South Africa, and to solicit assistance. In the past few years he had worked in secondary education, in Australia and in Tonga, and he was doing some teaching at the Normal College in Johannesburg, but, he wrote, 'of course I should prefer to stick to ethnology'. A position as ethnologist at the Transvaal

Museum in Pretoria was one possibility. He had also picked up a tantalising rumour that the Union government might be prepared to establish an ethnographic research unit.

> The man who can do this is Smuts. If you know of any means of approaching Smuts and putting the matter before him I think it would be well worth doing and would probably be successful . . . . I hope to meet Smuts, but of course I cannot well urge the needs of ethnology for it will be obvious that I am hunting for a job. So I hope that you will be able to do something.[3]

J.C. Smuts was at that time Prime Minister of the Union of South Africa, but he had been a student at Cambridge, and was an honorary fellow of Christ's College, to which Haddon belonged. Haddon had himself urged the establishment of a research bureau in ethnology during a visit to South Africa in 1905, and in response to Radcliffe-Brown's prodding he immediately wrote a letter to Smuts, urging two main reasons for the project: '(1) the advancement of scientific knowledge, and (2) the advantage which would accrue to the Government for the purpose of administration in having authoritative information concerning the sociology, manners and customs, and religion of the various tribes.' He went on to remark that 'It so happens that Mr A.R. Brown is at the present time in Johannesburg. . . . Thus you have on the spot the most brilliant and experienced of the younger students turned out by the Cambridge School of Ethnology, and I am sure that you could not get a more competent investigator from elsewhere.'[4]

Smuts passed Haddon's letter on to the Minister of Native Affairs, who forwarded it to the liberal parliamentarian John X. Merriman, with the remark that it 'arrives at an opportune time'. Several South African scholars were also busily lobbying for a school of African studies,[5] but Haddon's initiative coincided fortuitously with the first major parliamentary crisis on the question of what was termed Native policy. In the aftermath of World War I, African politics became more radical, and white politicians began to debate native policy with new urgency. In 1920, the Smuts government enacted the Native Affairs Act, which set up native councils in the reserves with local government powers, and established mechanisms for consultation between white and black leaders. The legislation precipitated a confrontation between segregationists and more liberal politicians (or, in the view of some historians, between more and less extreme segregationists).

Precisely what weight Haddon's intervention may have carried in this complex situation is uncertain, but in any case the authorities decided to fund a School of African Life and Languages, and to establish it at the University of Cape Town. A professor of African languages was appointed in 1920. In the following year the University advertised a chair in social anthropology, the first established chair in the subject in Britain or in the British Empire.

But what sort of scholar should be appointed to this novel position? The South Africans who lobbied for anthropology – some administrators and politicians, and missionaries – expected, naturally enough, that an authority on South African ethnology would be appointed. However, the university followed the advice of an English advisory committee – in which Haddon participated, together with Frazer, Marett and Rivers – who took it for granted that what was needed was a theoretically trained anthropologist. They recommended Radcliffe-Brown, on the grounds of his scientific standing. The fact that his field experience was entirely in the Andaman Islands and in Australia was a secondary matter. Radcliffe-Brown was duly appointed, though it was made clear that long-term funding could not be counted upon.[6]

Radcliffe-Brown's science was, however, very different from that of the established British anthropologists who recommended him for the Cape Town chair. Influenced by Durkheim, he had broken with the evolutionism of Frazer and the diffusionism of Rivers. He advocated a science that would be based on 'general laws of sociology and psychology', and he claimed that such a scientific anthropology would be more likely 'to lead to results of practical value to South Africa' than historical, ethnological studies.[7] In his inaugural lecture, in 1921, the new professor summarised in lay terms the principles of his science. The subject of social anthropology was social structure, and social structures were integrated systems. Any change, in any part, would have repercussions for the rest of the system. He remarked that great changes had been in train for generations in South Africa. The traditional social systems of the African people had been transformed by European interventions: 'we inaugurated something that must change the whole of their social life'. From the principles of structural-functionalism an ineluctable conclusion followed: 'Segregation was impossible.' Radcliffe-Brown also advised legislators to take note of the fact that the various communities might apply different moral principles to evaluate laws. Finally, he remarked that it was necessary to consider what future 'white civilization' might have in South Africa, since the institutions of the whites would also, inevitably, be subject to change in the emergent social system.[8]

Radcliffe-Brown regularly insisted that the social anthropologist should provide facts and scientific appreciations, rather than political opinions, but he could have had no illusions about the political sensitivity of his analysis. It is hardly surprising that only a couple of months after taking up the post, the new professor was complaining to Haddon:

> It is a detestable nuisance having this work mixed up with the kind of politics that we have out here. Beattie [the Vice-Chancellor of the University of Cape Town] tells me that there was much opposition amongst Smuts's followers to making the grant. They were prepared to withdraw their opposition if a member of the Dutch Reformed Church (!) was appointed to one of the professorships . . . . So Smuts anticipates very violent opposition to the renewal of the grant in three year's time.[9]

Radcliffe-Brown also turned his guns on the established, evolutionist anthropology of the leading Southern African specialists, notably Henri Junod. Indeed, his famous lecture counterposing the sociology of the present, the study of social structure, to the speculative history of the evolutionists and diffusionists was delivered and published in South Africa.[10] He was, in short, determined to stir things up, but for the same reasons he also found allies, among them perhaps the leading African intellectual of the day, Professor D.D.T. Jabavu, who was a Professor at Fort Hare Native College. Jabavu attended some of Radcliffe-Brown's vacation schools (run for missionaries and civil servants) and wrote lyrically about his inspiring lectures and his 'unbiased racial outlook'; and he endorsed Radcliffe-Brown's call for 'research on Bantu Social Anthropology.'[11] Jabavu was later to offer courses in anthropology at Fort Hare (where one of his students was the young Nelson Mandela).[12]

In 1926, Radcliffe-Brown departed for Sydney, urging in a final public lecture that 'South African nationalism must be a nationalism composed of both black and white'.[13] Despite the opposition Radcliffe-Brown had aroused in some quarters, the chair itself was maintained. His successor was T.T. Barnard, another Cambridge student of Haddon and Rivers, who lost interest in anthropology and took to horticulture. In 1935 Barnard gracefully handed over the chair to Isaac Schapera, on the grounds that he was the best man for the position. Before Radcliffe-Brown's departure, teaching in social anthropology had also been established in three other universities (the University of the Witwatersrand, in Johannesburg, and the Afrikaans-medium Universities of Stellenbosch and Pretoria). In 1925 an ethnological section was established in the government's Native Affairs Department, under G.P. Lestrade. A small official fund was also established for academic research (smaller, it was noted, than the fund for prehistory, which interested Smuts rather more). However, government support was peripheral, and it ended when a new, right-wing government came to power just as the Depression was at its height.

This is not surprising, for the government had made little use of anthropology. In 1927 the Native Administration Act extended the application of so-called traditional law, and the jurisdiction of chiefs' courts, but the South African anthropologists were not called upon to participate in this initiative.

(In contrast, the Bechuanaland Government commissioned a review of customary law from Schapera.) As late as 1934, at a time when Lugard's policy of Indirect Rule was beginning to direct the attention of colonial administrators to modern anthropological ideas, Schapera noted that South Africa was the only country in Africa that did not require its native administrators to receive any professional training, and that policy makers did not call on anthropological expertise.[14]

In 1929 the race question dominated what came to be called the 'black peril' elections, and an Afrikaner nationalist government came to power. It was sympathetic to the European fascist movements of the 1930s, but the South African situation had its own very particular characteristics. The crucial issue for white South African politicians was the so-called 'Poor White Problem', the development of a growing population of unemployed, largely Afrikaans-speaking whites. The Afrikaner nationalists blamed their plight on 'English' capitalists, who were prepared to sacrifice the interests of white workers for the sake of cheaper black labour. This economic analysis was subsumed within an ethnic politics. The Afrikaner nation, defeated on the battlefield a generation earlier, was now oppressed economically by its old enemies. Moreover, poor whites might be assimilated into the black proletariat. Miscegenation would lead to the end of racial identity. The solution was an Afrikaner cultural revival, ethnic mobilisation in politics, job reservation for whites, and racial segregation. A national debate was launched on the future of South Africa, and on the place of the African population within it.

Two broad and fiercely opposed discourses on the race question were already established. One drew on the notion that civilization and Christianity would transform the African societies, and that a liberal policy of individual rights would ultimately prevail. The educated Africans 'are ranged on the side of civilization,' Jabavu assured a parliamentary select committee in 1927.

Our interests are intertwined with civilized interests. We would not like to go back naked to the Kraals and live a barbarous life. We have renounced that life once and for all. In fact, if today there were a war between barbarism and civilization, we would be on the side of civilization.[15]

Some argued the the industrialisation of South Africa would lead ineluctably to the modernisation of all sectors of the society, and to a liberal political settlement. The most radical version of this theory was advanced by the historian W.M. Macmillan, and was memorably summed up by his student C.W. de Kiewiet, who noted that the 1936 census found that there were over half a million more natives outside the reserves than within them, and concluded: 'Segregation is a myth, a fancy, anything but a fact. As a word it describes a hope or a policy but not a real situation . . . . What has been twisted together by history cannot be readily disentangled by laws. To unwind the woven cord of native and European life is simply to require history to retrace its steps.'[16]

The alternative view opposed culture to civilization, insisting, in the tradition of German romanticism, that interests were shaped by primordial cultural identities, and that if the integrity of a culture was undermined then social disintegration would follow. The main point of reference for this theory was, of course, the Afrikaner nation itself: and this was the period in which modern Afrikaner nationalism was taking shape. However, it could also be applied to the African population. This was the standpoint of leading Afrikaner ethnologists, who had typically taken their advanced degrees in Germany in the 1920s and 1930s, and who now supported segregation. W.W.M. Eiselen, the professor of ethnology at Stellenbosch, argued that policy should aim to foster 'higher Bantu culture and not at producing black Europeans'.[17] Giving evidence to the new government's Native Economic Commission, in 1931, Gérard Lestrade, Professor of Ethnology at the University of Pretoria, presented a 'scientific' case against assimilation and in favour of a segregationist, or what he termed an 'adaptationist' approach, that 'would take out of the Bantu past what was good, and even what was merely neutral, and together with what is good of European culture for the Bantu, build up a

Bantu future'.[18] Lestrade's intervention provoked Macmillan to issue a root-and-branch denunciation of anthropologists as 'paralysed conservatives',[19] but in fact the small community of anthropologists were divided.

The underlying assumptions of the segregationist ideology were opposed by Agnes Winifred Hoernlé, a close associate of Radcliffe-Brown,[20] who taught at the University of the Witwatersrand, and by Isaac Schapera at Cape Town. Winifred Hoernlé was one of the founders of a liberal think-tank, the South African Institute of Race Relations, in 1929. She also supervised the first ethnographic studies of African urban slums, studies that must be seen not only as examples of a classic reformist genre of 'social problems', or even as adaptations of the urban studies of the Chicago school, but perhaps above all as attempts to direct attention to the life of the so-called 'detribalised natives', the bane of the segregationists.[21]

Schapera published an edited book in 1934, entitled *Western Civilization and the Natives of South Africa* (London: George Routledge and Sons), which took for its subject the rapidly changing situation of black South Africans. In his preface, Schapera directly confronted the segregationist arguments of the Native Economic Commission, pointing out that there was no longer in South Africa the social basis for a policy of indirect rule. Moreover, and in contrast to every other contemporary academic symposium on Africa, he included a chapter by an African intellectual, written by D.D.T. Jabavu, and simply entitled 'Bantu Grievances'. Jabavu concentrated on land issues and the oppressive regulation of labour, but also covered a variety of topics from the 'travesty of justice' to the franchise.

A later volume, *The Bantu-Speaking Tribes of South Africa* (London: George Routledge and Sons, 1937), also edited by Schapera, included a chapter on 'The Imposition and Nature of European Control', by the liberal historian J.S. Marais, who concluded that 'the position of Natives throughout the country has become worse since 1910. Rights they formerly enjoyed have been abolished or have become precarious; the principle of anti-native discrimination has been extended into a number of new fields, and new ways of enforcing it have been devised.' Schapera's own chapter on 'Cultural Changes in Tribal Life' concluded with the observation that despite legislation promoting segregation, 'the Bantu are being drawn more and more into the common cultural life of South Africa', a conclusion, he noted, that was reinforced by the evidence presented in the chapters that followed, on Africans on the farms (by Monica Hunter) and in the towns (by Ellen Hellmann).

The Hertzog government suspended support for Africanist research in South Africa, in 1931, and an Inter-University Committee for African Studies was established. It was affiliated to the International Institute of African Languages and Cultures, so becoming eligible for the funds that the Rockefeller Foundation was making available, via the Institute, for ethnographic research. Among the beneficiaries were Monica Hunter, Eileen and Jack Krige, Hilda Kuper, and Z.K. Matthews, a black scholar from Fort Hare, who participated in Malinowski's seminar and undertook research on a characteristic 'social change' theme: 'The impact of Western Civilization on the Family Life of the the Bantu of South Africa.' Funding dried up again when World War II broke out, and the Inter-University Committee suspended its operations. At the same time, the Union Government closed the native reserves to anthropologists. Yet in this brief period in the late 1920s and 1930s, the classic ethnographic field studies of South Africa were undertaken, resulting in a magisterial series of publications including Schapera's books and articles on the Tswana, Monica Hunter's *Reaction to Conquest* (note the title), on the Pondo, and the works of the students directly influenced by Winifred Hoernlé, Hilda Kuper's monographs on the Swazi, J.D. and Eileen Krige on the Lovedu, and Max Gluckman's essays on the Zulu.

In South Africa, as in Europe, the 1930s was a politically charged decade. Jabavu, the first African intellectual to welcome the new anthropology to South Africa, became founding president of the All-African Convention, in 1936, set up to oppose the abolition of non-white voting rights in the Cape. In 1938, Winifred Hoernlé resigned from the University of the Witwatersrand to devote herself to activist work in race relations. The younger generation of students were steeped in politics. Max Gluckman and Hilda Kuper were close to the Communist Party at this time, but as Gluckman recalled, whether they considered themselves socialists or anti-segregationist liberals, the whole cohort of students to which he belonged: 'either before or after they did field research, believed in the integration of Africans and Whites – and other ethnic groups – within a single social system based on equality of all men.' Their work, he went on, put little emphasis on the supposed inner harmony of societies, 'and certainly very little on the uniqueness' of the cultures they studied.[22]

II

It was also in the 1930s that Malinowski began to influence the development of South African anthropology, and to be influenced in turn by its particular concerns.

Following in the footsteps of Schapera, the new generation of anthropologists at South Africa's English-speaking universities spent periods with Malinowski at the London School of Economics. In the 1930s, Malinowski's interests were shifting, partly in response to a flow of funds for African research from the Rockefeller Foundation. He also began to attract black African intellectuals to his seminars, including Jomo Kenyatta and the South African Z.K. Matthews. 'As an African,' Matthews recalled, 'I found it a great relief to come across a student of primitive cultures who did not have a purely antiquarian and static interest in them, but stressed the necessity of following each item of culture in its proper context . . . .'[23] The concerns of his Africanist students – and in particular the South Africans – were soon reflected in Malinowski's own publications, particularly after his first, and only, journey to Africa, in 1934.

After brief visits to Lucy Mair and Audrey Richards in the field, in Uganda and Northern Rhodesia, Malinowski went on to South Africa, as a guest speaker at a conference on

African education. Here he met the Swazi king, Sobhuza, who had already made contact with the liberal South African anthropologists. There was a specific issue at stake, which had brought the Swazi king to this conference. Sobhuza wished to revive the Swazi initiation ceremonies and to induct a new regiment, arguing that this would provide young Swazi with discipline, and foster respect for elders. His proposal was strongly opposed by the missionaries, and also by some educated, Christian Swazi, though it had support from within the Swaziland administration. Hoernlé and Schapera, however, had visited Swaziland earlier in 1934 and strongly recommended that the *ibutho* (regimental) system should be revived.

A young South African student of Malinowski's, Hilda Beemer (Kuper), was beginning her fieldwork in Swaziland, and Malinowski spent a fortnight with her at the Swazi court, and had several meetings with Sobhuza.[24] Sobhuza and Malinowski established a political alliance that survived for several years, and Malinowski submitted a report to the Swaziland Administration endorsing Hoernlé and Schapera's support for the revival of the regimental system. The two men found common ground in their view of the importance of ethnic cultural reassertion in a colonial context. They were both hostile to assimilation, and anti-colonial. Malinowski was sympathetic to 'a sophisticated nationalism or tribalism' that 'can still draw full strength from the enormous residues of old tradition' which remain alive 'not only in the tribal areas but also among the partly detribalized communities',[25] and in Sobhuza he recognised a leader who was putting up an admirable struggle against Westernisation. (One might suggest that Malinowski saw a kinship between this form of nationalism and the nationalism of minorities in the Austro-Hungarian Empire.)[26] Sobhuza himself expected the liberal anthropologists to support his chosen course. In her 'Introduction' to *An African Aristocracy*, Hilda Kuper noted:

Most educated Africans, more particularly detribalized Africans and men with little standing in tribal life, distrust anthropology. They see it as a weapon to keep natives in their 'traditional milieu'(arbitrarily stripped of action judged 'barbarous' by Europeans) and to prevent them on pseudo-scientific grounds – retaining the 'soul of the people', their 'primitive mentality' – from assimilating European culture. Sohbuza, on the other hand, is interested in anthropology; he has read a number of books on the subject, subscribes to anthropological journals, enjoys descriptions of the customs of other people, and is proud of his own. He one day explained, 'Anthropology makes possible comparison and selection of lines of further development. European culture is not all good; our is often better. We must be able to choose how to live, and for that we must see how others live. I do not want my people to be imitation Europeans, but to be respected for their own laws and customs'.[27]

Malinowski's reading of African development was, however, by no means accepted by all his students. This became evident with the publication in 1938 of a series of essays, entitled *Methods of Study of Culture Contact in Africa* (London: International African Institute) – the first theoretical symposium in British social anthropology devoted to social change. In his introduction, Malinowski insisted that it was impossible to recover the pre-contact 'baseline' African cultures. The investigator was faced rather with a process, in which three foci could be identified: a complex of traditional institutions, beliefs and practices, that were, however, probably far removed from the pre-conquest institutions; the powerful overlay of white power, economic enterprises, and Christianity; and an emerging third force, a new, synthetic, urban culture, which was not an amalgam of the traditional and the western but a genuinely independent development.[28] Classical functionalism was inappropriate in such a context, Malinowski concluded. What was required was a renewed functionalism, that took for its subject the effect that changes in religion, or land rights, or employment had on other practices.

But although Malinowski's perspective was more dynamic, more celebratory of hybridisation than the contemporary

American work of Herskovits,[29] the South African participants in the symposium – Hunter, Fortes, and especially Schapera – preferred to represent the South African
situation in more sociological terms. Even a remote rural
community in Bechuanaland was integrated in a wider social
field, Schapera insisted:

> The missionary, administrator, trader and labour recruiter
> must be regarded as factors in the tribal life in the same
> way as are the chief and the magician. Christianity . . .
> must be studied like any other form of cult . . . .
> So, too, the trading store, the labour recruiter and the
> agricultural demonstrator must be considered integral
> parts of the modern economic life, the school as part
> of the routine educational development of the children,
> and the [Colonial] Administration as part of the existing
> political system.[30]

In his Presidential Address to the Royal Anthropological
Institute in 1940, Radcliffe-Brown dismissed Malinowski's
suggestion that a 'plural society' should be studied as an
arena in which two or more 'cultures' interacted. European
settlers and administrators impelled willy-nilly the development of a new kind of society.

> For what is happening in South Africa, for example, is
> not the interaction of British culture, and Afrikander (or
> Boer) culture, Hottentot culture, various Bantu cultures
> and Indian culture, but the interaction of individuals and
> groups within an established social structure which is itself
> in process of change. What is happening in a Transkeian
> tribe, for example, can only be described by recognising
> that the tribe has been incorporated into a wide political
> and economic structural system.[31]

Delivering the Hoernlé Memorial Lecture in 1953 for the
South African Institute of Race Relations, he remarked that:
'To talk of letting the Native peoples of South Africa develop
along their own lines was nonsense – their own traditional

system had been hacked to pieces and not much of it could be reconstructed.'[32]

In 1940, from the same perspective that Radcliffe-Brown outlined before the Royal Anthropological Institute, Max Gluckman published powerful case-studies on the sociology of Zululand. He demonstrated not only that chiefs and native commissioners were actors in a single social drama, but that they represented opposed interests. The dominant cleavage in the system ran between white and black, and shaped all the institutions on both sides of the divide.[33] It was above all money that 'established social cohesion by creating common, if dissimilar, interests in a single economic and political system, though it is one with many irreconcilable conflicts'. The tension at the heart of the system was only just contained by a series of countervailing practices and institutions. Perhaps unsurprisingly, the local government officials prevented his return to Zululand after 1939.[34]

III

Gluckman later devoted a long essay to a critique of Malinowski's theory of cultural change,[35] but Malinowski's approach also had its adherents in South Africa, and some Afrikaner ethnologists made approving references to his writings. A few were cautiously sympathetic to Sobhuza's policy, or even to that of the Zulu Cultural Society, founded in 1937 by Albert Luthuli.

Intellectually, the key figure in the Afrikaner school was W.W.M. Eiselen, who in 1932 became the first professor of ethnology at an Afrikaans-medium university, the University of Stellenbosch. Broadly educated, familiar with British, American and German theories, Eiselen was no simple racist or reactionary. He did not deny that changes had transformed the conditions of life in the African reserves. Indeed, he emphasised that the 'relatively simple social organization of the South African Bantu has, in a limited space of time, undergone two major changes'.[36] Subordination to the Europeans had undermined tribal institutions.

The modern educational system had reinforced 'the transmission of ideas, values, attitudes and skills which have not been developed in Bantu society and are often not in harmony with its institutions'. Both the organisational and ideological coherence of the Bantu system had therefore been breached. He recognised that one option was to accept these changes and to promote integration, but Eiselen believed that it would be better to check and even to reverse the tendency towards acculturation. The solution was, first of all, to develop the reserves: 'if the Reserves can be developed economically and culturally those who come to labour centres will have a background sufficiently rich and respected to prevent their demoralisation'. Secondly, an appropriate form of education must be developed which did not alienate a child from his own culture. In short, Eiselen drew on a functionalist mode of argument, but in a very different spirit from Radcliffe-Brown and his students, who concluded from their functionalist analysis that the changes in tribal life were irreversible.

In 1948, a radicalised Afrikaner Nationalist Party came to power, dedicated to a thorough-going policy of segregation, or, as it came to be called, *Apartheid*. Eiselen chaired the new government's commission of enquiry into Bantu education that recommended an educational policy founded on traditional institutions and values. These 'contain in themselves the seeds from which can develop a modern Bantu culture fully able to satisfy the aspirations of the Bantu and to deal with the conditions of the modern world'. He was later secretary to the Tomlinson Commission, which produced the blue-print for the Apartheid system, and he became the civil servant in charge of the Ministry of Native Affairs, to which his former professorial colleague from the University of Stellenbosch, H.F. Verwoerd, was soon appointed as Minister.

The other Afrikaner anthropologists were also by and large committed to the Afrikaner Nationalist movement in which the universities, like the churches, had traditionally been regarded as leading actors. During the five decades that the Afrikaner Nationalists ruled South Africa, the departments of *Volkekunde* in the Afrikaans-speaking universities were expected to contribute to the theory and practice of Apartheid, and in general they did what was expected of them.

The intellectual course of Afrikaans anthropology was set by a student of Eiselen, P.J. Coertze, who moved to a Chair at the University of Pretoria in 1951, where he was to remain until his retirement in 1972 (when he was succeeded, in good African style, by his son). From this eminence he ruled Afrikaans academic anthropology for two decades, establishing a tightly-disciplined cadre of ethnologists at the Afrikaans-medium universities. Like Coertze himself, every single professor of ethnology at these Universities was reputedly a member of the Broederbond.

Coertze and his school propagated what they called ethnos theory,[37] which asserted the primordial identity of national groups, and the enduring significance of cultural differ-ence. The ethnos was a cultural group, but it tended to be endogamous, and so developed significant racial traits. Ethnos theory has been described as a sanitised racism, as a version of German romantic cultural theory, and as a Calvinist anthropology, based on the conviction that dif-ferent peoples had been divinely elected to play their own particular part in history. However, it also had a certain explicit affinity to the culturalist movement in American anthropology, and Melville Herskovits and Ruth Benedict, especially, were frequently cited, as was Malinowski, if only as a counterweight to the South African social anthropologists who insisted on the inevitable development of a single South African society. The Afrikaner ethnologists none the less denounced Malinowski's research methods as subjective and unscientific. Participant observation required an intimacy of living that they found uncomfortable, preferring to rely on formal interviews with authority figures.

IV

Within South Africa, the two traditions, the Afrikaans and the

Anglophone, became polarised, and each developed its own national association.[38] But while the Nationalist ethnologists flourished with the development of the Apartheid state after 1948, the liberal, Anglophone South African anthropologists went into retreat, or moved abroad. Schapera left in 1950 for the London School of Economics. Z.K. Matthews was one of the defendants in the Treason Trial in 1956, and in 1962 he went into exile. At the same time, Hilda Kuper migrated to the United States. Many of the younger anthropologists also left South Africa, including most of the rising generation of black anthropologists, notably Absolom Vilakazi, Bernard Magubane and, later, Archie Mafeje and Harriet Ngubane.

Gluckman spent the war years in Northern Rhodesia at the Rhodes-Livingstone Institute. The new research programme that he introduced derived from the radical South African anthropology of the 1930s. When, after the War, he went to Manchester to establish a new department of social anthropology he brought the South African critique of functionalism into the heart of British social anthropology. In the 1970s, reacting against the flirtation of some British colleagues with cultural approaches, Gluckman again drew on his South African experience:

> It is possible in the cloistered seclusion of King's College, Cambridge (or Merton College, Oxford . . .), to put the main emphasis on the obstinate differences; it was not possible for 'liberal' South Africans confronted with the policy of segregation within a nation into which 'the others' had been brought, and treated as different – and inferior.[39]

But despite the departure of Gluckman, Schapera and others, important new initiatives were developed within South African anthropology. Philip Mayer organised a major study of urbanisation in East London, an industrial city on the borders of the Transkei, which developed the situational model of ethnicity that had been broached by some of Gluckman's associates on the Copperbelt in the 1950s.[40] Monica Wilson and Archie Mafeje published a parallel study of Langa, the African location in Cape Town.[41] A Swedish missionary, Bengt Sundkler, published a path-breaking study of African independent churches, *Bantu Prophets in South Africa*, in 1948, which stimulated a whole new stream of research on the Africanisation of Christianity. Monica Wilson also began a collaboration with historians. This was, however, soon overtaken by a new wave of African history, which represented in many ways the most stimulating research project in South African studies in this period.

The years between about 1960 and 1985 were the most painful and difficult of the Apartheid era, as the African opposition was crushed and its leaders imprisoned or exiled. The terrible machinery of the pass laws, forced resettlement, and Bantu Education ground relentlessly on. This was a period of ideological ferment among opposition intellectuals. The black opposition became polarised between a black power movement, initiated by a linguist at the University of the Witwatersrand, Robert Sobukwe, and developed by Steve Biko, and the increasingly Marxist orientation of the ANC in exile.

The liberal universities were forced to accept the imposition of a racial test on entry, and the liberal tradition appeared to be impotent. Social scientists and historians in the major English-speaking universities now developed a neo-Marxist account of South Africa, which included a critique of anthropology as conservative, and overly concerned with cultural difference. Ethnicity was false consciousness, manipulated by the régime. It was world capitalism that in truth shaped South African society. All anthropologists could effectively contribute was a critique of the discourse of cultural identity, and the documentation of the terrible effects of government policy.

The old structure of Afrikaner anthropology began to break up as the failure of *Apartheid* became apparent. When the great split in Afrikanerdom occurred at the end of the 1970s, Coertze and his son, his right-hand man, left the Nationalist Party to join the Conservative Party, which was committed to the resurrection of Apartheid. His son, an equally *verkrampte* figure, succeeded to his chair in Pretoria, but their empire crumbled. Kotze, a former student, who became Professor of Ethnology at the Rand Afrikaans University, was one of the first to break publicly with the ethnos theory. He and the handful of other ethnographers who led the break within Afrikaans anthropology were distinguished by the fact that they had earlier made a methodological move, embracing the suspect method of participant observation. This was both cause and effect of their change of sympathies. The first public expression of their defection was their attendance at meetings of the Anglophone and multi-racial Association of South African Anthropologists in the late 1970s.

Like a number of other radical intellectuals in the English-medium universities, some of the anthropologists came to the conclusion that they had to become actively involved in the resistance to *Apartheid*, and they faced the cruel dilemma of the activist-academic. David Webster, one of the outstanding social anthropologists, turned more and more towards activism, and in 1989 he was assassinated by a secret hit squad.[42] One activist, however, moved in the other direction, towards anthropology. Mamphela Ramphele, then a young doctor, colleague and lover of Steve Biko, was exiled to a remote country district after Biko's murder. When her banning order was lifted in the early 1980s, she moved to a position at the University of Cape Town, and chose to associate herself with the department of social anthropology. Here she carried out a study, typical of the time and place, documenting the desperate conditions in a workers' hostel in Cape Town. 'Learning to do research in a methodical way was taxing for one more accustomed to the world of activism', she recalls, but she also found that participant observation had parallels with the intuitive approach of the activist, working her way into a community, assessing the problems, trying to identify the leaders and the factions. None the less, academic work was criticised as a diversion by activists, and anthropology in particular was widely associated with colonialism. Thabo Mbeki challenged her, but 'I replied confidently that he needed to distinguish between good and bad Anthropology'.

Although a particularly vicious form of Anthropology operated in some Afrikaans-speaking universities, which provided ethnological justification for segregation, there was also another tradition that had earned South African Anthropology a place of honour internationally. Radcliffe-Brown, Monica Wilson, the Mayers and many others had done valuable work which had led to a greater and more sophisticated understanding of South African society.[43]

In the new South Africa, some old questions have returned. When Mamphela Ramphele visited Mandela in prison, shortly before his release, she had a fierce debate with him about the ANC's policy of recognising and working with established chiefs.[44] She is now Vice-Chancellor of the University of Cape Town. Another social anthropologist at the University of Cape Town, Harriet Ngubane, was, in contrast, a leading member of the neo-traditionalist, largely Zulu, Inkatha Freedom Party, and she is now a Member of Parliament. Their thinking about the role of traditional authorities is diametrically opposed.

Not only is the position of chiefs a live issue once more. Shortly after the establishment of the ANC government, an official commission of enquiry was set up to investigate witchcraft in the Northern Transvaal. Its chairman was an anthropologist, Victor Raloshai. It seems that the debates that shaped South African anthropology remain relevant to the new South Africa. Perhaps for that reason, it has become a very popular undergraduate option among black students. In the late 1980s several Afrikaans-medium universities closed their departments of ethnology, reasoning that there would no longer be a call for the services of their graduates in the new government. However, they are being obliged to reopen them, because of the demand from the black students. Today there are so many calls on anthropologists to act as consultants, and to carry out applied research, that fundamental ethnographic research is suffering.

This has been a hasty sketch of a single case, and I hesitate to impose a general moral on such a partial and particular story. A few points might nevertheless be worth a mention in conclusion. First, we must surely move on from the generalised accounts of colonial anthropology that represent it as part of the ideological apparatus of Empire, or the reflection of colonial interests. We should rather consider the ways in which not only the politics of the day but also the nature of their encounters in the field could form the minds of anthropologists and influence the theoretical discourse. More generally, while none of the scholars I have been discussing were detached from current political debates, only a small number were ideologues. Radcliffe-Brown, Malinowski, Schapera, Hoernlé, Jabavu, Matthews, Gluckman, Ngubane and Ramphele all had in common both an engagement with public issues and a belief in the value of scholarship and scientific detachment.

But political experiences, and the formative influence of ethnographic studies, are only part of the story. The impact of metropolitan theories must also be considered, but keeping two reservations in mind. First, there were competing theories in the great centres – in the 1930s, the South African anthropologists argued about Malinowski's ideas as against those of Radcliffe-Brown, and also for and against the British tendencies as opposed to alternative theories which came from Germany and the USA. Secondly, the periphery could also influence the centre: the case of South African anthropology in the 1930s shows this very clearly.

Finally, there are indications that the tradition of debate and investigation initiated in the 1920s will continue, and may even flourish. In the 1990s, with the end of the academic boycott, there is at last a flow of foreign anthropologists doing research in South Africa. They will have to engage with the concerns of their South African colleagues, and will surely, once more, carry ideas both to and from the international scholarly community.

Notes

1 Recently there has been a flow – almost a flood – of contributions to the history of South African anthropology, and more are in the works. Several specialised studies will be cited in

the text. For overviews see: W.D. Hammond-Tooke (1997) *Imperfect Interpreters: South Africa's Anthropologists*, Johannesburg: Witwatersrand University Press; Saul Dubow (1989) *Racial Segregation and the Origins of Apartheid in South Africa, 1919-36*, New York: St Martin's Press; Robert Gordon (1990) 'Early Social Anthropology in South Africa', *African Studies*, 49: 15-48; Bettina Schmidt (1996) *Creating Order: Culture as Politics in 19th and 20th Century South Africa*, The Hague: CIP; and George Stocking (1995) *After Tylor: British Social Anthropology 1888-1951*, Madison: University of Wisconsin Press, pp. 323-38. An important doctoral thesis is being completed by Paul Cocks. A review of contemporary developments may be found in Robert Gordon and A. Spiegel (1993) 'South African anthropology revisited', *Annual Review of Anthropology*, 22: 83-105, and for a recent commentary on South African liberal anthropology under Apartheid, see Jim Kiernan (1997) 'David in the path of Goliath: South African anthropology in the shadow of Apartheid' in Patrick McAllister (ed.) *Culture and the Commonplace*, Johannesburg: Witwatersrand University Press, pp. 53-68).

2 In the early 1920s he was beginning to use the form A. Radcliffe Brown in preference to A.R. Brown. In a post-script to a letter to Haddon (Haddon papers, Cambridge University, Letter from Brown to Haddon, 12 November 1921), he reported: 'As there are so many Browns in the world (there is an A. Brown at the University here) I have been obliged to find some way of distinguishing myself and have taken the name of Radcliffe Brown.' The hyphen came soon after.

3 Letter from A.R. Brown to A.C. Haddon, 13 March 1920, Haddon papers, Cambridge University Library.

4 Haddon to Smuts, 16 April 1920, Haddon papers.

5 See I. Schapera (1934) 'The Present State and Future Development of Ethnographical Research in South Africa', *Bantu Studies*, 8: 226-7. Cf. Hammond-Tooke, *Imperfect Interpreters*, pp. 20-1.

6 See I. Schapera (1990) 'The appointment of Radcliffe Brown to the Chair of Social Anthropology at the University of Cape Town', *African Studies*, 49: 1-13. Marett refused to join the others in recommending Radcliffe-Brown without qualification, preferring the Oxford candidate, F.E. Williams, and remarking that Brown 'seemed rather conceited and unso-

ciable when I knew him slightly some years ago' (Schapera, loc. cit.).

7 A.R. Radcliffe-Brown (1922) 'Some problems of Bantu sociology', *Bantu Studies*, 1: 38-46 (p. 40).

8 *Cape Times*, 25 August 1921, reprinted as an Appendix (pp. 35-9) to Robert Gordon (1990) 'Early Social Anthropology in South Africa'.

9 Radcliffe-Brown to Haddon, 12 November 1921, Haddon papers.

10 Radcliffe-Brown (1923) 'The methods of Ethnology and Social Anthropology', *South African Journal of Science*, 22: 124-47.

11 D.D.T. Jabavu (1924) 'Science and the Native', *Cape Times*, 24 March 1924, cited in Gordon, 'Early Social Anthropology in South Africa', pp. 20-1.

12 Mandela wrote about Jabavu with some awe in (1994) *Long Walk to Freedom*, London: Little Brown, pp. 52-3.

13 Cited by Stocking, *After Tylor*, p. 327.

14 I. Schapera (1934) 'The Present state and future development of ethnographical research in South Africa', *Bantu Studies*, 8: 219-342 (pp.227-8).

15 Cited by Saul Dubow, *Racial Segregation and the Origins of Apartheid in South Africa*, p. 151.

16 C.W. De Kiewiet (1941) *A History of South Africa: Social and Economic*, London: Oxford University Press.

17 Cited by Robert Gordon (1988) 'Apartheid's anthropologists: Notes on the genealogy of Afrikaner *volkekundiges*', *American Ethnologist*, 15 (3): 535-53 (p. 540).

18 Cited by Saul Dubow, *Racial Segregation and the Origins of Apartheid*, p. 36.

19 H. Macmillan (1989) '"Paralyzed Conservatives": W. M. Macmillan, the Social Scientists and the Common Society, 1923-1948' in H. Macmillan and S. Marks (eds) *Africa and Empire: W. M. Macmillan, Historian and Social Critic*, London: Temple Smith.

20 For a useful intellectual biography see Peter Carstens, 'Introduction' to Winifred Hoernlé (1985) *The Social Organization of the Nama*, Johannesburg: Witwatersrand University Press.

21 Hoernlé's student, Ellen Hellmann, undertook the first study of an African slum, in 1934, and she was soon followed by two other Hoernlé students, E.J. Krige and Hilda Beemer (Kuper). Ellen Hellman (1948) *Rooiyard: A Sociological Survey of an Urban Native Slum Yard* (published in 1948, Livingstone:

Rhodes-Livingstone Papers no. 13, but produced as a thesis in 1934); E.J. Krige (1936) 'Changing conditions in marital relations and parental duties among urbanized natives', *Africa*, 9: 1-23; Hilda Kuper and S. Kaplan (1944) 'Voluntary associations in an urban township', *African Studies*, 3: 178-86.

22 Max Gluckman (1975) 'Anthropology and Apartheid: The work of South African anthropologists', in Meyer Fortes and Sheila Patterson (eds) *Studies in African Social Anthropology*, London: Academic Press. Gluckman gave a more detailed account of his own motivation in another essay, 'The tribal area in South and Central Africa' in Leo Kuper and M. G. Smith (eds) (1969) *Pluralism in Africa*, Berkeley: University of California Press. Cf. H. Macmillan (1995) 'Return to the Malungwana Drift – Max Gluckman, the Zulu nation and the common society', *African Affairs*, 94: 39-66.

23 Z.K. Matthews (1981) *Freedom for My People: The Autobiography of Z.K.Matthews*, London: Rex Collings, pp. 103-4.

24 See Hilda Kuper (1978) *Sobhuza II: Ngwenyama and King of Swaziland*, London: Duckworth, pp. 3-10.

25 B. Malinowski (1945) *Dynamics of Culture Change*, New Haven: Yale University Press, p. 158.

26 Ernest Gellner has emphasised the influence on Malinowski of the multi-national model of the Austro-Hungarian empire, and his sympathy for it. See, e.g., his essay 'Zeno of Cracow' in his collection (1987) *Culture, Identity and Politics*, Cambridge: Cambridge University Press.

27 Hilda Kuper (1947) *An African Aristocracy: Rank Among the Swazi*, London: Oxford University Press, p. 1. For the conflicting views held by traditional and modernising African élites about anthropology, see Benoit de L'Estoile (1997) 'Au nom des "vrais Africains": Les élites scolarisées de l'Afrique coloniale face à l'anthropologie (1930-1950)', *Terrain*, 28: 87-102.

28 Malinowski visited urban slumyards in Johannesburg, and it is likely that he discussed these issues with Ellen Hellmann. Certainly the conclusion to her *Rooiyard* sounds the same note:

even among the Natives of Rooiyard – an outcast and, technically, a criminal population – there is a constant struggle to maintain or reaffirm standards or to create new standards . . . It seems probable that out of the chaos and confusion which exists in this transition period, there will emerge a people who will adopt such elements of European culture as may enable them to attain to an ordered and economically secure social life.

29   M.J. Herskovits (1938) *Acculturation: The Study of Culture Contact*, New York: Augustin. Cf. R. Redfield, R. Linton and M. Herskovits (1936) 'Memorandum for the study of acculturation', *American Anthropologist*, 38: 149-52.

30   I. Schapera, 'Contact between European and native in South Africa: Bechuanaland' in *Methods of Study of Culture Contact in Africa*, London: Oxford University Press for the International African Institute, p. 27.

31   A.R. Radcliffe-Brown (1940) 'On social structure', *Journal of the Royal Anthropological Institute* 70: 1-12.

32   Cited by Gordon, 'Early Social Anthropology in South Africa', p. 29.

33   Max Gluckman (1940) 'Analysis of a social situation in modern Zululand', *Bantu Studies*, 4: 1-30 and 147-74; 'The Kingdom of the Zulu of South Africa' in M. Fortes and E.E. Evans-Pritchards (eds) (1940) *African Political Systems*, London: Oxford University Press; A fascinating account of the genesis of the 'Analysis of a social situation' is provided by H. Macmillan (1995) 'Return to the Malungwana Drift – Max Gluckman, the Zulu Nation and the common society', *African Affairs*, 94: 39-66.

34   Hugh Macmillan (1995) 'Return to the Malungwana Drift – Max Gluckman, The Zulu nation and the common society', *African Affairs*, 94: 39-66. See pp.41-2 for the precise reasons for his exclusion from Zululand.

35   Max Gluckman (1947) 'Malinowski's "functional" analysis of social change', *African Studies*, Vol. 6.

36   This citation and those following are drawn from R. Gordon, 'Apartheid's anthropologists'.

37   For discussions of ethnos theory see Robert Gordon, 'Apartheid's anthropologists', W.D. Hammond-Tooke, *Imperfect Interpreters*, chapter six; John Sharp (1981) 'The roots and development of "Volkekunde" in South Africa', *Journal of Southern African Studies*, 8: 16-36.

38   See John Sharp, 'The roots and development of *volkekunde* in South Africa'.

39   Max Gluckman, 'Anthropology and Apartheid', p. 29. The veiled reference is to two of his main opponents. Edmund Leach was a fellow of King's College, Cambridge, and Rodney Needham of Merton College, Oxford.

40 See the introduction to Philip Mayer (1961) *Townsmen or Tribesmen*, London: Oxford University Press.

41 M. Wilson and A. Mafeje (1963) *Langa: A Study of Social Groups in an African Township*, Cape Town: Oxford University Press.

42 See Jim Kiernan (1997) 'David in the path of Goliath: South African anthropology in the shadow of Apartheid' in Patrick McAllister (ed.) *Culture and the Commonplace*, Johannesburg: Witwatersrand University Press, pp. 53-68.

43 Mamphela Ramphele (1995) *A Life*, Cape Town: David Philip, pp. 164-7.

44 Ramphele loc.cit., pp. 202-3.

10
Machiavelli in Precolonial Southern Africa

I

Of all the possible readings of Machiavelli, the most straight-forward is that he offered a ruler's guide to *realpolitik*. Rooted in Machiavelli's own experience of Italian politics, supported by reflections on history, especially ancient history, *The Prince* was designed to provide practical guidance. It is 'passionately driven forward', Quentin Skinner remarks, 'by a sense of what must realistically be said and done if political success is to be achieved'.[1]

Machiavelli's prescriptions hinged on an opposition between the dictates of common morality and the means necessary to maintain power. The ruler must act in the knowledge that 'doing some things that seem virtuous may result in one's ruin, whereas doing other things that seem vicious may strengthen one's position and cause one to flourish'. Since some of his rivals will be prepared to go to any lengths to seize power (for 'how men live is so different from how they should live'), the Prince cannot allow himself to be shackled by ordinary ethics. 'If a ruler who wants always to act honourably is surrounded by many unscrupulous men his downfall is inevitable. Therefore, a ruler who wishes to maintain his power must be prepared to act immorally when this becomes necessary'.[2]

It need hardly be said that Machiavelli's ethical reflections, and also his strategic analysis, are culturally specific. His writings are part of an elaborate Renaissance tradition of political discourse. Moreover, his main subject is the politics of his own day, of fifteenth and sixteenth century Italian city states, in which he played a significant part. Yet Machiavelli drew upon history, and not only Italian history. ('When evening comes,' he wrote from his rural exile to the Florentine envoy to the Holy See in December, 1513, 'I enter the ancient courts of the men of old, in which I am received affectionately by them. . . . There I do not hesitate to converse with them, and ask them why they acted as they did; and out of kindness they respond.')[3] His ambition was to transcend the immediate situation of Florence or Rome, and a measure of his success is the fact that Machiavellian principles have been invoked, Machiavellian strategies applied, even by princes who never heard his name, or read his – or indeed any other – books. Leading chiefs in nineteenth century South Africa took for granted the basic Machiavellian principles. On a few occasions they are on record formulating these principles in distinctly Machiavellian style.

II

The chiefdoms in nineteenth century South Africa were typically made up of diverse populations, yoked together by a leader. They were extremely unstable, seldom surviving a generation without major splits, liable to sudden and total collapse. The great missionary observer Eugene Casalis put it succinctly: 'It is . . . in the nature of these little African states to divide into an indefinite number of fractions, under the influence of peace and prosperous circumstances'.[4]

There were two great fault-lines in these systems. One ran within the royal family, pitting against each other the different 'houses' of the main wives, each of which could harbour a pretender to the succession. Throughout a reign, younger brothers and sons of the chief would be grouping themselves to make a grab for the succession. Catastrophic internal conflicts were regularly triggered by the death of a chief. The rules of succession were notoriously ambiguous and open to challenge, and there were usually several well-supported rivals with a legitimate claim. And no chief could sit back comfortably. Schapera cites a series of relevant adages. 'The king should not eat with his brothers, lest they poison him', say the Zulu; 'princes make restless subjects,' say the Swazi; 'nobles are the chief's killers', say the Tswana; and the universal and much-quoted proverb, 'There cannot be two bulls in one kraal'.[5] These lines of fissure continued beyond the royal family, dividing the whole population, since every faction had to recruit a following. 'We pay homage to all the chief's sons', says the cynical Pedi proverb, 'since which one of them will finally become chief is uncertain'.[6]

The second fault-line ran between the core ethnic group of the chief and immigrant or conquered populations. Some conquered leaders retained a following, and incorporated populations were always ready to secede. As Casalis explained:

> The chief who is called to govern several tribes, however great may be the respect and fear he inspires, seldom succeeds in assimilating them sufficiently to subject them to the same customs, and to avoid the difficulties which are constantly arising from the ideas of independence connected with recollections of origin. The elements of which the nation is composed have a tendency to separate, and are only held together by means of a system of concessions and acts of rigour, skilfully combined but seldom based upon a foundation of strict justice.[7]

Loyalty had to paid for, and cattle were the coin of the system. Cattle were loaned to dependents, binding them as followers. Chiefs were reluctant to allow individuals outside the immediate royal circle to establish independent herds. Every cattle herd was the nucleus of an independent political grouping, and so powerful chiefs ruthlessly cut down any subject who built up a substantial herd of his own. Writing in 1841, Casalis noted: 'With the exception of a few individuals who have succeeded in preserving their herd in the past wars, the people depend entirely on Moshesh and his sons for their means of subsistence'.[8]

But the consequence of this policy was that chiefs were themselves bound to increase their own cattle holdings if they wanted to hold or increase their followings. An ambitious chief was always raiding neighbours and stealing their cattle. In a large raid, tens of thousands of cattle could be captured. The victims of these raids might be so impoverished that they were obliged to become followers, to whom cattle were then loaned. Of course, their loyalty was tenuous, depending above all on the continued ability of the chief to deliver success in raiding and to punish individual accumulation.

Although cattle were the main form of wealth, pastoralism was everywhere combined with agriculture. Chiefs were polygamists, and profited from the agricultural labour of their wives, and the alliances which their marriages cemented. A chief allocated land to each married man, and women provided most of the labour in the fields. However, both agriculture and the marriage system itself were functions of the pastoral political economy. Wives were acquired by the payment of bridewealth cattle, and clients who were granted loans of cattle returned wives to their patron.

Elsewhere in Africa in the eighteenth and nineteenth centuries, chieftainship rested on the control of trade, particularly the slave trade. The chiefs in Southern Africa directed most of the significant trade, but the slave trade was of marginal importance south of Delagoa Bay, and although the shifting demand for ivory and for cattle sometimes offered great opportunities, nowhere in southern Africa could a chief duplicate the trade-power of the old Zimbabwe state, with its monopoly on supplying the Portguese on the east coast with ivory and slaves. The acquisition of trade goods was a useful complement to power in some cases, but never its foundation. Manpower was the basis of military strength, but armies which were employed to accumulate cattle also had to be satisfied by continual allocations of stock, and they were fed chiefly on beef. The system was largely driven by the resources of the pastoral economy.

Given the fissive nature of local politics, parties of armed white and Hottentot bands were early sought as allies. Even a small party might intervene in a political dispute with decisive effect, but increasingly in the second half of the nineteenth century white military forces were imposing permanent changes in the political landscape rather than just temporarily tilting the local balance of power. By the 1870s the English and the Boers were the decisive forces in South African politics well beyond the borders of the Colony. Both before and after conquest much of the success and failure of individual chiefs depended on luck and skill in manipulating whites.

III

The two major Southern Bantu cultural traditions are the Nguni and the Sotho-Tswana. The Zulu and the Basotho are classic representatives of the two traditions. Each was effectively the creation of a single chief, respectively Shaka and Moshoeshoe, in the early nineteenth century. These two hero-founders have usually been represented as polar opposites. Thompson, for example, wrote:

> The quality of Moshoeshoe's achievement is highlighted when it is compared with that of Shaka . . . the Zulu and the MoSotho created two diametrically different types of states. Shaka's was militarized and predatory: Moshoeshoe's pacific and self-sufficient. Shaka ruled by fear: Moshoeshoe by consent. Shaka broke brutally with the past: Moshoeshoe built a bridge between the past and the future. The Zulu's career was cut short by assassination at the hands of his kinsmen: the MoSotho was to die peacefully of old age. [9]

Shaka and Moshoeshoe are thus taken to represent two polar political strategies in the conditions of nineteenth century Southern Africa. The first strategy was to depend on aggressive, continuous expansion. This was Shaka's method. The second was to attract as dependents defeated, small groups with their remaining herds, while maintaining a flexible, defensive posture when faced with a dangerous opponent. This was a strategy particularly associated with Moshoeshoe. These are, of course, famous political alternatives: they were identified by Machiavelli as the strategies of the lion and the fox.

In the eighteenth chapter of *The Prince*, Machiavelli extends the distinction between morality and the proper expediency of princes to one between culture and nature. He remarks 'that there are two ways of contending: one by using laws, the other, force. The first is appropriate for men, the second for animals; but because the former is often ineffective, one must have recourse to the latter. Therefore, a ruler must know well how to imitate beasts as well as employing properly human means.' He then cites the classical myth that 'Achilles and many other ancient rulers were entrusted to Chiron the centaur. . . . Having a mentor who was half-beast and half-man signifies that a ruler needs to use both natures, and that one without the other is not effective'. This reflection leads on to the conclusion that a ruler 'must know how to act like a beast', and specifically that 'he should imitate both the fox and the lion, for the lion is liable to be trapped, whereas the fox cannot ward off wolves. One needs, then, to be a fox to recognise traps, and a lion to frighten away wolves.'[10]

Moshoeshoe was born about 1786, son of a minor Sotho chieftain.[11] His father, with a few hundred followers, was formally subordinate to a senior chief, Mpiti, and jostled by an elder brother, Libe (who famously compared commoners to flies, which gathered round a fresh pan of milk and disappeared when it was empty). Moshoeshoe made his mark as a cattle raider, and then, after some years, defied Mpiti, who had claimed some of his booty from a raid. Against his own father's orders, Moshoeshoe robbed Mpiti of his confiscated stock, and more beside, so destroying the old chief's authority.

At about this time Moshoeshoe outlined his long-term strategy to his closest associate, who recalled it in a conversation with a French missionary some twenty years later, in the 1840s.

You are my right hand. Together we will found a new empire. Let us first render ourselves popular by mighty deeds, and afterwards we will speak of peace and clemency. In the disputes of others let us always put ourselves on the side of the strongest. If we would become rich in men and cattle, we cannot help making enemies; but they will not roar forever. Motlume has carried out to a great extent the important system of polygamy, we must go beyond him even in this. He considered that it often was better to entreat enemies than to fight them; – this too we must follow out when necessary.[12]

Moshoeshoe was a successful cattle raider in his youth, and as a young chief he was ready to be ruthless even to his own followers. Yet for many years he remained vulnerable. Early in the *mfecane* he suffered severe reverses and was lucky to survive as a leader at all, but in 1823 he was able to rebuild his fortunes in the classic manner, by a series of cattle raids. Manipulating a web of shifting alliances he won several military victories. He only achieved a long-term strategic breakthrough, however, when he settled in a mountain fortress, Thaba Bosiu, in 1824. It was here that he built up his empire: but it was a defensive empire, men and cattle coming to him largely as refugees from the war-torn Highveld. They were incorporated as vassals, being given back a portion of their own cattle (but only in trust), and surrendering their political independence. Beginning with a few hundred supporters, he had 25,000 people under his control in 1836, 40,000 in 1843, 80,000 in 1848, 100,000 in the 1850s, and 150,000 in 1865.[13]

Moshoeshoe's reputation as a diplomat and peace-maker attach largely to the second part of his career, when he established a defensive state: and it could be argued that this represented a tactical switch to profit from his possession of a refuge at a time when every community in the open veld was prey to ravaging armies. However, even at the peak of his power he was by no means in complete control of his people. His brothers and sons had their own followings and played the same game of shifting allegiances that Moshoeshoe had always favoured, the more powerful sons quarrelling and attempting to assert their autonomy, even plotting a grab for power at the centre. His son Tsehelo twice tried to assassinate Moshoeshoe himself, and there are Basotho sources which assert that Moshoeshoe killed one of his sons.

Shaka, born about 1787, so perhaps a year after Moshoeshoe, was also a son of a minor chieftain, and he made his
reputation as a warrior leader in the service of Dingiswayo,
chief of one of the large political blocs in northern Natal,
the Mthethwa.[14] Shaka's father died in about 1816, and
with the help of Mthethwa warriors Shaka assassinated his
father's heir and assumed the chieftainship of the Zulu.
Two years later, Dingiswayo was defeated in a confrontation
with another political bloc, the Ndwandwe. The Mthethwa
army was dispersed and the Mthethwa chieftaincy mor-
tally wounded. Now Shaka attracted Mthethwa refugees
to his standard, and challenged and defeated Zwide, the
Ndwandwe leader. The Ndwandwe bloc dissolved in turn,
even more completely than the Mthethwa. These had been
chiefdoms capable of fielding armies of many thousands on
the eve of their destruction. Shaka now rapidly built up a
following, conquering and incorporating or driving off his
neighbours, and year after year launching large-scale stock
raids. Shaka began with a few hundred soldiers in 1816, but
by 1819 the Zulu army was estimated at 20,000 men.

His was a state at war, and military discipline was fero-
ciously maintained. There were regular – certainly weekly
– executions at the royal camp. Dissent was bloodily sup-
pressed. A few leaders did break away and establish their
own military states, in one or two cases coming almost to
rival Shaka, though at a safe distance; but the army was
generally kept under tight control. Returning from even a
successful engagement, soldiers trembled in the knowledge
that 'cowards' would be instantly despatched.

Shaka had no children himself, and so protected himself
against the classic form of challenge, that would be orches-
trated by the maternal uncles of leading princes. Indeed, he
reportedly killed any of his women who became pregnant.
However, he did not kill his brothers, and in 1828 Shaka was
assassinated by two of his brothers, Dingane and Mhlangana.
Dingane then had Mhlangana killed, and initiated a new
policy of peace-time administration, allowing the soldiers to
marry and suspending campaigns. But he soon reverted to a
Shakan policy, taking it yet further by killing his remaining

brothers, sparing only one, Mpande, the Zulu Claudius, who was regarded as too simple to pose a threat. However, Mpande established an independent following, seceded, and returned to defeat Dingane in 1840 with the support of a Boer commando.

Mpande's was a more peaceful reign, and the mature Mpande/Cetshwayo state was organised on much the same administrative principles as Moshoeshoe's mature chiefdom, the more powerful barons being permitted considerable autonomy.[15] The new order endured effectively until the Anglo-Zulu war in 1879, though it was troubled throughout by a succession conflict, which erupted in Mpande's own life-time in a bloody battle between two of his sons. One authority comments that according to Zulu tradition, 'Mpande had brought on the fight between the most powerful of his sons, and that he had a third, more malleable, candidate for succession to the Zulu throne in mind.'[16]

The fissiparous character of these chiefdoms can hardly be overstated. Although there were periods during which the Zulu and Basotho states enjoyed a measure of political calm, neither was stable in terms of population, ethnic composition, or territory. Every decade saw effectively a fresh configuration of peoples submitting to the chief's authority. Every twenty years at least there was a near catastrophic reconstitution. Guy remarks that 'perhaps there is no greater indication of the real nature of the Zulu kingdom in 1879 than the fact that when faced with invasion, the Zulu king could put 30,000 men into the field in an attempt to preserve the Zulu state'.[17] Yet as Guy himself has shown, although the great battle with the British ended in a stalemate, with the Zulu authorities still in a strong position, within five years the Zulu had been devastated by a civil war. The royals routinely divided even in the face of dangerous outside challenges. Previously marginal chiefs united to defeat the – itself divided – royal house. Under the shadow of the Boer threat, Mpande had turned against Dingane, 'breaking the rope' which bound the nation, as the Zulu say. When his son, Cetshwayo, was faced with the ultimate and fatal provocation of the British, some of his closest relatives, including his uncle

Hamu, sided with the enemy.

In 1820 the Basuto had themselves been defeated by the
Zulu. 'It would have been easy for those attacked to repulse
the enemy', Casalis remarks, 'had they joined and made
common cause.' They did not.

> The inferior chiefs were at that time possessed of great
> wealth, and though they approved of a policy founded
> upon simple common sense, not one of them would join
> the ranks, so entirely were they absorbed with the idea that
> evil consequences might accrue to their flocks should they
> gather round a common centre, and that their possessions
> might, in the general confusion, fall into the power of one
> master.[18]

It was even less likely that enemy chiefs would make
common cause against the whites. In 1852 Moshoeshoe sent
this remarkable message to his bitter enemy, Sekonyela:

> We are both black and of one nation – it is now our duty
> and interest to sympathise with each other – to lay aside
> all hostile feelings, and henceforth to be united, and only
> to keep a jealous eye on enemies of another colour. – It
> never was my wish to make war on you, but your constant
> depredations have driven me reluctantly to do what I have
> done.[19]

However, this remains an isolated if not unique initiative.
Sekonyela did not respond, and it is possible that the inspiration behind the appeal came from the sophisticated local
representatives of the Paris Evangelical Mission Society, who
served as a virtual foreign office secretariat for Moshoeshoe
at this period.

Max Gluckman emphasised the conflicts within the chiefdoms, but argued that they might nevertheless achieve stability: indeed, that certain forms of conflict actually sustained
the structure. 'Periodic civil wars', for example, 'strength-
ened the system by canalizing tendencies to segment, and by
stating that the main goal of leaders was the sacred kingship
itself.'[20] Isaac Schapera countered with numerous examples

in which conflicts of this sort resulted in permanent fission. Rebels might indeed aim at the chieftaincy, but 'the outcome of their attempts almost always was the flight or secession of one section.'[21]

Schapera is surely correct, and yet despite endemic conflict the Zulu and Basotho states survived and even prospered for much of the nineteenth century (though with constantly changing boundaries and much accretion and secession of population and, in the Zulu case at least, regular coups and coup attempts). A number of comparable stories could be told about the same period – of the Pedi, the Ngwaketse, the Ndebele, for example – but there are many more instances of powerful tribal agglomerations which were defeated and disintegrated – as Moshoeshoe's Basotho so nearly did in 1823, or the Zulu themselves in the early years after Shaka's murder, and as Dingiswayo's Mthethwa had done when defeated by Zwide's Ndwandwe, and as the Ndwandwe did when defeated in turn by Shaka.

Peter Sanders has contrasted Moshoeshoe with Sekonyela, chief of the Tlokwa, another Sotho group in the Highveld.[22] While Sekonyela pursued a more aggressive course than Moshoeshoe, he also established a mountain fortress, Marabeng, and succeeded in building up almost as large a following until he was defeated by Moshoeshoe in 1853, his fortress captured and his people dispersed. In 1824, when the two leaders were roughly equal in strength, Sekonyela came within an ace of destroying Moshoeshoe. It was only when Moshoeshoe pulled off two extremely successful raids against the Thembu that he accumulated a large herd and with it a stable basis for power. As the missionary Arbousset remarked, 'The people, seeing him comparatively rich, attached themselves to him'.[23] Sekonyela had poorer luck, coming up against the Griqua who were armed with guns.

In short, followings were fluid, dependent on constant success, dissolving swiftly when chiefs were beaten and herds dispersed. *When the milk is finished, the flies vanish.* There is little evidence that national identity or loyalty were major political forces, except in the immediate crisis of a colonial war, and even then not always. Only the members of the core community identified with the chiefly house, and in a large chiefdom they were a minority. Moreover, the chiefly house itself was almost always divided between rival factions. Few leaders could expect to survive a period of adversity.

The Zulu and Basotho stories must therefore be placed in the context of a continuous cycle of the rise and fall of chiefs and their systems. Where a particular political bloc seems to survive a generation in the nineteenth century, this is only if we ignore its shifts in composition, size, and territory, and emphasise that one chief's son reigned after him – though usually only over some of his subjects, and quite commonly in another country. It is only in the late nineteenth century, with colonial overrule, that some states were frozen and then transformed into colonial provinces.

IV

One of the great questions that faces a Prince, according to Machiavelli, is whether it is better to be feared or loved. 'My view,' he wrote, 'is that it is desirable to be both loved and feared; but it is difficult to achieve both and, if one of them has to be lacking, it is much safer to be feared than loved'.[24] The Zulu kings, notoriously, chose to be feared, and their courts were places of terror. Regular public executions were carried out as a matter of deliberate policy. A political scientist, E.V.Walter, has even described the Shakan state as a prime instance of a political system based on a systematic reign of terror.[25] He drew mostly on the overblown accounts of white contemporaries, which must be discounted largely as propaganda. Nevertheless, it is clear that the Zulu kings regarded executions as a vital resource of power. Shaka explained to his young friend Maclean that the Zulu were 'a bad people; I am obliged to kill a few to gratify the rest; and if I were not to do it, they would think me an old woman, a coward, and kill me themselves.'[26] When Shepstone, the Zulu expert of the Natal government, was using this bloodthirsty reputation to undermine the legitimacy of the Zulu King,

Cetshwayo wrote provocatively: 'Did I ever tell Mr Shepstone I would not kill? . . . I do kill but I do not consider that I have done anything yet in the way of killing. Why do the white people start at nothing? I have not yet begun. I have yet to kill, it is the custom of our nation, and I shall not depart from it.'[27]

Another telling anecdote comes on the authority of Jantshi Ka Nongila, whose father was a spy under all the Zulu Kings from Senzangakona to Mpande. The Zulu kings each had an *isiGodhlo*, a secluded womens' quarter, in their main settlements. The women here were reserved for the king, and no other man might enter, or have anything to do with them. Shaka once massacred a whole band of young boys who were accused of taking liberties with the *isiGodhlo* women. When Dingane succeeded he is reported to have said that he did not wish to maintain the *isiGodhlo* since 'it is the cause of people always being put to death. It is a bad institution'. His counsellor, Nzobo, replied: 'The killing of people is a proper practice, for if no killing is done there will be no fear' – an argument that persuaded Dingane.[28]

The contrast with Moshoeshoe is striking. He was noted for his judicious administration of the law, for his clemency, and for his regard for the opinion of his people. 'Freedom of thought and freedom of speech are the foundation and the guarantee of the national rights of his subjects,' Casalis reported from Morija in 1834. 'They are allowed to express their opinion on the chief's conduct quite openly; if they disapprove of it, they say so with a virile and eloquent boldness which the most fiery Roman tribune would have envied.'[29]

Far from bloodthirsty, the Basotho king hated killing. 'During the twenty-three years I spent among the Basutos,' Casalis reported, 'the chief put no one to death from personal motives; and nothing like an attempt upon his life was ever made'. On one occasion, while they were walking together, Moshoeshoe pointed out to Casalis a precipice over which two rebels had been thrown, and said he had often repented of the act. 'More than once, when trouble has come upon me, I have attributed the cause of it to this act of severity.'[30]

Where the Zulu king was approached on bended knee and any untoward gesture could be punished by execution, people flocked happily to meet Moshoeshoe. 'His affability did not flag for an instant,' the missionary Arbousset reported. 'Warmth, gaiety, nothing is lacking. He talks to everyone without distinction of age or rank. He even amuses himself with the children as if he were one himself; and, still, more astonishing, his memory is so good he seems to know the name and history of each of his subjects.'[31]

There was a striking contrast in the use of ritual, most obviously in the way that the first-fruit ceremony was celebrated. This was the central ritual of chieftaincy in the whole region. The elaborate Nguni first-fruit ceremonies (most famously the Swazi *ncwala*) is the main evidence for any 'sacred' element in Southern Bantu kingship. The Zulu first-fruits ceremony was, like that of the Swazi, a massive affair, bringing together tens of thousands of soldiers at the King's settlement and whipping up emotions surrounding the King. Among the Sotho-Tswana, however, as Casalis noted, the right of the chief to control the agricultural cycle 'is confirmed afresh every year by a very simple ceremony'.

When the first-fruits of the earth are ripe, the eldest of the reigning family gathers a pumpkin, of which he eats the first morsel, and divides the rest between his brothers and other collateral relations, according to the order of their birth. When this is done, heralds are sent round to proclaim that the Morena [Chief] has eaten the first-fruits. The same ceremony is repeated in all the ramifications of the tribe, and then each one is at liberty to gather in its fruits.[32]

The most fundamental contrast has to do with the place of the military in each of these states. The Zulu state was virtually a military camp, its army employed in annual campaigns through much of the reigns of Shaka and Dingane. Moshoeshoe had no standing army, and fought mainly defensive campaigns after 1823. It is reasonable to expect a military leader to rely particularly on force. Strict discipline is required to control an army of predators. Machiavelli remarks approvingly that Hannibal never experienced unrest among his troops. 'This could be accounted for only by his inhuman cruelty which, together with his many good qualities, made him always respected and greatly feared by his troops'.[33]

The Zulu were virtually always on the offensive. They had constantly to recruit fighting men, and they used the regimental system as 'both an instrument of internal social control and a means of external control'. Young men of conquered chiefdoms

> were compulsorily drawn into the Zulu *amabutho*, segre-gated into specially-built royal homesteads or *amakhanda*, and forbidden to marry without the permission of the Zulu king. The *amabutho* system thus gave the Zulu state the means to divert the labour-power of young men from their fathers' homesteads and turn it to state purposes, and to socialize young men into identifying the Zulu king as their ritual leader and the source of their welfare.[34]

Moshoeshoe was a master of the defensive alliance, and while he insisted on cooperation against external foes, he allowed considerable autonomy to local leaders, left local communities in effective control of their land, and tolerated the distinctive language and practices of Nguni communities within the state. The Zulu, in contrast, scorned foreign habits and discriminated systematically against non-Zulu.

Finally, there was a striking difference in the treatment of the inevitable, endemic conflicts within the royal family. Among the Zulu they were settled by infanticide, assassina-tion and civil war; among the Basotho more commonly by judicious intermarriage and compromise.

The African peoples of Southern Africa would have recognised Machiavelli's characterisation of two opposed types of prince as lions and foxes. The Zulu chiefs dressed in the skins of predators and they gloried in comparisons with marauding lions and elephants: metaphors which their subjects, however, occasionally turned against them. In con-trast, the gentle Moshoeshoe is more usually compared in his praise poems to a cow; once to a frog, which comes with the rain (associated with all Sotho-Tswana chiefs); and only occasionally to a hyena or a lion – and then according to one poem:

> It has no teeth, the Binder's lion,
> As for the people, it only nibbles them![35]

V

Two kinds of explanation are usually offered to account for these contrasts in policy. One is cultural. The Southern Bantu languages fall into two closely related families, the Nguni (including the Zulu language) and the Sotho-Tswana (including Sesotho, the language of the Basotho). These language families are commonly associated with two cultural traditions, marked by distinctive settlement patterns, pottery forms, marriage regulations and so forth (although it should be emphasised that there are many common themes, and the two traditions (like the two language families) are best regarded as closely related variants of a common, deeper tradition).

When it comes to politics, a militaristic Nguni – or northern Nguni – tradition is sometimes contrasted to a pacific Sotho-Tswana tradition. Certainly there are grounds for this distinction, the Sotho-Tswana chiefs generally being less dictatorial, their power less ritualised, their councils more influential than was the case for the Nguni chiefs. However, Shakan strategies were followed by some Sotho chiefs, most notably perhaps Sebetwane (whose Kololo followed a bloody trajectory similar to that of Mzilikatse's Ndebele) and Moshoeshoe's local rival, the Tlokoa chief Sekonyela. Sekonyela and his mother were famously aggressive warrior chiefs, and when he was finally defeated local missionaries blamed 'the systematic robbery practised by the Chief Sekonyela upon his neighbours' and remarked that 'His prevailing disposition is to plunder'.[36]

For their part, not all Zulu leaders modelled themselves on Shaka. Dingane briefly seemed to consider instituting a more pacific policy after the murder of Shaka, and his successor, Mpande, was noted for shifty compromise rather than the ruthless use of force. Perhaps he had little room for manoeuvre. A modern historian suggests that 'a lack of alternatives drove the Zulu kingship to diplomacy. Frequently, Mpande had no choice but to feign innocence, weakness, and a willingness to co-operate.'[37] The Swazi kings, however, were often noted for diplomatic skills and political flexibility, and some southern Nguni leaders were celebrated for their respect for law, tendency to compromise, and pacific policies. In short, the explanation from cultural tradition is inadequate.

The other conventional explanation appeals to the character of the rulers concerned. There is obviously something in this, though very little is known about Shaka or Dingane as people, compared, for example, with Moshoeshoe or even Mpande. But as Machiavelli insisted, 'we are successful when our ways are suited to the times and circumstances, and unsuccessful when they are not'.[38] It is therefore worthwhile to evaluate strategies without speculating about character.

I have suggested that similar structural problems faced all the chiefs in nineteenth century Southern Africa: they had to deal with endemic competition within the royal family, the tendency of defeated peoples to rise or secede, the necessity to accumulate cattle by force, and the increasing challenge from whites and other immigrant groups. The two pure strategies were those of the lion and the fox, and Shaka (and Dingane) and the mature Moshoeshoe incorporated these in remarkably pure form, following through the logic of their choices in every area of policy. Other leaders experimented, shifted, with more or less success depending on various circumstances including, most obviously, what Machiavelli called fortune. Moreover, it should be apparent that the strategies of lion and fox are complementary, since lions create foxes, and foxes flourish precisely because they have discovered a way of resisting the force of the lions. My conclusion is that the behaviour of the princes of precolonial Southern Africa is best understood in terms not of individual character or cultural tradition but rather through a rational assessment of the options available to them.

In reaching this conclusion I have drawn on Machiavelli, and I hope that I have illustrated that Machiavelli may be read with profit as a comparative sociologist – or an anthropological theorist – in the same way as we are accustomed to reading Durkheim or Weber. Of course, like all theorists he was culturally biased (by his experiences, by his milieu, and by the sources available to him). Nevertheless the basic law of politics that he adduced fits the South African case. The prince must be prepared to use every means to secure his position, for rivals and enemies will be doing their best to undermine him, and to exploit the fault lines that are built into every regime.

Machiavelli also described the strategies that were open to the prince in a variety of circumstances, and even in these practical matters, where one might expect to find the greatest degree of cultural specificity, his observations are often of very general relevance. The problems faced by the Southern African princes were hardly unique, and the strategies they chose were often familiar, Machiavellian strategies. If these South African chiefs were true Machiavellians, that must advance the argument for a realistic, cross-cultural political anthropology, a political anthropology that takes as its starting-point the constraints on leaders, and the options open to them.

Notes

1 Quentin Skinner (1988) 'Introduction' to Quentin Skinner and Russell Price (eds) *Machiavelli: The Prince*, Cambridge: Cambridge University Press, p. xxiv.

2 I have used the edition of *The Prince* edited by Quentin Skinner and Russell Price (1988) Cambridge: Cambridge University Press, Cambridge Texts in the History of Political Thought. Citations here from pp. 54-5.

3 Loc. cit. p. 93.

4 E. Casalis (1861) *The Basutos*, London: Nisbet, p. 212.

5 I. Schapera, (1956) *Government and Politics in Tribal Societies*, London: Watts, p. 169.

6 Loc. cit., p. 175.

7 Casalis, loc.cit., p. 212.
8 Quoted by Peter Sanders (1975) *Moshoeshoe, Chief of the Sotho,* London: Heinemann, p. 451.
9 Leonard Thompson (1975) *Survival in Two Worlds: Moshoeshoe of Lesotho 1786-1870,* Oxford: Oxford University Press, p. 216.
10 *The Prince,* p. 61.
11 Two excellent biographies of Moshoeshoe appeared simultaneously in 1975: Peter Saunders, *Moshoeshoe,* London: Heinemann and Leonard Thompson *Survival in Two Worlds: Moshoeshoe of Lesotho,* Oxford: Oxford University Press.
12 T. Arbousset and F. Daumas (1846) *Narrative of an Exploratory Tour to the North-east of the Colony of the Capte of Good Hope,* Cape Town: Robertson, p. 293.
13 These estimates are drawn from Saunders *Moshoeshoe,* passim.
14 For a valuable synthesis of Zulu history in the preconquest period see Andrew Duminy and Bill Guest (eds) (1989) *Natal and Zululand from Earliest Times to 1910,* Pietermaritzburg: University of Natal Press.
15 See Peter Colenbrander (1989) 'The Zulu kingdom, 1828-79' in Duminy and Guest, loc. cit., and J.J. Guy (1979) *The Destruction of the Zulu Kingdom,* London: Longman.
16 Guy, loc. cit., p. 13.
17 Guy, loc. cit., p. 39.
18 Casalis, *The Basutos,* p. 213.
19 P. Sanders (1969) 'Sekonyela and Moshweshwe: Failure and success in the aftermath of the Difaqane', *Journal of African History,* 10: 439-55, p. 449.
20 Max Gluckman (1954) *Rituals of Rebellion in South-East Africa,* Manchester: Manchester University Press, p. 25.
21 I. Schapera (1956) *Government and Politics in Tribal Societies,* London: Watts, p. 175.
22 Sanders, 'Sekonyela and Moshweshwe'.
23 Loc.cit., p. 443.
24 *The Prince,* p. 59.
25 E.V. Walter (1969) *Terror and Resistance: A Study of Political Violence,* New York: Oxford University Press.
26 Charles Rawden Maclean (1992) *The Natal papers of 'John Ross',* edited by Stephen Gray, Pietermaritzburg: University of Natal Press, p. 72.
27 R.L. Cope (1985) 'Political power within the Zulu kingdom and the "coronation laws" of 1873', *Journal of Natal and Zulu History,* VIII: 11-31 (p. 16).

28 C. de B. Webb and J.B. Wright (eds) (1976) *The James Stuart Archive*, Volume One, Pietermaritzburg: University of Natal Press, pp. 196-7.
29 R. C. Germond (ed.) (1967) *Chronicles of Basutoland: A Running Commentary on the Events of the Years 1830-1902 by the French Protestant Missionaries in Southern Africa*, Morija, Lesotho: Morija Sesuto Book Depot, p. 517.
30 Casalis, *The Basutos*, p. 220.
31 Germond, loc.cit., p. 196.
32 Casalis, *The Basutos*, p. 215.
33 *The Prince*, p. 60.
34 John Wright and Carolyn Hamilton (1989) 'The Phongolo-Mzimkhulu region in the late eighteenth and early nineteenth centuries', in Andrew Duminy and Bill Guest (eds) *Natal and Zululand from Earliest Times to 1910*, Pietermaritzburg: University of Natal Press, p. 69.
35 M. Damane and P.B. Sanders (1974) *Lithoko: Sotho Praise Poems*, Oxford: Oxford University Press, p. 71.
36 Thompson, *Survival in Two Worlds*, p. 113. On Sebetwane see Edwin Smith (1956) 'Sebetwane and the Makololo', *African Studies*, 15/2: 49-74. On Sekonyela see Peter Sanders (1969) 'Sekonyela and Moshweshwe: failure and success in the aftermath of the Difaqane', *Journal of African History*, X: 439-55.
37 See Phillip A. Kennedy (1981) 'Mpande and the Zulu kingship', *Journal of Natal and Zulu History*, IV: 21-38, p. 37.
38 *The Prince*, p. 85.

11
The Death of Piet Retief

I

The very process of fieldwork has become a testing-ground for the question that haunts modern anthropology: to what extent is it possible to make sense of another way of life? Behind that lurk other, more philosophical issues – most obviously, in whose terms must the sense be made? This is a question that can be rephrased in moral terms: if we are once able to grasp the principles by which others operate, are we then to judge them by our own standards or by theirs? It is obvious, too, that these questions all have great political implications.

The ethnographic field is not, of course, the only laboratory for enquiries of this kind. Historians and anthropologists have posed similar questions with respect to what is sometimes called 'first contact', the dramas of cultural confrontation that occurred when the agents of Western colonialism met the native peoples who lived beyond the frontiers of the great states and empires of the modern world. On this stage there operated – on each side – proto-ethnographers, trying to grasp what the other party was after. Their interpretations, and misinterpretations, were sometimes a matter of life and death.

The death of Captain Cook on the beach of Kealakekua Bay on February 14th, 1779 is one of the most famous stories of the era of European exploration, but it is in consequence of Sahlins' analysis that it has become, for many anthropologists, the paradigm of first contact, a tragic and ironic instance of cultural misapprehension. According to Sahlins, Captain Cook was killed as an incident in Hawaiian myth and ritual: more precisely, he was the victim of a dispute about the meaning of a mythological event.

To the Hawaiian priests, Cook was always the ancient god Lono, even when he unexpectedly came back; whereas, to the king, the god who appears out of season becomes a dangerous rival. The two Hawaiian parties, out of their own self-conceptions, conceived different (proportional) relations in the same event, whence their own conflict in the structure of the conjuncture whose outcome was Cook's death.[1]

In other words, the Hawaiians cast the unfortunate Cook in a play they had already written. Cultures operate by scripts, myths shape perceptions, actions are ritualised performances. Even Western colonialism is today sometimes analysed as though it was an enactment of an ideology of domination, or perhaps even an attempt to restage the dramas of Kipling and Rider Haggard.

And yet there are growing doubts even about the paradigmatic case of the death of Cook. This was not a pure case of 'first contact'. Cook already had considerable Polynesian experience and indeed he had touched the Hawaiian islands earlier on his third voyage; and the Hawaiians must have begun to gather intelligence about their visitors. There was therefore room on both sides for something more than sheer misapprehension of the other. After all, exchange relationships had quickly been organised. Moreover, there are other possible interpretations of Cook's murder by a mob on the beach, some of them advanced by eyewitnesses. Beaglehole, who has written the standard modern biography of Cook, presents the death as the climax of a series of isolated violent incidents, caused in part by Cook's loss of perspective and increasing weariness and irritability.[2] Obeyesekere has criticised various aspects of Sahlins' account, and suggested that Cook was actually named for a category of high chief, also known as Lono, and that he was only deified and enshrined in Hawaiian mythology after he had been killed. Sahlins has responded robustly to Obeyesekere, and the debate shows every sign of continuing for some time.[3]

Whatever the merits of the case, one reason for the influence of Sahlins's account was that it summed up in a single iconic – almost mythical – story of culture contact a major theoretical proposition of the day. Its message is that culture – more specifically, religious and mythical ideas – determines behaviour and shapes history. The implications are many. If true, then political events may not yield to an analysis that assumes rational, material motives. We can understand other people, if at all, only in their own terms, and these terms will be culturally specific. Cross-cultural understanding is accordingly rare, and difficult to achieve; and contacts across cultural barriers are fragile, constantly at risk from mutual misunderstandings. The perspective challenges the perhaps more obvious presumption that opportunities for profit and influence are quickly grasped even on first contact, and that even total strangers may quickly come to understand each other only too well.

The moral implications are also evident. Cultural determinism implies cultural relativism, which makes it difficult to avoid moral relativity. Who can blame the Hawaiians if they are acting according to their lights? On this argument, who, indeed, could blame even the *Conquistadores?* But if we prefer a *realpolitik* interpretation of inter-cultural encounters, then the moral ground shifts beneath us in a different direction. If the protagonists do indeed understand one another but act only by a Machiavellian calculus – which assumes that one cannot afford scruples where power is at stake – then how are moral judgments to be formulated, if at all? The actors may well denounce the morality of their opponents, but this is just part of the political game.

My path into this debate is an indirect one. I shall discuss a case that in some ways parallels the end of Captain Cook. This is the murder of the Voortrekker Piet Retief and his companions by the Zulu chief Dingane on 6th February, 1838, at the Zulu capital, Mgungundhlovu.

II

The rise of the Zulu as a power in South-East Africa had been rapid and recent. Shaka became Zulu chief in a coup around

1816, and he built up the Zulu army virtually from scratch. He quickly became the dominant war-lord on the east coast of South Africa, but he was murdered by his half-brother, Dingane, in 1828. Dingane had then taken over the Zulu war machine.

Piet Retief became one of the leaders of the small groups of Boers who had trekked out of the Cape Colony in 1836. They left in protest against British colonial rule, and in particular the emancipation of the slaves; and in search of land in the interior of Southern Africa. Retief's own manifesto, issued in 1837 when he joined the trekkers, emphasised discontent with Britain's relatively liberal native policy in the frontier region, where he was a district leader.[4]

South and west of the Zulu state was a large area claimed by Dingane, but not directly controlled by him. According to a number of contemporary sources it was not heavily populated, since this border zone was a dangerous place to settle. Piet Retief and another Trekboer leader, Gerrit Maritz, visited Dingane in November 1837 to ask for a grant of land in this region. The land was also claimed by English settlers at Port Natal, who had negotiated a vague and disputed agreement with Shaka. However, Dingane indicated that he would consider the Boer request on condition that Retief recovered cattle that had been apparently taken from him by a rival, Sekonyela. Dingane had been informed that the theft was the work of Boers, and he told Retief that only if he returned the cattle – and brought in the thief – could he clear his people.

Retief successfully undertook the task, tricking Sekonyela into allowing himself to be handcuffed, and then holding him hostage for the restoration of the stolen stock. When he returned to interview Dingane once more, he came with a company of 66 armed Boers and 30 servants, and he left a substantial following on the edge of Zulu country. He also brought a small proportion of the stock taken from Sekonyela, but to Dingane's disappointment did not hand over Sekonyela himself.[5]

Arriving at Mgungundhlovu, Retief's party rode into the cattle byre shooting their muskets into the air and making sham charges and salutes. They were allocated a camping place below the main kraal. For four days they petitioned Dingane. At last Dingane invited them for a farewell celebratory dance, asking them to come unarmed and promising that the Zulu soldiers would also dance without their weapons. As the dance reached a climax, Dingane gave a signal – whistling and calling out, '*Bulalani abathakathi* – kill the witches.' The soldiers then fell on the Boers and dragged them off to the place of execution, on a ridge north-east of the capital. Here they were clubbed to death, and left, as was customary, unburied. Retief was forced to watch while his followers (including his son) were killed, before he was himself put to death, his body mutilated. A party of warriors was immediately dispatched to wipe out the main body of Voortrekkers, and on the following morning they almost annihilated the easternmost camps, killing some four hundred people, including many women and children, and (a fact glossed over in many accounts) perhaps two hundred coloured servants of the Boers.[6] The more westerly camps rallied, however, and held them off.

In the last weeks of 1838 the Boer had their revenge. Andries Pretorius, a more prudent man than Retief, was appointed Commandant-General, and in December he advanced on the Zulu capital with a commando of 500 men. On the 16th of December they engaged and defeated a large Zulu army, killing an estimated 3,000 men. There were no Boer losses. They then marched on and took Mgungundhlovu, and among the skeletons on execution hill they may have discovered a purse of Piet Retief containing a treaty signed by Dingane, ceding them land. Shortly afterwards, Dingane's half-brother Mpande allied himself to the Boers and in a combined action in January 1840 Dingane was finally defeated, and Mpande became Zulu chief.

III

The standard Boer account of this episode presents it as a betrayal, in the first place by Dingane, then, more generally, by black people. Dingane made false promises, rejected the proffered hand of friendship, lured the Boers into a trap, and then massacred defenceless women and children. In some versions, the missionaries and the English colonists based at Port Natal were implicated, accused of having incited Dingane to his action. The charge against the English is that they were afraid that the Boers would dominate their settlement and take from them some of the lucrative trade they enjoyed in the Zulu domains. They therefore led Dingane to believe that the killing of the Boers would be welcomed by the British authorities.

In the last quarter of the nineteenth century, the massacre and the subsequent counter-attack at what the Boers called Blood River became a central focus of Afrikaner mythology. However, the participants themselves did not engage in mythological excursions. The oath taken before the Battle of Blood River was evidently not remembered by Pretorius or most of his followers, but with the growth of Afrikaner nationalism it was recast in the second half of the nineteenth century as a Covenant between the Boer people and God. In the twentieth century the Day of the Covenant (formerly, Dingaan's Day) came to be celebrated every year on December 16th as a great national occasion.

Later generations thus recast the murder of Retief and his party as a morality tale that legitimated the Afrikaner conquest of Black South Africa. God had elected the Boers as His Chosen People in South Africa. The execution of Piet Retief took on something of the aura of a martyrdom. The deed that may or may not have been found near Retief's bones became a charter in which black South Africans ceded their land to the whites. In short, this episode became one of the central myths of Afrikaner nationalism, but it was not itself *caused* by mystical Boer ideas of their special destiny.[7]

IV

The Zulu have not invested in a comparably elaborate reinterpretation of Retief's death or of the Boer revenge.

The political movement Inkatha, for example, prefers to highlight the warrior deeds of Shaka and the great battles against British troops in 1879. (They also stress the friendly relations maintained by Shaka with the whites at Port Natal.)

At the time, however, Dingane was eager to explain himself to the British, most immediately to the missionaries who were working in areas under his control. He had reluctantly admitted the first missionaries in 1831. Four others followed in 1836, one of whom, Owen, had been allowed to establish a post on a hill overlooking Dingane's headquarters, Mgungundhlovu itself. On February 6th, 1838, two Zulu councillors called on Owen with a message from Dingane. 'He sent to tell me not to be frightened, as he was going to kill the Boers. This news came like a thunderstroke to myself and to every successive member of my family as they heard it. The reason assigned for this treacherous act was that they [the Boers] were going to kill him [Dingane]; that they had had come here, and that he had now learnt all their plans.'[8] Owen was in a frightful dilemma: would it be possible to warn the Boers without bringing immediate destruction on his own household? He ran out and seized his telescope, but saw that the slaughter was already beginning.

The following day Dingane again sent messengers to tell Owen and his family that they were in no danger, and to justify the action against Retief and his party. They explained that the Boers had been implicated in cattle-raiding adventures, and that they had regularly resorted to treachery. They were suspected of harbouring designs on Dingane's own cattle. The Boers had also been provocative, mounting a show of force at Mgungundhlovu. Finally, there was evidence that they had designs on the life of Dingane himself.

These were by no means frivolous, trumped-up charges and excuses. The Highveld was the stage for huge cattle-raids at this period, and Boer parties had quickly become embroiled in these. Their record was by no means clean, and Retief had retained cattle claimed by Dingane that had come into his hands as a result of the expedition Dingane had sent him on against Sekonyela. The mock charge mounted by the

Boers on their arrival at Mgungundhlovu was undoubtedly
provocative. In the Zulu area, war-dances were not per-
formed at the home of a foreign chief as a gesture of
friendship. According to one Zulu source, Dingane was so
agitated that he placed a double in the arena to represent
him. Moreover, Retief had proved himself a tricky and
ruthless enemy of various Highveld chiefs, and he had
sent a threatening letter to Dingane. (Retief's menace was
couched in religious terms. 'From God's great Book we learn,
that kings who do such things as Matselikatse [Mzilikazi] has
done are severely punished, and not suffered long to live and
reign.')[9]

There is an interesting contemporary assessment of Dingane's behaviour by Henry Francis Fynn, who had observed
Shaka and Dingane over many years and spoke good Zulu.
(Fynn was something of an anthropologist himself, and
was described by a high colonial official as 'a retrograde
Christian and a progressive barbarian'.)[10] In Fynn's view,
Dingane had decided at once to eliminate Retief, and the
mission to Sikonyela was a ruse. (There is evidence that a
subordinate chief was in fact ordered to kill Retief as he
returned from his first visit to Dingane.)[11] Moreover, Fynn
noted that: 'Dingane could, without the possibility of failure,
have defeated the tribe under Siqonyela [Sikonyela] without
the aid of the Boers.' He reflected that:

> Few European diplomatists could have planned a more
> perfect mode of destroying an enemy than that conceived
> by Dingane. The very idea of so powerfully an armed force
> anticipating the occupation of so close a neighbourhood
> at once alarmed him. He therefore assented to cede the
> country to the Boers on the condition that they would
> attack and retake cattle which had been taken from his
> country by the roving chief Siqonyela . . . Dingane had
> attached to Retief's force some of his own followers, and,
> knowing the Zulu chief as I do, I conclude his object was
> that his followers were sent to observe the Boers' mode of
> fighting and the result, in which it might be possible the
> Boers might be defeated, thus saving him the necessity of

their destruction, or, on the other hand, enable him to judge how he might defeat them himself.

Fynn also pointed to the parallels between Retief's deception of Sekonyela, and Dingane's deception of Retief. 'It is, however, certain that he adopted the same mode of treachery as Retief had done when he enticed Siqonyela into Mr. Allison's garden and, making him a prisoner, put him in irons until he refunded the cattle.'[12]

These strands of evidence combine to suggest that Dingane was activated by considerations of *realpolitik*. But what of the insistent claim that he feared the Boers were witches or sorcerers, out to kill him? The accusation that the Boers were sorcerers was not taken seriously by Owen himself, but his young interpreter, William Wood, says that this was the first charge made by the Zulu. (Wood, incidentally, sent a message back with the Zulu emissaries to say that Dingane had acted correctly, and that if he had not killed them the Boers would have killed him.)[13]

Zulu witnesses, recorded later in the century by Stuart, were agreed that the Boers did act like witches, specifically by riding their horses at night around the perimeter of the capital. Cetywayo, son of Dingane's half-brother Mpande, and the Zulu leader at the time of the war against the British, summed up the royal Zulu view in a statement in 1881. The Boers had ridden round Dingane's settlement at night to see if they could encircle it, 'and next morning Dingane's sentinels reported to him the trail of horses which they had seen round the kraal, whereupon Dingane decided to have the Boers killed, as he considered that they intended to kill him instead of treating with him, as they had said. Dingana considered them Abathakathi [witches], because they moved around at night. . . .'[14]

The most sophisticated assessment of Dingane's thinking was provided by James Stuart, a man who devoted a lifetime to the collection of Zulu historical texts. In a lecture delivered in the early nineteen thirties, he tried to recover the motive for what whites had come to see as an act of incomprehensible barbarism. Carefully sifting a number of possible reasons for the killing of Retief and his men, Stuart concluded that the most important precipitating factor was indeed that identification of the Boers as *abathakathi* after they had ridden round Mgungundhlovu at night. He explained that the Zulu term 'means a doer of diabolical evil, a fiend incarnate, one addicted to secretly poisoning others, or practicing witchcraft or villainy of a kind calculated to compass stealthily and at a safe distance, the destruction of others'.[15] Anyone caught wandering around a sensitive area by night would immediately be suspected of witchcraft. Moreover, Stuart pointed out that horses were still a novely to the Zulu, and he suggested that they may well have imagined that these creatures had functions still unknown to them. I think it likely that horses were associated with the class of animal familiars that witches were supposed to use for their evil work.

The notion that the Boers were practicing sorcery was not, however, simply a piece of bad luck, resulting from the misinterpretation of innocent behaviour. (And why *were* some of Retief's party following horses, or riding them, around Dingane's capital by night?) Rather, the conclusion fitted perfectly with other, very well-founded suspicions of Boer intentions. Dingane had come to believe that Retief was out for his land, his cattle, and even his life: and the precise methods that the Boers intended to use to gain their ends was a secondary matter. All efficient enemies, after all, were expected to pursue their purposes with every means to hand – including weapons of war, trickery, and what whites might consider magical techniques.

It is nevertheless possible that the accusation of witchcraft may have crystallised Dingane's suspicions, and forced him to act. There is evidence that he was wavering, since while Retief's party was at Mgungundhlovu he summoned another interpreter, Brownlee, saying that he was dissatisfied with the young Port Natalian, Thomas Halstead, who was interpreting for Retief. This suggests that even two days before the massacre Dingane had not finally decided to kill the party, and that he decided on this course only after hearing the report of his night police that Retief's men were acting as witches.

It is also important to remember that the killing of enemies and rivals, and indeed of witches, was routine in Dingane's capital. Wood recorded that he and Owen counted an average of fourteen executions of witches every week at Mgungundhlovu.[16] Other enemies were routinely despatched, including many Zulu royals and local chiefs; and as Stuart pointed out, the families and dependents of traitors and witches were also commonly killed. Dingane's praise poems do not give any motive for the killing of Retief, but it is significant that the killing is laconically celebrated along with the execution of many other enemies.

> Ford of Ndaba,
> That had slippery rocks;
> Which proved slippery for Pieter and [his] son;
> He devoured two whites,
> One was Pieter and the other was Noziwawa.[17]

In short, the identification of Retief and his party as witches may simply have reinforced Dingane's shrewd suspicion that Retief was out to take his land, his cattle, and perhaps his life. At the very least, as Fynn pointed out, Dingane quickly realised that the settlement of Retief's party in his vicinity would represent a threat to his power. Once this conclusion was reached, the killing of Retief and his party had to be contemplated. Owen commented in his diary, 'Many other causes were then assigned for their slaughter. . . . Some of the other reasons I could not well understand, nor did I trouble myself about them, as there was but one true reason - the dread of their [i.e. the Boer's] power.'[18]

There was, however, a further important political consideration behind Dingane's actions. He may have killed Retief not only from fear of the Boers, but also out of respect for the British.

V

A small trading colony had existed in Port Natal (the modern Durban) since 1824. Established by lawless freebooters of mainly British extraction, some two dozen white men occupied the settlement at the time of Retief's arrival, together with Zulu and Hottentot wives and, by now, many children. They also had several thousand Zulu followers, mainly refugees from Shaka and Dingane. The presence of these disaffected Zulu had troubled Shaka and become an increasing source of concern to Dingane. For some time he had exerted pressure on the settlers to return refugees to his jurisdiction.

The official British attitude to Port Natal was not favourable, but in 1835 a retired British Navy officer, Allen Gardiner, came to the area as a missionary, and with a commission from the British authorities to bring the settlement under some sort of discipline. He negotiated terms with Dingane, who was prepared to countenance some missionary activity if the whites in Natal promised to send all refugees back to him. In 1837 Gardiner returned to Port Natal, accompanied by the missionary Owen, and he despatched a number of refugees to be executed by Dingane. The Port Natal settlers were, however, unwilling to accept Gardiner's authority, and they were infuriated by his determination to prevent them running guns across the Tugela and to restrict their hunting forays.

They were also ambivalent about Piet Retief's ambition to establish a Boer republic in Natal. Some felt, at least initially, that the Voortrekkers would strengthen the settlement and allow them to make a bid for sovereignty. However, they soon came to suspect that Retief planned to appropriate the lands that they claimed and that he would threaten their trading monopoly. This rabble of adventurers were by no means capable of a fixed policy – 'The wonder is that they have not cut one another's throats long ago,' Captain Gardiner once remarked.[19] Without question there were men among them who would take risks and do dirty deeds if there was advantage to be gained. Boer contemporaries claimed that men from Port Natal egged Dingane on to kill

Retief and his party, urging that he would be rewarded by the British Government. This cannot be proved, but the charge is plausible.

VI

On the Zulu side, there were two men with personal experience of the whites, who greatly influenced Dingane's assessment of Retief. One was the leading *induna*, Sotobe, who had twice been sent as an emissary to the British, and who was deeply suspicious of the Port Natal party. Another key actor in this interface between Zulu and British was Jacob Sumbili, who Shaka named Hlambamanzi (denoting a strong swimmer), since he had come ashore in Port Natal from a shipwreck. His ghostly voice was without question a major factor in determining the fate of Retief.

A Xhosa cattle-rustler, Jacob had been imprisoned on Robben Island. In 1823 he was freed to serve as an interpreter to a British Naval captain making a survey of the East Coast. The expedition was shipwrecked at Port Natal, and Jacob, after a quarrel, fled inland and became an interpreter for Shaka. He served as an important intermediary between the whites at Port Natal and the Zulu court under both Shaka and Dingane, and rose to a position of considerable influence on the strength of his expertise on the British. Shaka included him, together with Sotobe, in a failed embassy to the British in 1828, and Dingane, equally eager to come to terms with the British, sent Jacob and men from Port Natal, together with Sotobe, on a similar embassy in 1830. They were treated with disdain by the British at Grahamstown.

What was perhaps even more important for the future, however, was the fact that Jacob met a Xhosa-speaker in Grahamstown who warned him about the tactics and goals of the whites. They first came and took part of the land, then encroached more and more, then built houses – missionary establishments – for the purpose of subduing their enemies by witchcraft. Some four chiefs had recently died as a result of witchcraft practised by missionaries. Then came the soldiers, who would build forts and finally take the country. Moreover, Jacob was told, soldiers had recently been enquiring about the Zulu region.[20] Jacob's report greatly troubled Shaka and also Dingane and their councillors, although the British at Port Natal mobilised all their resources to discredit him. Dingane eventually permitted them to murder Jacob, in January, 1832, but even after his death his reports were often cited by Zulu councillors. Dingane's options were limited, however. Neither he nor Shaka ever contemplated a direct confrontation with the British, and Dingane was fully aware of the disparity of force available to them.

Dingane's great fear was that refugees from his rule would form the nucleus of an army and attack him. This had happened before, most notably in the cases of Mzilikazi and Soshangana, Zulu generals who had struck out on their own. Indeed, his brother Mpande was to make Dingane's worst nightmares come true by decamping into Natal with a great horde of followers and allying himself with the Boers. That is why he had made Gardiner undertake to return refugees to be dealt with by him, as a price for permitting missionary activity in his domains.

However, he had a shrewd appreciation of official British attitudes towards the Boers, and towards the motley settlers of Port Natal, who had only recently forced the resignation of Gardiner as justice of the peace. As Dingane saw it – perhaps encouraged by British elements at Port Natal – the Boers were fleeing the jurisdiction of King George. There are reports that he questioned missionaries and Englishmen from Port Natal about the Boers, and was told that they were rebels against King George, who had fled his jurisdiction. It seems likely that just as he had made Gardiner promise to return fugitives from his justice, so he thought he would be doing the British a favour by checking the advances of their own fugitives.

VII

My conclusion is that the parties had a shrewd understanding of each other, and that their motives were on the whole obvious to their opponents, and immediately comprehensible. One of the striking themes of all the first-hand accounts of the courts of Shaka and Dingane is the way in which visitors were interrogated about European institutions and particularly military techniques. The first Englishman had visited Shaka in 1824, only some eight years after his accession to power, but early visitors also found Portuguese envoys from Delagoa Bay at court. Very soon Shaka and Dingane were dictating and receiving letters to British authorities. Their spies reported in detail on life in Port Natal, as in foreign tribal capitals. For their part, the English settlers in Port Natal maintained a detailed watch on the Zulu court. This does not mean that they, or the Zulus, always grasped precisely what others were aiming at, but in general they may be said to have miscalculated rather than misinterpreted each other. When Retief was making his second visit to Dingane, the American missionary Champion warned him that he was taking a foolish risk. Retief retorted that the Boers understand the blacks, and that he would not take advice on the matter from an Englishman. Champion pointed out that he was in fact an American, but Retief's hubris was not be punctured.[21] However, even other Boer leaders had warned Retief that he was being foolhardy, and a number of his followers peeled off at the last moment. For his part, Dingane certainly miscalculated, but it is more than likely that he was encouraged to do so by British settlers. Moreover, he had an accurate strategic appreciation of the threat posed by the Boers, the British, and Zulu refugees in Natal.

Boer covenants with God, missionary faith in Jesus, Zulu belief in witches do not, I think, greatly complicate the story. It is a grim tale of power. The story could also be rewritten in the Rashamon mode, each witness recasting it in a different light: but, again, I think that the result is to add further layers to our understanding rather than to confront us with irreconcilable perpectives.

But if my reading of this episode is resolutely Machiavellian, I would not argue that it should be taken as the type-case of early colonial conflict, or even as a better instance of the nature of 'first contact' than the Captain Cook story. (Should either episode be termed a 'first contact'? The concept cries out for deconstruction.) My object is more modest. First, I want to emphasise that the Captain Cook episode was not typical, and that there is something wrong with an anthropology that reads it as a type-case not only of first contact, but of cultural contacts, and inter-cultural relations more generally. Very often people of different cultural backgrounds understand each other very well indeed, even on the basis of very limited acquaintance. Jacob Hlambamanzi, a proto-anthropologist, interpreted between two cultures with great accuracy and acumen, as did Fynn on the other side of the divide.

But second, even if we are less pessimistic about the possibility of inter-cultural understanding, we will not find ourselves back on the safe shores of moral certainties. What grounds are there for choosing between the Zulu tyrant, the English and Boer freebooters, the calculating British officials? We might wish to sympathise with the Zulu, but it is hard to justify Dingane. He came to power in a bloody coup, ruled largely by fear, and when his half-brother Mpande allied himself with the Boers and defeated him, he ushered in the first generation of comparative calm that had been experienced in the area since the rise of Shaka. It was only after Mpande's death that the coalitions he built up collapsed and the Zulu were finally defeated, the British forces sweeping across the land in 1879, just as Jacob Hlambamanzi had predicted.

Notes

1 Marshall Sahlins (1985) *Islands of History*, Chicago: University of Chicago Press, p. xvii.
2 J.C. Beaglehole (1974) *The Life of Captain James Cook*, Stanford: Stanford University Press, chapter XXV, especially pp. 662-72.
3 Gananath Obeyesekere (1992) *The Apotheosis of Captain Cook: European Mythmaking in the Pacific*, Princeton, NJ: Princeton University Press; Marshall Sahlins (1995) *How 'Natives' Think: About Captain Cook, For Example*, Chicago: University of Chicago

Press. For a good review of the debate see Robert Borofsky (1997) 'Cook, Lono, Obeysekere, and Sahlins' (*Current Anthropology*, 38 (2): 255-82. My own review of the case can be found in chapter six of my *Culture: The Anthropologists' Account*, Cambridge MA: Harvard University Press, 1999.

4 J.C. Chase (ed.) (1843) *The Natal Papers*, Grahamstown: Godlonton, pp. 83-4.

5 See Ogle's statement in John W. Colenso (1982) *Bringing Forth Light*, Ruth Edgecombe (ed.), Pietermaritzburg: University of Natal Press, p. 132.

6 Chase, loc.cit., p. 11 note 8.

7 See Leonard Thompson (1985) *The Political Mythology of Apartheid*, New Haven: Yale University Press, chapter five.

8 Owen's diary extracts are in J. Bird (ed.) (1888) *Annals of Natal 1495-1845*, Pietermaritzburg: P.Davis and Sons, vol. 1 pp. 347-50.

9 Chase, loc. cit., p. 132.

10 B.T.T. Leverton (ed.) (1984) *Records of Natal*, Pretoria: Government Printer, Vol. 3, p. 6.

11 See, e.g., the letter from the American missionaries, 2 April 1838, in Bird loc. cit. 1: 212. Kirkman, an interpreter with the American missionaries in the Zulu region, reported that the chief, Silwebana 'had been ordered to kill Mr. Retief and the five men who had accompanied him, on his way to Natal. Mr Retief had to pass that Kaffir's kraal, and orders had been sent to him to invite Mr. Retief and his party into the kraal, to entertain them with a dance, milk and beer, and, whilst so engaged, fall on the whites and kill them.' Silwebana had refused to carry out the order, and he and many of his people had then been slaughtered on Dingane's orders. (J.D. Kirkman 'Life of Mr Joseph Kirkman in Zululand 1836-40', Joseph Kirkman Papers, File 1, Killie Campbell Library, Durban. No date.)

12 James Stuart and D. McK. Malcolm (eds) (1969) *The Diary of Henry Francis Fynn*, Pietermaritzburg: Shuter and Shooter, pp. 314-15.

13 William Wood (1840) *Statements respecting Dingaan, King of the Zoolahs, With some particulars relative to the massacres of Messrs. Retief and Biggars, and their parties*, Cape Town: Collard and Co.

14 R.C.A. Samuelson (1929) *Long, Long Ago*, Durban: Knox, p. 215.

15 James Stuart 'The massacre of Piet Retief and party', Type-script, Stuart Papers, Killie Campbell Africana Library, Durban (no date. ?1932) pp. 32-3.
16 Wood, loc. cit.
17 D.K. Rycroft and A.B. Ngcobo (eds) (1988) *The Praises of Dingane*, Pietermaritzburg: University of Natal Press, pp. 74-5. Cf. pp. 125-7 for a commentary and alternative texts. The editors note that Noziwawe was a Khumalo chief, and they cannot account for the linking of his name here with that of Retief.
18 Bird, loc. cit., p. 350.
19 See Kirkman loc. cit. p. 1. Cf. G.E. Cory (1926) *The Diary of the Rev. Francis Owen*, Cape Town: Van Riebeeck Society, p. 157.
20 Bird, loc. cit., p. 279.
21 See Kirkman, loc. cit., p.1. Cf. Cory, loc. cit., p. 157.

Sources

Chapter two. 'Postmodernism, Cambridge and the Great Kalahari Debate', *Social Anthropology*, 1992, 1:1a: 57-71.

Chapter three. 'Culture, identity and the project of a cosmopolitan anthropology' *Man*, 1994, 29(3): 537-54.

Chapter four. 'On human nature: Darwin and the anthropologists', in M. Teich, R. Porter and B. Gustafsson (eds) (1997) *Nature and Society*, Cambridge: Cambridge University Press, pp.274-90.

Chapter five. 'Psychology and anthropology: the British experience', *History of the Human Sciences*, 1990, 3:3: 397-413.

Chapter six. 'Symbols in myths and dreams: Freud v. Lévi-Strauss', *Encounter*, March 1989, pp. 26-31.

Chapter seven. 'Audrey Richards', in Carmen Blacker and Edward Shils (eds) (1996) *Cambridge Women*, Cambridge: Cambridge University Press, pp.221-44.

Chapter eight. 'A seeker of truth – Ernest Gellner, Anthropology and Politics', *Times Higher Education Supplement*, 25 October 1996, p. 23. 'Ernest Gellner: The last of the Central Europeans', *Anthropology Today*, 1996, 12 (1): 19-20.

Chapter nine. Bradford Morse Distinguished Lecture at the Boston University African Studies Center, April 1997.

Chapter ten. 'Machiavelli in precolonial Southern Africa' *Social Anthropology*, 1995, 3 (1): 1-13.

Chapter eleven. 'The death of Piet Retief', *Social Anthropology*, 1996, 4:2: 133-43.

Index

Abu-Lughod, Lila, 45, 50
American anthropology, 16, 32, 45; cultural theory in, 38-42; post-modernism in, 42-45; and the Boasian tradition, 39-41, 56; and Freudian theory, 79, 94
Annan, Noel, 115
Apartheid, 2, 159-160, 162-163
Appiah, Kwame Anthony, 49
Arnold, Matthew, 9

Barnard, Alan, 28
Bartlett, F. C., 86, 93
Bastian, Adolf, 83
Benedict, Ruth, 39, 79, 160
Bird, Nurit, 29
Boas, Franz, 39, 44, 51, 83
Bourdieu, Pierre, 11
British social anthropology, 24-25, 145; and Darwin, 59-60; and psychology, 79-97; and British national character, 80
    See also Cambridge University, London School of Economics, Malinowski, Radcliffe-Brown, Richards
Burke, Kenneth, 41, 42
Burrow, J. W., 59-61, 63

Cambridge University, social anthropology at, 19-21, 129
Cape Town, University of,

social anthropology at, 147, 148, 149, 163, 164
Carrithers, Michael, 17
Casalis, Eugene, 172, 173, 180, 183
Clifford, James, 17, 43
Coertze, P. J., 160, 162
Cook, Captain James, 191-192, 206
Crapanzano, Vincent, 45
culture, a major issue again, 2, 37; in the United States, 2, 3, 4-5, 7; in South Africa, 3-4, 7, 150-152; German and French approaches to culture, 4, 7-8, 39; in American anthropology, 5-6, 38-42; cultural determinism, 5-6; race and culture, 6-7, 12; and British social anthropology, 7; humanist conception, 9; Geertz on, 16, 40-41; high vs. authentic, 11, 38-39; Boas on, 39; as text, 42, 50-51; culture and personality school, 79; Malinowski on, 92, 167-157

Darnell, Regna, 40
Darwin, Charles, 59-77; and the Fuegians, 63-67; and cultural selection, 68-72; on race, 70-72; on mating, 72, 75-76; and evolutionist

anthropology, 59-63, 76-77
DeVore, Irvine, 22-24, 26, 27
Dingane, 178, 179, 183, 184,
186, 187; and Retief, 193-206
dreams, 90; Rivers on, 85;
Freud on, 99, 100-102,
108-110; the dream of Irma's
injection, 108-110
Durkheim, Emile, 88, 89, 92,
94, 147, 188

Eiselen, W. W. M., 151, 158-160
Elias, Norbert, 8
Eliot, T. S., 9
ethnographic fieldwork,
13, 20-21, 26-27, 51-52;
interdisciplinary, 53-54
ethnography, 15-18, 37, 43;
Geertz on, 41, 42; foreign vs.
nativist, 45-50, 54; who buys
it? 55-57
ethnicity, 48, 56
Evans-Pritchard, E. E., 15, 21,
79-80, 124
evolutionist anthropology, 23,
39, 149; and Darwin, 59-63,
76-77; and marriage, 72-76

Faber, T., 130, 133
Feldman, A., 45
Firth, Raymond, 125, 133
Fortes, Meyer, 19-20, 124,
129, 157
Fortune, Reo, 19
Frazer, James, 38, 62, 81, 89,
93, 147
Freud, Sigmund, 76; on
folktales 98-100; on dreams,
99, 100-102, 106-107,
108-110; Freudian theory,
79, 85, 90-91, 94, 95, 110,
140; Malinowski on Oedipus

complex, 90-92; Freud on
symbolism, 99-102, 104, 106-
107, 112, 113; Lévi-Strauss
on Freudian theory, 100-102,
104, 107, 111-112, 113-114
Fynn, Henry Francis, 198-199,
201, 206

Galton, Francis, 61
Gardiner, Allen, 202, 204
Geertz, Clifford, 15, 16, 17, 18,
40-42, 131
Gellner, Ernest, 138-144
Gefou-Madianou, Dimitra,
48-49
Gluckman, Max, 153, 154, 158,
161, 165, 180
Goody, Jack, 19, 20, 21
Gore-Brown, Lorna, 122-123
Gramsci, Antonio, 11
Griaule, Marcel, 51, 52
Gudeman, S., 52-53, 56

Habermas, J., viii
Haddon, A. C., 62-63, 81-82,
87, 149; and Radcliffe-
Brown, 145-147, 148
Hearnshaw, L. S., 95
Hellmann, Ellen, 153, 167, 168
Herskovits, Melville, 157, 160
Herzfeld, Michael, 46
history of anthropology,
ix-x, 12-13
Hoernlé, A. W., 152, 153-154,
155, 165, 167
Howell, Nancy, 27
Huntington, Samuel, 3
Huxley, Thomas, 67

Jabavu, D. D. T., 149, 150-151,
153, 165
Jahoda, Gustav, 95